Humana Festival '97
The Complete Plays

Humana Inc. is one of the nation's largest
managed health care companies
with 6 million members in its health care plans.

The Humana Foundation was established in 1981
to support the educational, social, medical and cultural development
of communities in ways that reflect
Humana's commitment to social responsibility
and an improved quality of life.

SMITH AND KRAUS
Contemporary Playwrights: Collections

Humana Festival '97
The Complete Plays

Edited by Michael Bigelow Dixon
and Liz Engelman

Contemporary Playwrights Series

SK
A Smith and Kraus Book

A Smith and Kraus Book
Published by Smith and Kraus, Inc.
PO Box 127, Lyme, NH 03768

Manufactured in the United States of America

Cover and Text Design by Julia Hill
Text Conversion and Layout by Joel A. Smith
Cover artwork © Wiktor Sadowski

First Edition: November 1997
10 9 8 7 6 5 4 3 2 1

Library of Congress Cataloguing-in-Publication Data
Contemporary Playwrights Series
ISSN 1067-9510

Contents

Acknowledgements

Thanks to the following persons for their invaluable assistance in compiling this volume:

Miriam Brown
Monica Bueno
Kathleen Early
Emily Gnadinger
Charles Forbes
Debra Renauer
Jeff Rodgers
Jenny Sandman
Joel A. Smith
Val Smith
Alexander Speer
Emily Vail

Judy Boals
Jason Fogelson
Robert Freedman
Peter Hagan
Joyce Ketay
Sarah Jane Leigh
Helen Merrill
Carl Mulert
Jill Westmoreland

Foreword

This seems to be the festival of uneasy laughter. The jokes, and there are slews of them, all seem to be riffs on what we used to call "morally ambiguous" behavior. Underneath all the comic tensions of marriages betrayed, drugs provided, trust misplaced, satirical optimism and hysterical pessimism, there is a subtext of the old virtues of family, romantic love, home, and respectable work, but it just seems that it wouldn't be cool for these characters to reveal up front that they feel those nostalgias.

While the characters are uneasy and angst ridden, the words are delicious. From Steven Dietz's phantasmagoria of disloyalty to Naomi Iizuka's street theatre poem of emptiness, sensation, desire, and fear, right through Benjie Aerenson's staccato take on the dark side of horse racing, the language is playful, piercing, wildly rhythmic and satisfying. Shaw could have liked these plays and, given the right drugs, might even have written one or two. There seems here to be more faith in language itself than in the moralities devolved from it.

These plays are highly theatrical, but oddly enough, would also make great radio because they are filled with sea tides, Mozart, pounding hoofs and the music of the streets. They have a sense of sweep but at key moments they pull down into deeply intimate two-character scenes as if trying to get these smallest human units right before moving on to something larger.

I enjoy their intimacy, their despairing humor and their trust that words are still the heart of the theatre. These are truly plays where the writers hope we will laugh ourselves well.

Jon Jory
Producing Director
Actors Theatre of Louisville

Editors' Note

A book like this plays a significant role in the national environs of new play development. First, it records what happened in the 21st Annual Humana Festival of New American Plays. Second, it marks the completion of dramaturgical work on these scripts at Actors Theatre of Louisville, a collaboration that may have lasted six months or more. And third, it assists other theatres in finding new plays to produce. Plays, of course, are written to be *seen*, but first they need to be *read*, and this cycle of reading / production / reading / production characterizes the journey of a play's development through the American theatre.

In addition to making these plays available to a wider public, this book provides an opportunity for us to share our enthusiasm for the reading phase of the play development cycle. Ours is an interesting job: to read 2,900 new scripts a year and respond responsibly to so many sensibilities. From this, we've learned that plays speak in many different ways. Some pop up and shout Boy Howdy, some play cat and mouse, some simply bowl you over, some whisper and seduce, while others tickle and delight. The trick to reading any play, we think, is listening—to the characters, to the playwright, to your own thoughts as you go. The challenge is to find the writer's wavelength and tune in.

So here's the theatre chart's top nine singles for 1997, as different from one another as hard rock, jazz, funk, reggae and country western. And it's all brought to you by the Humana Foundation and Radio Free ATL—where we play the hits from coast to coast for your listening (reading) pleasure.

Liz Engelman & Michael Bigelow Dixon

Humana Festival '97
The Complete Plays

Lighting Up The Two-Year Old
by Benjie Aerenson

BIOGRAPHY

Benjie Aerenson grew up in Miami and lives in New York City. His play, The *Possum Play*, received a staged reading directed by Bill Hart at the Joseph Papp Theater and a workshop production, featuring Mariette Hartley and directed by Stanley Soble, at the 1994 New Works Festival of the Mark Taper Forum. It also won the 1997 Arnold L. Weissberger Award from New Dramatists. Aerenson's work has appeared in the East Village literary magazine *Between C&D* and in *National Lampoon*. He graduated from M.I.T. and the University of Miami School of Law, and practiced law in New York. His play *When Cuba Opens Up* premiered at the Florida Shakespeare Theatre in Miami in 1997.

HUMANA FESTIVAL PRODUCTION

Lighting Up the Two-Year Old was first performed at the Humana Festival of New American Plays, March 1997. It was directed by Laszlo Marton with the following cast:

Carl . . . . Bob Burrus
Bud. . . . . Lou Sumrall
George . . . . Allen Fitzpatrick
Junior . . . . George Kisslinger

and the following production staff:

Scenic Designer . . . . Paul Owen
Costume Designer . . . . David Zinn
Lighting Designer . . . . Ed McCarthy
Properties Designer . . . . Ron Riall
Stage Manager . . . . Christine Lomaka
Assistant Stage Manager. . . . . Megan Wanlass
Dramaturg . . . . Michael Bigelow Dixon
Casting . . . . Laura Richin Casting

CHARACTERS

CARL: a horse trainer around sixty
BUD: a groom and stablehand in his later twenties
GEORGE: a man around forty; the owner's son
JUNIOR: the owner around sixty-five; George's father

TIME AND PLACE

The play is set on a horse farm in north central Florida and in a house in Miami in the present.

Lighting Up The Two-Year Old

ACT ONE
SCENE 1

In the tack room of the stables; blankets and saddles, etc. are arranged and hung; Bud is at work. Carl enters.

CARL: Neat

BUD: It is

CARL: You keep a neat room

BUD: I fold the blankets in here. I don't just leave them out where the dust can get to them
(Carl points to the blankets running along the wall.)

CARL: You got those stripes lined up all the way across, and I see you arrange the leather by length

BUD: Not too many people notice

CARL: I notice

BUD: But most people...

CARL: Boss don't notice. Hell, how often do they wheel him down here anyway...wheelchair get stuck in the mud, and even if he did notice, he couldn't tell you

BUD: Terrible to be in a chair with wheels

CARL: Clean too

BUD: Huh

CARL: The place

BUD: Swept

CARL: Some people are neat but not clean

BUD: I'm both

CARL: And some people are clean but not neat. But you're both
(Pause. Carl sights along the straight lines of blankets.)

CARL: You wanted to see me?

BUD: Yeah see there's this doctor and he says...

CARL: Some men you meet, they're very clear, very organized in the way they live

BUD: ...he says...

CARL: ...in the way they dress

BUD: I keep myself neat

CARL: I know you do, and other guys live like pigs
     (Pause.)

CARL: But some guys on the outside they're neat and clean, but inside their mind it's a tornado. They live like pigs inside their mind

BUD: Pigs are clean about themselves

CARL: What did you want to see me about

BUD: This doctor, I went to see him about my shoulder and he says...

CARL: But sometimes no matter how neat and clean you keep a place, you got to get out once in awhile, am I right

BUD: Right

CARL: But you go to Daytona, cruise the Boardwalk, tie one on, never know where the hell you'll end up the next morning

BUD: I like to stick close by

CARL: But sticking close by, you find something to do

BUD: I stay out of trouble
     (Carl begins shifting around the hanging blankets and adjusting the length of the hanging leather straps.)

BUD: What are you doing

CARL: Redecorating

BUD: But I had it just so

CARL: So you'll put it back
     (Pause.)

CARL: ...maybe get in a card game

BUD: I don't play cards anymore
     (Pause.)

CARL: They call it gambling

BUD: I don't, none o' that

CARL: I mean when you play cards they call it gambling

BUD: I don't play

CARL: But when the bosses lose money on a deal they call it business

BUD: Right, I saw this doctor...

CARL: They're losing money on this place, they're bleeding

BUD: ...about my shoulder, and what he said was...

CARL: Do you see it coming

BUD: What

CARL: Losing, in a card game

BUD: I don't play

CARL: I mean when you did

    (Pause.)

BUD: You got to think positive

CARL: I suppose you do. Same with a place like this, everybody was thinking positive, but when they had to shoot that three-year old...

BUD: That was too bad

CARL: Frozen track

BUD: I heard about that, that was awful

CARL: You felt bad

BUD: I did

CARL: ...to hear about that happening

BUD: It stinks

CARL: Poor fucking animal

BUD: Yeah

CARL: But did you feel bad

BUD: It's a horse

    (Pause.)

CARL: Where were you before here

BUD: Over on the edge of the woods, I was...

CARL: I mean before before

BUD: He says I need this work on my shoulder

CARL: Where

    (Pause.)

BUD: The carnival

CARL: Puttin' the kids on the merry-go-round

BUD: Dump the clown in the water

CARL: You were the clown?

BUD: Yeah

CARL: That's funny. And then you got a taste for the real ones

BUD: Huh?

CARL: Horses. You put the kids on the merry-go-round and then got a taste for the real horses

BUD: Yeah and so this doctor says that this pain in my shoulder, this pain it's got to do with ligaments, it's involving tendons, this thing I got with my shoulder has got to be worked on

CARL: So get it worked on

BUD: Yeah but

CARL: We got medical, the pay might not be great but we got medical

BUD: But see that's the thing the doctor can't do anything

CARL: I thought you just said he said it's got to be worked on

BUD: But he can't work on it, it's got to be like massaged and that's not covered

(Pause.)

BUD: Massaged regular

CARL: Wouldn't you know that what you need isn't covered

BUD: Yeah and not just the massage but like for the massage to work they tell you you need all these vitamins and diet supplements

CARL: Wouldn't you know it

BUD: Yeah and that stuff costs

CARL: But you need it 'cause you got this pain in your shoulder

BUD: I do

CARL: And pain can wear you down

BUD: It can

CARL: Chronic pain can piss you off

BUD: Can it

CARL: Don't ask me, you're the one with the pain

BUD: It can

CARL: Horses don't understand that. They're too fucking dumb

BUD: They're not so dumb

CARL: Aren't they?

BUD: They know what they're doing

CARL: Do they

BUD: It costs...

CARL: And sometimes when you're mad 'cause you've got this chronic pain and you've got this dumb animal standing in front of you who knows what he's doing, I bet you just want to...hey, I bet I know how you screwed up your shoulder

(Pause.)

CARL: That throwing motion, throwing all that money into the middle of the table without bringing any back. See, it's that one-way throwing out the arm and nothing coming back...

BUD: I told you I'm all through with that

CARL: That's funny, out and back out and back. I bet that's the only time you see the Doc, when you're studyin' his face above five Bees wonderin' what he's holdin'

(Pause.)

CARL: Or do you boys play with the Hawaiian titty deck

BUD: A thousand dollars, I mean for all this massage and the supplements and...

CARL: A thousand dollars. For two you could chop it off and buy a new arm

(Pause. Carl steps back and studies how he's got the blankets rearranged.)

CARL: You been moving around a little

BUD: I like to travel

CARL: You like to gamble so you have to travel. Why did you say you left the carnival

BUD: You said

CARL: Why'd I say

BUD: To be near real horses

CARL: But I was wrong, wasn't I

(Pause.)

CARL: The way I heard it you had some trouble with a house

BUD: I lived in a trailer

CARL: A full house when you were holding three of a kind

BUD: Is that what you heard

CARL: Is that what it was

BUD: Sure

CARL: What was it

BUD: Nothing like that. I got up to take a piss in the middle of the night and when I came back a coupla goons were going at these three bedrolls with baseball bats. My buddies were in two of them, but I wasn't in the third

CARL: You got any idea why

BUD: Some people are just mean

CARL: Probably on their way home from a Minor League game

BUD: Huh

CARL: It would explain the bats

BUD: I didn't even hear them scream, just bones crushing...and where their heads were, it was this cracking sound

(Pause.)

CARL: If you bunk in the bunkhouse, I think I'll sleep in the woods

BUD: It wasn't about me

CARL: What the hell was it about then

(Pause.)

BUD: This sore shoulder really makes it hard to work

CARL: I got something for that

BUD: I really need this therapy, and I'm tellin' you it's expensive

CARL: Is it

BUD: I told you

CARL: Things get a little out of hand for fellas like you and everybody in the vicinity gets hurt

(Pause.)

CARL: But what the hell, it's their fault for being in the vicinity

BUD: I got to get back to my work

CARL: I don't want to keep you from your work

(Carl starts to leave.)

BUD: Hey, I wouldn't play cards with those guys. Their cards smell like horse, and after you play with them you got the smell all over your hands

CARL: How about the money, the money smell like horse

BUD: It all smells like horse, and if you have a date afterward...

CARL: You wouldn't know about the money because you never touch the money after, only before, as it's on its way out

BUD: I won a few, I haven't done bad

CARL: You don't like horses very much, do you

BUD: I groom them

CARL: But you don't like them

BUD: I don't like their smell all over me when I don't want it

(Pause.)

BUD: What does it mean when blood comes out of somebody's ear

CARL: It means their ear is bleeding

BUD: Or does it mean their brain is bleeding out their ear

CARL: They sting you with that baseball bat?

BUD: I hit this guy in the Imperial the other night

CARL: And he started bleeding from the ear?

BUD: I met this girl

CARL: Girls like you

BUD: I do okay, I was doing okay with this one, we were getting along fine, talking, you know, she was turned to me on the barstool and I had my knee up toward her cunt, and then like I brought my hand up toward her face and I could see the way she looked, her face turned and kind of twisted 'cause it must've smelled like horse, and I said wait, but she was trying to get away and I took her face and turned it back toward me and this guy reaches and I hit him on the side of the head

(Pause.)

BUD: And he looks funny and this blood starts coming out of his ear

CARL: What did you do

BUD: I got the hell out of there

CARL: How hard did you hit him

BUD: I didn't hit him hard

(Pause.)

BUD: I hit him so fucking hard the inside of his brain must smell like a horse shit inside it

CARL: They say Duran once knocked out a horse with his fist

BUD: What do you think

CARL: Could you do that

BUD: I mean about the guy in the bar

CARL: I once saw you almost take the legs out from under one with the back of a brush

(Pause.)

CARL: Where are you going to go after this

BUD: You firing me for hitting a horse

CARL: I'm not firing you

BUD: I do my job

CARL: I mean when I don't give you the money for the vitamins and you got to get the hell out of town

BUD: I don't have to get out of town

CARL: You don't

BUD: No

CARL: Whatever you say

(Pause.)

BUD: Sometimes a little shot is the only thing they understand

CARL: Sure

BUD: Like when a jockey has to use the crop

CARL: Of course

BUD: It's the only way they'll do anything

CARL: But the funny thing is, sometimes I see you come in there before the horse does a thing and just give it a shot

BUD: I must've asked it to do something and you didn't hear

CARL: Is that it

BUD: Must've been

CARL: I think it's something you brought with you down to the barn. I think that you come down to the barn and suddenly some horse is on the other side of an argument without ever knowing how he got there...poor sonofabitch, he's got no opinion besides what you give him
(Pause.)

CARL: Whoa, the horse says, I got no position in this matter. But see you give him a position and he just can't shake loose of it

BUD: I don't give him anything

CARL: That's okay, sometimes it's like that with the old man, sitting like that in the wheelchair, staring straight ahead, you give him opinions

BUD: Tough

CARL: Sure it is, whole fucking thing ready to go to hell, balanced like a needle on water

BUD: Can you balance a needle on water

CARL: Sure you can, if you do it gently. Sometimes the whole thing balanced on one horse

BUD: One horse

CARL: When the three-year old took that spill and they shot her, I think that's when

BUD: Do you

CARL: I think so, and sometimes to bring things back, to get things going again, it's the hair of the dog that bit you

BUD: What do you mean

CARL: Nothing, I mean horses die

BUD: Everything dies

CARL: Most people can't believe how long a horse lives. It makes you think

BUD: What

CARL: That it's unnatural how long a horse lives
(Pause.)

CARL: But you wouldn't do that

BUD: Do what

CARL: ...have a horse die sooner

BUD: Are you crazy

CARL: It happens

BUD: I've never heard of that

CARL: But have you heard of it

BUD: Maybe I've heard of it

CARL: You know, I was just thinking of something funny

BUD: What

CARL: Nothing

BUD: What

CARL: I was thinking you should just play poker with the horses, but I think they'd beat you. That's funny
(Pause.)

CARL: You wouldn't do that, would you

BUD: You can't play poker with horses

CARL: I mean kill a horse for the insurance

BUD: Are you crazy

CARL: But would you
(Carl looks at the blankets hanging.)

CARL: Hell, I think I'm going to have to redo the whole thing
(Pause.)

CARL: They want us to bring the stables back, to bring home winners, but they don't give us anything to work with

BUD: They want us to work with shit

CARL: You can say that again, I mean they don't invest in the place

BUD: You can't make a champion out of a dog

CARL: You need something to start with

BUD: You can't make a pig out of a tree

CARL: If he wants to be wheeled into the winner's circle, he's got to ante up

BUD: That's right

CARL: You ante up every chance you get, you been into every game between here and Daytona

BUD: I told you...

CARL: And the boys from Daytona, when you're into the fellas from Daytona...

BUD: They know I'm good for it, they give me time

CARL: At least until spring training
(Carl gestures as if swinging a baseball bat.)

CARL: So say you had to kill a horse to raise this money, which one would it be

BUD: I wouldn't

CARL: But let's just say you did, which one

BUD: Buttermilk

CARL: Dale Evans would hate you

(Pause.)

CARL: But that two-year old has some insurance on him. He showed early promise but he's fallen off his game

BUD: He could still develop

CARL: I'm sorry kid, I'd like him to develop into a concert pianist, but I just don't have that kind of time

BUD: People don't do things like that

CARL: It happens

BUD: But I mean people don't

CARL: Some people do

BUD: You do and then you're one of those people

(Pause.)

BUD: All's I need is a thousand dollars

CARL: That's all you need today

BUD: That's all I need

CARL: I'm kinda short myself

BUD: But these guys...

CARL: And I might have to let you go, the way you treat the horses

BUD: There's nothing wrong with how I treat them, and here you are talking about...

CARL: So what about it, are you going to kill this horse so you can get a coupla thousand bucks and not have your head stoved in

BUD: A coupla thousand...

(Pause.)

CARL: Look, I know this is tough for you, but that's why I asked you. Do you think I want to deal with some kind of animal

BUD: I don't kill horses

CARL: I know, that's what I mean, in the ordinary course of things you wouldn't. But you'll sacrifice one to save the others

BUD: But...

CARL: I want to deal with someone who knows its value, who it means something to, who wouldn't kill it for no reason but who when the scales are weighed, tips in favor of killing it

(Pause.)

BUD: Maybe you could just have to give me a thousand dollars or I'd tell them what you're up to

CARL: Make your best deal. But you got to figure if they'd believe you

BUD: You want to take that chance?

CARL: You got to figure how many people know you owe the boys from Daytona

(Pause.)

BUD: Three thousand

CARL: Twenty-five hundred. Look, I'm giving you a chance. There's plenty of guys would kill a horse

BUD: You said you didn't want an animal

CARL: I was pulling your chain

(Pause.)

CARL: Look, you go out, you have a few drinks, get loosened up, then you come back and light up the two-year old

BUD: How

CARL: Split an electrical cord, attach one to his ear and one to his ass, and then plug it in

BUD: I don't know

CARL: C'mon, kid, one to the ear, one to the ass, two to the bank, what do you say

BUD: Maybe I could just break his leg

CARL: You don't have the skill to make it look like he kicked his stall. This is the only thing to do. Just don't touch the wire to the hay, don't want to set the barn on fire

BUD: I didn't say I was going to do it

CARL: Look, it's just so fuckin' easy it's not like something you have to do, it's just like something that's going to happen and you're not going to get in the way of

(Pause.)

CARL: One cocky horse worth more dead than alive. Fuckin' thing should shoot itself if it had a heart

BUD: Why don't you do it yourself

CARL: That's not my job

(Pause.)

BUD: Just clip one to his ear one to his ass?

CARL: Easy as plugging in a lamp

BUD: And...and it's like teaching me a lesson, teaching me not to play cards...see, it's like this horse has to die because of my card playing...see, if it didn't have any consequences I might still keep playing...but now that a horse has to die for it, I'll quit for sure

(Pause.)

CARL: Kid, you're a genius

(Lights down and they exit. Through a dim corridor of light, Junior wheels himself across the tack room. Lights down.)

SCENE 2

Same; Carl and George are talking.

CARL: So what do you think

GEORGE: About what

CARL: About how the old man looks

GEORGE: He looks good

CARL: Does he

GEORGE: Sure he does. You don't think he does?

CARL: I didn't say anything

GEORGE: I don't like that, I don't like somebody around him all the time who doesn't think he looks good

CARL: I didn't say that

GEORGE: I don't like it

CARL: What difference would it make

GEORGE: He senses it

CARL: Can he

GEORGE: He can, and I can see, in his eyes, back behind his eyes. I can see there's a lot going on

CARL: Tell me what

GEORGE: A lot

CARL: Tell me where

GEORGE: Back there. I can talk to him, I still get advice from him, from his eyes

CARL: When he gave you advice from his mouth, you didn't take it

GEORGE: I was young, I was a kid

CARL: 'Course he didn't really give you advice, he just beat you up

GEORGE: He was strong

CARL: He was abusive

GEORGE: To weak men, he seemed...

CARL: Not to me. I mean to you. To me the old man was a peach
   (Pause.)

CARL: I'm glad you came up here, I needed to talk to you

GEORGE: You could've called me

CARL: I wanted to see you

GEORGE: You could've come down to Miami

CARL: I don't like to go down there. South Florida doesn't hold much for me,
   ever since they stole the good dates away from Hialeah ...

GEORGE: We've got some promising horses, wouldn't you say

CARL: I don't know

GEORGE: The two-year old

CARL: He hasn't done so well

GEORGE: He's been in the money

CARL: He's been in a lot less money than has been put in him

GEORGE: And Financier

CARL: That jockey didn't know what to do with her

GEORGE: That was your doing

CARL: Your dad's

GEORGE: I thought you said...

CARL: I didn't say a thing, I was asking you

GEORGE: You don't take responsibility, that's why you're where you are, that's
   why all this is his

CARL: All what
   (Pause.)

CARL: You bought a new house down there

GEORGE: You should come see it

CARL: Right in town

GEORGE: Miami's a city

CARL: I mean you live right inside of it

GEORGE: ...more a sprawl

CARL: I mean right inside the sprawl that's the city. How's the boat business

GEORGE: Boat business is good

CARL: People buying boats?

GEORGE: They got water, they got money

CARL: And you got that Chris Craft

GEORGE: It's a Post, you were on it

CARL: Sure, a few times, with you and your dad. He still likes that, I think it soothes him, the motion of the water comin' up through him. You should take him out more

GEORGE: It's tough

CARL: You like that fishing, fighting a marlin, giving him slack, pulling him in, giving him slack, pulling him in. Of course, once you get him in mid-air, you could just shoot him. But I guess that would take the sport out of it, sport of sticking the gaff into the side of his mouth, dragging him into the bottom of the boat and clubbing him until he stops complaining

GEORGE: We eat them. You eat them

CARL: Never cared much for the water, boat's more trouble than it's worth

GEORGE: That's why you got to have a good captain, and they're tough to get, independent as hell, they drink your beer and if you ask them to replace it, they're gone

CARL: Those captains got you by the balls

(Pause.)

CARL: I don't care for sand and swamp and where the land goes flat, I just don't care for it. I like the turf under my feet, someplace that will take the print of a horse. Water doesn't remember...

GEORGE: Remember what

CARL: But it's been good for you, the boat business, nice and simple. Hell you can see what we go through with horses

GEORGE: I told him he should get out of it

CARL: I know you did, you were the smart one, keeping away from horses, tacklin' something easy

GEORGE: Simple but not easy

CARL: Whatever. Not like your Daddy, good to know your limits

GEORGE: I run a simple business, I make more than I spend. I don't know if he knew

CARL: What

GEORGE: His limits

CARL: He was a helluva man

GEORGE: But he bit off more than he could chew

CARL: He had a helluva reach

GEORGE: Sometimes I think it was too far

CARL: Do you think so

GEORGE: I keep it simple, he made it complicated

CARL: He had ambition

GEORGE: He tried to do too many things at once

CARL: He had imagination

GEORGE: It's not good to have too much imagination, you got to stick with something

CARL: You did

GEORGE: I did

CARL: With that little boat business he gave you

(Pause.)

GEORGE: He needed someone to run it. He asked me to come in and see if I could keep it afloat

CARL: Keep it afloat, that's funny

GEORGE: You need to know where you're at, you need to keep track, I know where I'm at

CARL: He's in the shithouse

GEORGE: What

CARL: Just what I said. But we got it covered, we got it covered

(Pause.)

GEORGE: Do you

CARL: Sure we do

GEORGE: You've got that two-year old

CARL: We've been disappointed in him

GEORGE: He's got promise

CARL: He had. He's not living up to it

GEORGE: He still might

CARL: Might...but when you got one with unfulfilled promise, that's when you got something. That's why he's the one I picked to kill

GEORGE: What

CARL: I mean we got to kill one of them, so I figure we plant the two-year old and the crops will grow

GEORGE: You're kidding

CARL: Of course I am

(Pause.)

CARL: He reads the paper cover to cover

GEORGE: But he doesn't talk about it

CARL: You know he can't talk

GEORGE: You talk about it to him

CARL: Not really

GEORGE: Then how do you know

CARL: The way his eyes move across it, they don't just lay on it, they move

GEORGE: But do they read what they're moving across

(Pause.)

CARL: Sometimes I think we should've done what you did, move from flesh into fiberglass

GEORGE: It's got its rewards

CARL: Boats are sleek as horses, but none of the complications

GEORGE: Right

CARL: As soon as you got blood and breath, you got complications

GEORGE: And what the hell are they, assets, same as boats

CARL: So you won't mind when we kill one

GEORGE: You said that once

CARL: There I said it again

(Pause.)

CARL: He wouldn't listen, not even to me, that's why we're where we are

GEORGE: Where

CARL: In the shithouse, just where I told you

GEORGE: You're in the shithouse only since he's in that chair

CARL: No, he's in the chair only since we're in the shithouse. He blew a fuse so the lights would go out before he'd have to see the state he was in

GEORGE: That's not true

CARL: The hell

GEORGE: Two fucking years, how could the place go to hell in two years

CARL: Because it had a running start, that's how, a flying start

GEORGE: That's not what I was told

CARL: He kept you in the dark, just turned the light on long enough for you to sign on the dotted line. He bought horses, Georgie

GEORGE: It's a horse farm

CARL: He bought them but he didn't sell them

GEORGE: He got attached

CARL: He wasn't attached to anything, he was just too arrogant to admit he had to sell one. So rather than sell, he borrowed against them, he put them deeper in hock

GEORGE: He ran the place, he built the place, he found ways, he would've still found ways

(Pause.)

GEORGE: You're in charge now, Carl, you're the one in charge

CARL: I'm the trainer, I'm not the businessman

GEORGE: You don't take the responsibility you mean, you don't make the tough decisions

CARL: I'm taking the responsibilty for this one

GEORGE: For what one

CARL: For killing the horse

GEORGE: You're serious

(Pause.)

GEORGE: You even had to call somebody in on that

CARL: There's no other way, look at the books

GEORGE: I will

CARL: Talk to the accountant

GEORGE: I'll do that too. I'll look over the whole operation

CARL: Go ahead

(Pause.)

CARL: On second thought, maybe you shouldn't

GEORGE: Why not

CARL: Maybe what's going to happen is going to happen one way or another and you shouldn't be too close

GEORGE: Or maybe you've been screwing around

CARL: I'm the fucking trainer. I'm down with the horses

GEORGE: If he had kept a closer eye...

CARL: He got tired of them

GEORGE: He loved them

CARL: He found a game he was good at for awhile, then he got tired of it

GEORGE: You didn't bring him home winners

CARL: That's where he wanted to be, in the clubhouse and the winner's circle. The horses are in the barn

GEORGE: Winners are in the winner's circle

CARL: He shoulda been in the boat business, instead of just setting you up in it

GEORGE: I told you...

CARL: And I told you...the two-year old's going to have a sudden attack of colic. I'll lay you odds he won't recover

(Pause.)

GEORGE: Why do you go and do that

CARL: There's no other way

GEORGE: I mean get me all the way up here to see you humiliate yourself

(Pause.)

GEORGE: He said you were weak

CARL: Your old man thinks everybody's weak

GEORGE: Not everybody

CARL: He thinks you're weak

(Pause.)

CARL: No, he doesn't. You're like him

GEORGE: Strong

CARL: Not strong, strong-willed

(Pause.)

GEORGE: I'm going to tell him

CARL: You are

GEORGE: You bet I am, I'm going to tell him he's got a criminal working for him

CARL: Go on

GEORGE: Maybe I won't

CARL: I didn't think you would

GEORGE: I don't want to upset him. I'll just fire you myself. Just pack up your things and get out. Don't talk to him, don't even look in his direction

CARL: Is that how it's going to be

GEORGE: That's how. I don't even want him to know. If not for him you'd be in jail by now. He always said you were weak, but he always thought you were straight. But a weak person can only be straight while things are good, isn't that right. Once they go bad...

CARL: You'd be doing me a favor

GEORGE: I think I would

CARL: Of course, you're on the note

GEORGE: The note...

CARL: The note, the note. You're personally on the note

(Pause.)

CARL: It all goes down the drain, houses, cars, boats, horses, all going down in one big whirlpool

GEORGE: We'll go to the bank

CARL: We been to the bank

GEORGE: There's other lenders, sure they take a bigger piece, but hell they'll...

CARL: They all got their bigger piece already

GEORGE: There's...

CARL: Don't you think we tried everything, do you really think I'd go for something like this if there was any other way

(Pause.)

GEORGE: You never brought it home for him

CARL: He never gave me anything to work with, he bought horses, but he cut corners

GEORGE: He depended on you to bring it home and you never did

CARL: If he would've let me do it my way

GEORGE: You disappointed, besides everything else...

(Pause.)

CARL: Besides, they say this whole place grew on a dead horse, like Indian corn on a fish

(Pause.)

CARL: You never heard about that? I believe your daddy visited the barn at night himself a long time ago

(George grabs him. They lock stares.)

CARL: What happened to you

(Carl shoves him off.)

CARL: What happened to you, Junior

GEORGE: Get out

CARL: Isn't it funny, they don't call you Junior. Your daddy they call Junior and you they call George

GEORGE: I want you out of here

CARL: Your mother was a beautiful woman

GEORGE: Forget her

CARL: I'm sure she's still beautiful, wherever the hell she is. Your daddy was never an early riser. Hell you'd have to be a fool to be an early riser with a woman like that in the hay. I was up early though, I was walking the horses

GEORGE: You were the trainer

CARL: I was in love with her

(Pause.)

CARL: You know that, there's no secret about that. Just knowing he was in bed with her I had to get the hell out and walk them. Those were the bad hours, those were the tough hours I had to get through. But eventually she left him

GEORGE: She just walked out

CARL: I knew she'd leave, I was just hoping she'd stop by the bunkhouse and pick me up on the way

GEORGE: So you tried to take his wife too

CARL: I didn't say that

GEORGE: You tried to take his wife and then you let the place go to hell

CARL: Innocent on both counts

    (Pause.)

GEORGE: My manager can handle things down in Miami. I'm going to stay up here for awhile, get things straightened out. Before you leave, I'd like you to at least show me where the books are, give me a list of the five largest lenders, tell me who we deal with at each one

CARL: You sure you want to see?

GEORGE: I want to see

CARL: We're cross-collateralized

GEORGE: So that's normal. Your problem is you're not a businessman so when things look bad, you don't know what to do, you get scared, but these are problems of business. Maybe you're not crooked after all, you just panic

CARL: ...without them knowing it

GEORGE: What

CARL: Come to think of it, I don't think they call it cross-collateralized. I mean we put up the same property for more than one loan, for a lot of loans...without bothering to tell the lenders. *(He points to a saddle.)* That saddle's got so much debt riding on it, if there was a horse underneath, his knees would buckle

GEORGE: That's fraud, Carl

CARL: Make a list of your five largest assets, house boat business car kids education, they're all going away

    (Pause.)

GEORGE: We can hold them off, we can renegotiate

CARL: Renegotiate, we can't renegotiate...this is the last stop, this is the last time we can do anything and have a prayer of getting away with it. Later on it will be too obvious

GEORGE: Have we been paying

CARL: We been missing

GEORGE: How many

CARL: A few

GEORGE: So, a few is alright

CARL: A few...and then a few more, and one day Tom from River National is talking to Dick from Citizen's Bank over at the Kiwanis lunch and he says Junior's missed a few payments, are they having trouble over there...none that I heard about but I don't care 'cause I'm secured up the

wazoo, I got a first on every fuckin' stirrup...how can you have a first, I
have a first...and Harry from the mortgage company leans over and says
the fuck you do, I got a lien on every weed before it even pops out of the
ground...and before you know it their jaws are hanging slack and their
mashed potatoes are getting cold
(Pause.)

CARL: We are hocked and hocked and hocked and hocked, we're in so deep,
Georgie, the only things that live down here are blind. It's now or never
(Pause.)

GEORGE: You never had anything of your own, did you, never had a house,
never married, never had a wife...never even had your own horse

CARL: I got a kid

GEORGE: You got a kid? I didn't know you had a kid

CARL: I mean a kid who will light up the two-year old. It's the only way

GEORGE: Were you with my mother. Just tell me
(Pause.)

CARL: You don't ask what happened to her, why'd she leave, was she unhappy,
what was she like, did she love her boy. You ask, was I with her

GEORGE: He was good to her, he provided for her

CARL: He provided for you, but he used to come down on you, it didn't matter who was around

GEORGE: Because he was strong, he was a perfectionist

CARL: I stood up for you

GEORGE: Because you were weak, you wanted to think I was weak, you wanted
to think I was like you, but I was like him

CARL: You had a window back there, a time you could have left, why didn't
you

GEORGE: I did leave, I went into the boat business in Miami
(Pause.)

GEORGE: I'm not your son, you don't have a son

CARL: I taught you to ride, remember that, when I taught you to ride
(Pause.)

CARL: You were good, you were good with the horses, you used to be good
with living things

GEORGE: I liked horses

CARL: You took to it, and you had a spark, but of course you deny it, you deny
it when you're not prepared to go forward with it, it's tough to admit

there was possibility that you did nothing about, better to say there was nothing possible at all. I think that's why I got you up here

GEORGE: Why

CARL: To talk me out of it

(Pause.)

CARL: But you got nothing to say

GEORGE: I told him to get rid of you

CARL: What'd he say

GEORGE: Where's he gonna go

CARL: I didn't mind her fucking around on him, he deserved it, but when she passed right over me to do it that's what pissed me off. That's what hurt

(Pause.)

CARL: Hey, maybe I could come down to Miami, what do you think, I could come down to Miami and sell those motorboats

(Pause.)

CARL: ...think I could do it?

GEORGE: Yachts

CARL: They call them yachts. How big does it have to be sizewise before it goes from motorboat to yacht

GEORGE: Speedboat

CARL: Beg your pardon

GEORGE: It goes from speedboat to yacht

CARL: Shit look at that, you got the lingo down, whole other world, horse is still a horse though, how big

GEORGE: Forty feet

CARL: Is that all. I could do that, I mean it's different than training, training you're teaching something, you're taking care of something, selling you're putting one over on them

GEORGE: It's a good product

CARL: How good

GEORGE: Real good

CARL: But the price, the play is in the price, to sell it for better than it is...unless of course you've bought it for a lot worse than it is. So what do you think, would you give me a start

GEORGE: You're finished

CARL: That's why I need a start, I could forget about all this, come down there straightaway, as they say in the yachting world, and you know the thing of it is, I got a headstart

GEORGE: Why

CARL: Naming horses and naming boats very similar. What do you say

(Pause.)

GEORGE: You couldn't kill a horse

CARL: I've lost my feel for horses, I've lost my love for them. They don't mean anything to me

GEORGE: But you couldn't kill one

CARL: You haven't been listening. I said I got this kid who could kill one

GEORGE: You didn't mention me

CARL: Of course I didn't mention you

GEORGE: You mention me the deal's off

CARL: What deal

(Pause.)

CARL: Of course I'm not going to mention you

GEORGE: Then why'd you get me up here

CARL: To get you dirty. I wanted you to be near this thing. I wanted you to stand inside it and breathe its air

GEORGE: You used to protect me, you said that

CARL: But now I wanted to get you dirty, I wanted you to see what it felt like

GEORGE: I used to look up to you

CARL: When did you change

GEORGE: When I got old enough to see what you were

CARL: What was that

GEORGE: You didn't get me up here to get me dirty. You got me up here because even this decision you can't make. You're paralyzed with him in that wheelchair, you're even more paralyzed than he is

(Pause.)

GEORGE: So what about the kid

CARL: He can do it

GEORGE: How do you know

CARL: I know

GEORGE: Has he done it before

CARL: I doubt it

GEORGE: Then how do you know

CARL: I can see by the way his eyes lay on things that he can kill a horse. I'm not saying that he doesn't have a good heart, that he's not kind to animals, just that there's a place inside him where a dead horse can find shade...if you know what I mean, where he can kill a horse and look the other way

GEORGE: Why

CARL: Am I a psychiatrist

GEORGE: I mean why will he do it

CARL: Because he's in a tough position like yourself

GEORGE: But I'm not killing a horse

CARL: You can't, you're not that kind of man, but you can stand by while it happens. Each according to his abilities

(Pause.)

CARL: He owes people with baseball bats some money

GEORGE: He could run off

CARL: He could, but then he's got to find a new job and a new place and be looking over his shoulder all the while he's doing it. This is easier, all's he's got to do is kill a horse

GEORGE: Which one

CARL: The two-year old, I told you

(Pause.)

CARL: He's not such a pretty horse

GEORGE: He's your favorite horse

CARL: I didn't say he wasn't, I just said he's nothing unique. He didn't meet expectations

GEORGE: He didn't win

CARL: That's what I'm telling you. If you had a horse with no expectations, you wouldn't have him insured, and if you had one that met expectations, you wouldn't have him killed

(Pause.)

CARL: A horse in the middle is playing with dynamite

(Pause.)

CARL: But I like his markings

GEORGE: A good-looking horse

CARL: I didn't say that

GEORGE: It sounded like that to me

CARL: It wasn't what I said

GEORGE: You said...

CARL: I said I like his markings, they appeal to me personally but I didn't say they'd appeal to anyone else

GEORGE: He's a beautiful horse

CARL: Do you believe that or are you just saying that because you know he's going to die

(Pause.)

CARL: See, now what did I tell you. Don't make a martyr out of the fucking horse

(Pause.)

CARL: Unless it helps you. If it helps you, do whatever the hell you want. Call him Saint Seabiscuit if that gets you through the night

GEORGE: I don't want to be around

CARL: I don't want you to be around

GEORGE: But I want to see the kid

CARL: I don't want you to meet him

GEORGE: I didn't say I want to meet him, I want to see him, I want you to point him out

CARL: I'll point him out

GEORGE: Without him seeing me

CARL: Fair enough

(Pause.)

GEORGE: What am I doing up here

CARL: You're visiting your dad

GEORGE: I mean what's my reason for being up here

CARL: To visit your dad

GEORGE: That's what I tell them

CARL: They're not going to ask

GEORGE: I mean if they do

CARL: They're not going to. This way we stay afloat

GEORGE: Are you sure

CARL: It's the only way

GEORGE: But do we stay afloat or are we doing it for nothing

CARL: We stay afloat

GEORGE: Have you worked it out, have you worked out the numbers

CARL: It will keep us afloat

GEORGE: For how long

CARL: Long enough for you to get off the note. Is that long enough

(Pause.)

GEORGE: I wasn't thinking of myself

CARL: You weren't thinking of Seabiscuit

GEORGE: I was thinking of my dad

CARL: Go see him. It's a nice afternoon, take him for a spin
  (Pause.)
GEORGE: He knew the horse business
CARL: He might not have known horses, but he knew the horse business. Sometimes I took a walk when I should've walked away
  (Pause.)
GEORGE: When did you take a walk
CARL: When they were talking...when they let the three-year old run, for instance, when they let him run so he could slip on the track. The bullet they put in him, that let the air out of the place, that was the beginning, that let the life out of your father
  (Pause.)
CARL: And you and me, we're both finished around horses, I guess you know that. They say the same soul moves through all the horses, so we're finished
GEORGE: I'm in the boat business
CARL: Maybe it moves through boats too. I mean I can still train them, but I'm finished around them. I'm persona non grata in the barn
  (Pause.)
CARL: How the ground accepts a horse's hoof, like they were separated and each step was a return...the air is shaped by the running of a horse, its gait calms down the sky...we're both finished around the excited air, the peaceful air, around the smells, the resting air, the wild air, have to find another air to breathe
GEORGE: I'll go see Dad
CARL: You do that
GEORGE: I'll take him for a spin
CARL: He'll like that
GEORGE: The air's fresh up here, it's a good time of year up here
CARL: It is. A time of year like this up here you don't get down there
GEORGE: It's chilly
CARL: He likes the chill, and you get some leaves, you get a few leaves, you can build a fire. You're in Florida but you get a little of the seasons...smell of burning leaves, he likes that
GEORGE: Everybody likes that
CARL: I didn't say they didn't. He likes it even now in his wheelchair wrapped in his blanket. You ever see a man in a wheelchair in Miami
GEORGE: I live in Miami

CARL: So you must've. They wrap them in blankets, they're in Miami but they wrap them in blankets. It's a bad place to be in a wheelchair. But up here, everybody loves this season, folks, folks in wheelchairs, horses, especially horses

GEORGE: All except for one

CARL: Don't kid yourself, he loves it too, he's too dumb not to love it

GEORGE: But he's gonna...

CARL: An animal doesn't see death coming

GEORGE: Who does

CARL: I mean he doesn't concern himself with it. That's the difference between us. We spend our life worrying about death

GEORGE: Is that it

CARL: In a nutshell

(Pause.)

CARL: He's livin' his life, he doesn't know a thing

GEORGE: He senses

CARL: He doesn't sense shit. You're just jerkin' yourself off is all it is, you're just jerkin' off a few tears in my direction

(Pause.)

GEORGE: He used to bow his head

CARL: What

GEORGE: ...when he'd see you coming down from the stable he'd kind of bow his head, like he was saying hello...

CARL: So

(Pause.)

GEORGE: And he'd keep it down so you could stroke him on the top of the head, you told me

CARL: So I told you

GEORGE: You liked that

CARL: So I liked it, so he came in Mr. Congeniality, but he didn't win place or show

(Pause.)

CARL: This is done, this is a done deal, over and done with so let's not dwell on the past. The thing we got to do is plan the changes, we got to figure out the changes we're going to make, because I'll tell you what the crime is...

GEORGE: Killing the horse and taking the insurance money

CARL: That's not the fucking crime, that crime is in the past, didn't I tell you.

(Pause.)

CARL: The crime is to light up the two-year old in vain, to piss away the money, not make it count. Because let me tell you, if you make it count you're gonna forget about killing it, but if you screw it up it's gonna be woulda shoulda coulda

(Pause.)

GEORGE: We should've stayed at the Sinclair station

CARL: What

GEORGE: You and me and Dad, when we came down from Richmond and broke down for two days...

CARL: Busted radiator, they were waiting for parts

GEORGE: I slept between you in the big bed

CARL: ...only one motel, only one bed

GEORGE: The dinosaur

CARL: You don't see them much anymore

GEORGE: The double sixes

CARL: The flying horse

(Pause.)

CARL: After the three-year old took that spill and they destroyed her, your mother wouldn't let him touch her, it was like the panic in that horse's eyes was spread all across her skin and she jumped from his touch...

(Pause.)

CARL: She blamed me

GEORGE: For what

CARL: For the three-year old

GEORGE: But

CARL: She expected that of me, she didn't expect it of him, compassion wasn't his department, but I gave in, like you said, I was a weak man

(Pause.)

CARL: I once knew a girl who thought it was cruel to ride a horse, can you imagine that, to even climb on his back

GEORGE: I want to hear him talk

CARL: But you know your dad can't...

GEORGE: The kid

(Pause.)

CARL: Just stray on over while we're talking. Make it look natural

GEORGE: I'll do that, I'll stray on over, I'll be looking at something else, I'll—

wait...wait...are we crazy, we can't do this, listen to us, listen to you...what are we talking about—we can't kill a horse

CARL: You're right, George, we can't...

(Pause.)

CARL: So don't look at it like we're killing him, look at it like we're cinching up his life a little

END OF ACT ONE

ACT TWO
SCENE 1

At George's house in Miami on an afternoon about a year later; in the Florida room which looks out through sliding glass doors onto a patio and a dock; Junior wheels himself across the Florida room through a dim corridor of light and out toward the patio. Lights up. Carl enters. George is sitting.

CARL: Done pretty well for yourself down here, George. Done real well. Got a place right on a canal

GEORGE: Waterway

CARL: Pardon

GEORGE: It's a waterway

(Carl peers.)

CARL: Now that you mention it, it does have the feel of a waterway. And we've done well too

GEORGE: You've done great

CARL: Hialeah, Calder, Gulfstream...

GEORGE: The way that horse came up from sixth in the seventh

CARL: He came up from seventh in the sixth

GEORGE: Pardon

CARL: He was back in seventh

GEORGE: I guess he was. But Carl...

CARL: And your daddy, when they wheeled him into the winner's circle and put those bouquets on him...It's a fortunate man who's covered with flowers before he's ready to be planted

(Pause.)

CARL: What do you call them, those flowers. You got them on the patio

GEORGE: Roses

CARL: No, the other ones

GEORGE: Gardenias

CARL: Gardenias, I didn't know they grew down here

GEORGE: All over

CARL: And their smell, you could choke to death on it. Is Junior okay

GEORGE: He's fine, he loves them

CARL: He loves everything down here, the sun, the water. I like it down here myself. What to you call this water, I mean its color

GEORGE: Turquoise

CARL: Yeah, turquoise, but more than turquoise. It's the color they're looking for when they settle for turquoise
(Carl moves toward the side so he can look at an angle through the sliding glass door.)
CARL: You can almost see the bay
(George moves toward Carl.)
GEORGE: You can, you can see all the way across. Here...
(George moves Carl.)
GEORGE: See
(They peer.)
CARL: I guess you can. And that motor...speedboat, you sell it?
GEORGE: That's a Chris Craft, I don't sell them
CARL: And that one...
GEORGE: That's out of Wilmington, it's not...
CARL: I bet you sold them all, I bet you hold the paper to every piece of flotsam and jetsam on the bay
GEORGE: I wouldn't say that
CARL: What would you say
(Pause.)
GEORGE: I think that corner lot is going to come up for sale
CARL: That's good, that's great. I guess you're in a position to take advantage of that
GEORGE: I will be
CARL: Nothing hanging over you
GEORGE: Nope
CARL: Look up, only the clear blue sky
GEORGE: It's a beautiful day
CARL: There's nothing hanging over you, is there
GEORGE: Nope
(Pause.)
CARL: Nothing hanging over Junior except some palm fronds. He's got the deed to the shade
GEORGE: He's doing well
CARL: In the winner's circle so much lately he's going to have to pay rent
GEORGE: ...pay rent
CARL: He will
GEORGE: That's funny
(Pause.)

GEORGE: So what are you doing down here, Carl

CARL: Came down with Junior

GEORGE: What's Junior doing

CARL: Came down with me. Need to look at some horses. When you're in the money, everybody's offering you horseflesh

GEORGE: But the fact is, Carl, you couldn't have come down at a worse time...this weekend with the boat show...

CARL: Don't I know it. It was hell getting a motel room. We're staying halfway to the Everglades

GEORGE: My boat should be here any minute to take Junior for a cruise. Why don't you go

(Carl refers to his jacket.)

CARL: Not dressed for it

GEORGE: Take off your jacket

CARL: You like it?

GEORGE: It's a nice blazer

CARL: Palm Beach. You do get the sun down here

GEORGE: That's why you have to stay in the water

CARL: Stay wet

GEORGE: That's the key

(Carl appears to be peering through the sliding glass doors.)

GEORGE: I just had those bougainvillea put in

CARL: I was looking at the doors. You got quite an expanse of glass. I'd be scared I'd go right through it

GEORGE: You get used to it

CARL: You could open them up

GEORGE: Got to keep them closed for the air conditioning

CARL: You do. It's tough to dress nice down here. Up there we get the heat in the summers, but even then you have the memory of cool. Inside your body, you have the cycle set up. Down here you don't have that. Cool just never comes around. You put on a nice blazer, go outside, get sweated up, come into the air conditioning and catch your death...

(Pause.)

CARL: Hey, remember that kid, that kid who used to work for Junior

GEORGE: What kid

CARL: That kid. The groom. You ever hear from him?

(Pause.)

GEORGE: Here's the boat now

(As they watch the boat tie up, Carl speaks.)

CARL: I was just wondering...you like this blazer, I like it, spending a lot of time in the clubhouse, at the rail, have to look the part...and Junior, well Junior is the elder statesman, and don't think he doesn't relish it, but he's in that chair, and so I...

(Bud enters after tying up the boat. Pause.)

CARL: I see the can—...waterway, but I don't see the stables

GEORGE: Bud's my right hand man

CARL: You didn't tell me he worked for you

GEORGE: I mentioned it

CARL: Did you

GEORGE: I think I did

CARL: I don't think so. I wouldn't've forgotten a think like that, the groom securing a position with a yacht broker. It's not something that would've slipped my mind

GEORGE: Carl was just asking about you

BUD: What was he asking

(Pause.)

BUD: So, you've been winning races

CARL: How long's this been going on

BUD: Hialeah...Calder

GEORGE: He's been working for me for three months

CARL: I didn't know you got that many ponies wanting to go for boat rides

(Pause.)

BUD: Is your dad all set

GEORGE: He's ready, and I told Carl maybe he'd like to go too

CARL: Didn't know you knew anything about boats

GEORGE: He learns fast

CARL: What does he learn

GEORGE: He drives them, he keeps them shipshape. He's even already working on the engines a little

CARL: Aren't you ever afraid he might touch two wires together and blow one up

(Pause.)

GEORGE: Carl, it's like I told you, with the boat show and everything...

CARL: You didn't tell me he worked for you

GEORGE: ...Bud has got to take these prospects out

CARL: You didn't tell—

GEORGE: So it slipped my mind
    (Pause.)

CARL: But one thing I don't get

GEORGE: What's that, Carl

CARL: One thing that's confusing me

GEORGE: What, Carl

CARL: *(To Bud.)* How do you keep the wind from blowing the cards out all
    across the Bay
    (Pause.)

BUD: None of that

CARL: Confine yourself to cockfights in Hialeah warehouses, do you

BUD: I don't have anything to do with that anymore

GEORGE: He takes out prospects, he does sales follow-up, he's my right hand
    man. Tell him about the tuxedo

BUD: You tell him

GEORGE: Go on and tell him, Bud

BUD: We've got this Cigarette, it glides, it hydroplanes, it flies low over the
    water, I don't care what kind of chop you got. So I pull up to the dock in
    a tuxedo and pick up the prospects. I tell them we're going to meet
    George at Pier 66 in Lauderdale. I open it up on the Intracoastal and I tell
    them, one drop on the tuxedo and the boat is yours
    (Pause.)

BUD: And the boat is yours

GEORGE: Are you listening to this

CARL: Lose many boats?

GEORGE: Not a one

BUD: I'm tearing the bay in half but not a drop on me

GEORGE: Because he's gliding over the water

BUD: And George closes them over dinner

CARL: You eat?

BUD: Sure I eat

CARL: But not with George and them

GEORGE: What's your problem, Carl

CARL: You never told me he worked for you
    (Pause.)

CARL: But that's good, that's fine, we're all doing well, in the money, in the
    winner's circle, in the blazer, in the tux, we all came out of this thing
    golden

GEORGE: What thing

CARL: This thing

(Pause.)

GEORGE: But Bud's really got to get busy, the boat show is like Derby Day for us, Carl

CARL: I didn't realize that

BUD: That's where we do our business, make our connections

GEORGE: And they've got these boats lashed together for a mile up the Intracoastal, you can just walk from one to the other, it's like a shopping mall, you can't do business like that

CARL: Can't you

GEORGE: Of course you can't, you got to get them on your boat out in the bay

CARL: Fuck or swim, is that it

GEORGE: What

CARL: That's what you used to say

GEORGE: I'm talking about getting them out on the bay, giving them the feel of a cruise

BUD: But you got to watch who you take, sometimes you get the sightseers, can we go past the cruise ships, which one's the Fountainbleau

CARL: Bet you want to drown them

BUD: Sometimes

CARL: It's funny, you can think about people drowning, but it's hard to think about drowning a horse, I mean it happens, they drown, but the snorting, the screaming, the eyes, seems like it should take a whole ocean to drown a horse

(Pause.)

CARL: But hell, some people do better with things that don't breathe in the first place

BUD: Excuse me

CARL: I mean you seem like you're in your element down here with the boats

BUD: I am, I'm...

CARL: And I'm glad, we're all doing good, doing good in the surf and doing good on the turf, and you know the first thing that happens when you're doing good, when you really got a good thing going, when you're finally out of the woods...

(Pause.)

CARL: They start calling you at dinner time

BUD: Who's calling

(Pause.)

CARL: But George, I guess they been calling you at dinner time for years

GEORGE: What are you talking about, Carl

CARL: How about you, Bud

BUD: Who is calling

CARL: I guess they haven't found you yet, kid

BUD: What's he talking about

CARL: The calls to buy stocks, buy bonds, buy condos, the calls to make contributions, George knows

GEORGE: Carl...

CARL: How do they do that, how do they know you're doing well even before you do, how do they get your name
(Pause.)

CARL: But I'll tell you what would be bad, I'll tell you what the worst would be

GEORGE: What would the worst be, Carl

CARL: The worst would be to find yourself back in the woods once you're out of it

GEORGE: Back in what woods

CARL: I mean after you're doing so good, after you're winning races, to find yourself back on your ass

GEORGE: Why would you do that

CARL: I didn't say I would. I just said it would be the worst, because before you didn't know no better, before you didn't know how the other half lived but now you do

GEORGE: And you like it

CARL: What's not to like

GEORGE: Then what's the problem

CARL: Who said there was a problem
(Pause.)

CARL: But I bet they'd still call you at dinner time, I bet that wouldn't stop

BUD: Who's calling

GEORGE: What happened now, Carl, what kind of trouble are you in

CARL: Who said I was in trouble

GEORGE: It's the calls at dinner time, isn't it, those boiler room operations and you were the sucker, they depend on guys like you, guys who don't know anything, who have new money in their pocket and are looking to make a quick buck, stupid guys so greedy they...

CARL: Oh, the call at dinner time, no, that wasn't from anybody trying to sell me anything

(Pause.)

CARL: That was from the insurance investigator

(Pause.)

CARL: I was wondering, does Bud ever get upset by the way the boat's lying in the water and just go apeshit on it. Because, as I understand it, it's amazing what a shovel will do to fiberglass

GEORGE: Carl

CARL: I don't like the way you're leanin' to starboard, wham

(Pause.)

GEORGE: What insurance investigator

(Pause.)

CARL: See, I thought like you did, that he was another hustler calling to sell me something, stocks...bonds...so when he says insurance, I figure life, and the receiver is about to go down, and then he says investigator

(Pause.)

GEORGE: They do follow-up...I'm sure it's...

CARL: Did he call you

GEORGE: No, he...

CARL: You, deckhand?

BUD: He didn't

CARL: Maybe he called you first and that's why they called me

GEORGE: He didn't call anybody

(Pause.)

GEORGE: What did he say

CARL: Oh, this and that

GEORGE: What

CARL: Just calling to follow-up, anytime a horse dies and they pay...you know...

GEORGE: What did I tell you, it's just follow-up, just doing their job

CARL: Did they call the stablehand and he came to you and you made him a deckhand

GEORGE: They didn't call anybody

CARL: And you made a deal

BUD: I didn't make any deal

(Pause.)

GEORGE: You still have the same problem, Carl. You panic

CARL: I panic

GEORGE: You do. You get a call and you run down here asking me to hold your hand

CARL: To hold my hand

GEORGE: Just like the last time. I shouldn't've come up there when you called the last time

CARL: You shouldn't've

GEORGE: No

CARL: I got you off the note

GEORGE: But you were up there. I was down here. I should have let you do it yourself. That's your problem, Carl, you've been taken care of. You're a sixty-year-old man who's been taken care of, first by Dad and then by me. And I blame myself

CARL: For what

GEORGE: For not throwing you in the deep end and telling you to swim

CARL: I swam alright, I kept the place afloat, I put him in the winner's circle

GEORGE: But you needed me to do it. And so now, at the first hint of trouble you panic, you pack Junior in the car and come running down to Miami

BUD: Trouble

GEORGE: There is no trouble

CARL: Is there any trouble, Bud

(Pause.)

BUD: There's no trouble

(Pause.)

CARL: I just thought of something funny. What if the deckhand just went at the waves with the shovel, forgot about the boat entirely and just tried to beat the hell out of the ocean. Now that would be something

GEORGE: Bud, why don't you get going

CARL: But if you do, just don't let the insurance investigator see you

BUD: What investigator

CARL: The one who called me around dinner time

GEORGE: What would he be doing down here, Carl, you didn't tell him anything about anything down here

(Pause.)

CARL: And if he takes you for a ride...

BUD: Why would he take me for a ride

CARL: I'm just saying if he does, I wouldn't want him to see the way your eyes lay on a horse. It would be a dead giveaway. So if you pass by a pasture, look the other way

(*Pause.*)

GEORGE: I asked you did you tell him anything

CARL: I didn't tell him a thing

GEORGE: Then what the hell would he be doing down here

CARL: You tell me, George, you tell me what deal you've made with the deckhand

GEORGE: No deal

CARL: You had some leverage coming into this, didn't you, Bud

BUD: I didn't have any leverage

CARL: What leverage, what did you tell them when they called

BUD: Nobody called

CARL: What did you tell them when they came to visit

(*Pause.*)

GEORGE: I hired Bud the same as Dad hired you

CARL: There was nothing the same about it

GEORGE: He came down and asked for a job

CARL: I didn't ask for a job, Junior needed me, Junior and I came up together

GEORGE: You didn't come up at all, Carl, you're still a hired hand at sixty

CARL: I run the show, I saved the place, Junior is in the chair, don't forget that. I'm the one taking care of business

(*Pause.*)

GEORGE: Bud's helping me take care of my business

BUD: I was polishing at first, that's all I was doing was polishing. But I did it well

GEORGE: He did

BUD: And soon I was taking the prospects out

GEORGE: He has a nice way with people

BUD: These Donzis sell themselves

CARL: Do they pay for themselves

GEORGE: We've got a well-to-do clientele, Carl

CARL: The rich didn't get rich by paying their bills

BUD: You should see the wads on them

CARL: Bet you have to shake it loose

BUD: I don't

CARL: Bet you have to board them, once in awhile, in your nice suit or your tuxedo

BUD: I said I don't

CARL: Bet you have to ask for it nice and then...

GEORGE: I told you, Carl, he's good with people
> *(Pause.)*

CARL: Some people are better with boats than horses

BUD: He said people, I'm good with people
> *(Pause.)*

BUD: And George is good with me

CARL: You don't have to say that. He doesn't have to say that, does he, George

BUD: He is

CARL: I know these people, Bud, they're a tough family to work for, I worked
> for his father, hell I still do, sometime we should have a talk you and me

BUD: I don't need to talk to you
> *(Pause.)*

CARL: Whose side are you on, Bud

BUD: You should go back up north

CARL: Who got you out of spring training

BUD: I work down here now

CARL: Up there down here it's all the same

BUD: It's different

CARL: It's no different
> *(Pause.)*

CARL: So come on, Bud, tell us how it was in the barn

BUD: It was fine. There was no problem in the barn

GEORGE: Forget about the barn. The barn is all over with

CARL: C'mon Bud, tell us, give us the play by play

GEORGE: He doesn't want to talk about this

CARL: Of course he does, he needs to. He needs to get it off his chest. Or did
> he get it off his chest already
> *(Pause.)*

BUD: I didn't get anything off my chest

CARL: You were a little drunk, weren't you

BUD: Who says I was drunk
> *(Pause.)*

BUD: Just a little, you have to be

CARL: Sure you do

BUD: I got nothing against a sleeping horse

CARL: Of course you don't. So you have to be drunk enough to do it but not so drunk that you fuck it up

GEORGE: Bud

CARL: You didn't get so drunk that you fucked it up, did you

(Pause.)

GEORGE: We've got work to do, Carl. We've got a boat show

CARL: We've got work to do?

GEORGE: Bud and me

CARL: Listen to him, he's made you a partner already. You own the bow and he the aft or vice versa? Tell me the truth, George, why do you keep him around

GEORGE: I told you

CARL: But tell me honest. Does he get the girls, is that why you keep him around

GEORGE: Carl...

CARL: C'mon, Bud, do you bring around some girls for George

BUD: George is married

CARL: So you keep them all to yourself. But you bring them around, it's nice to just have them around, especially down here where they don't wear much. Up there they have to wear clothes, I still remember this one you used to bring around

BUD: Which one

CARL: This one with the long dark hair

BUD: I had a few

GEORGE: Bud goes out

CARL: So you notice. I noticed, this one with this husky voice, and big chest. I used to think about her...when need be

(Pause.)

CARL: What the world has come to, George, your mother used to come down to the barn to visit me

GEORGE: Carl

CARL: I don't mean anything by it, she just used to. And now, I'm reduced to thinking of the stablehand's girls

BUD: I'm on the water, now

CARL: I'll put her in a bathing suit next time

(Pause.)

CARL: I...once I took my sweater off up over my head and I almost passed out...it was still so full of her...and I felt her lips on mine still kissing me, like when you think you're still wearing a hat but you've taken it off hours ago

(Pause.)

CARL: But these things, you can't talk about these things. Who the hell can you talk about them with. I could talk about them with Junior, but he can't talk

(Pause.)

CARL: So come on, Bud, when did they pick you up

BUD: Nobody picked me up

CARL: What was it for

BUD: They didn't pick me up

GEORGE: He told you, Carl

CARL: For the gambling, they find an IOU you signed?

BUD: I didn't sign any IOU

CARL: I know they picked you up, now are you going to tell me what it was for

GEORGE: How do you know they picked him up

CARL: I know because I know. They picked him up and he gave them my name

BUD: Who says I

CARL: Was it for the guy in the bar, for the guy you hit in the bar, you hurt him bad, you kill him is that what it was, you got some power in that arm, let me see that arm...I mean when you get mad, when you

(Bud is about to hit Carl.)

GEORGE: Bud!

BUD: I told you it was deep bleeding, I told you he was bleeding from the brain, you said he wasn't

GEORGE: Bud, don't talk to him, we have got things to do

CARL: You kill him?

BUD: I didn't kill anybody, all's I did was cuff him on the ear

CARL: An accident

BUD: You bet it was an accident but these guys they say attempted murder but...

GEORGE: What did you do

BUD: I told you, I...

CARL: And they had you for attempted murder but you had something else for them

BUD: I couldn't tell them about those guys, those guys would kill me you know that

GEORGE: So what did you do

BUD: I didn't do a thing, I didn't mention your name, you were nowhere near it, I didn't even think about your name I...It's just a fucking horse

(Pause.)

BUD: I told them about Carl

GEORGE: You stupid...

BUD: I told you, I left you out of it

GEORGE: Why the hell would you...

BUD: Attempted murder for cuffing him in the ear, you know how much time. And now I'm here doing a good job you said so, I clean them, I work on the engines

CARL: Now what did I tell you, George. I try to tell you what kind of men you have working for you

BUD: They start getting on you and getting on you till you can't see straight

GEORGE: Shut up

BUD: I told them I had a new life on the water but they start telling you about what it's like in jail and

GEORGE: I said...

BUD: What the hell do you want me to do

(Pause.)

CARL: I feel responsible, I'll take full responsibility, after all I introduced you, I found the kid

GEORGE: Full responsibility

CARL: For introducing you, for the introduction, I mean

(Pause.)

CARL: I mean for that, I'm not talking about anything else

GEORGE: Don't worry about it, Carl

CARL: I am worried

GEORGE: I'll take care of it

CARL: That's not like you, George

BUD: All's I did is I...

GEORGE: Don't worry, Bud, I said I'll take care of it

CARL: He means there'll still be a job waiting for you when you get out

BUD: Get out...I'm not going in

CARL: I bet he'll let you wear the captain's hat

BUD: I gave them Carl's name

CARL: You'll have to take it back

BUD: I'll give them yours, I'll give them—

GEORGE: I said don't worry

CARL: Look at the kind of men in your employ, George

(Pause.)

GEORGE: What are you getting so excited about, Carl...some kid gets picked up says anything to save his skin

CARL: Sure

GEORGE: What do they got on you, they got nothing. And the thing is, you never had an ownership interest, you never had any equity, you never had responsibility, that turns out to be the beauty of it

CARL: I don't follow

GEORGE: What motive would you have. You were never anything more than a hired hand...see, what would you have to gain

(Pause.)

GEORGE: It's funny how things work out

CARL: It's funny

GEORGE: See, now you came down here all bent out of shape, you talk it out, you see what happened, and now it will be taken care of

CARL: Right

GEORGE: I'm in the boat business, you're a hired hand, the kid's scared and makes up a crime...but there's no evidence, autopsies don't show a thing. The two-year old can't roll over on anybody

(Pause.)

CARL: And mum's the word on the bedside lamp

GEORGE: What bedside lamp

CARL: Bud knows what bedside lamp

BUD: I don't know what you're talking about

CARL: The one you pulled the cord from. Not that I blame you, I mean I never really knew a stablehand who read before bedtime. Mostly it's hit that sack and out like a light

BUD: I don't know what you're talking about

CARL: But wouldn't you know it, on the very night you take the cord from a bedside lamp some hotwalker is in the middle of a real page turner

(Pause.)

GEORGE: What are you getting at, Carl

CARL: Aah, it was probably just a girlie magazine and he wanted to get a better look at her pussy. But one way or the other that hotwalker needed the bedside lamp and when he checked to see if it was plugged in, there just wasn't any cord

GEORGE: What's he getting at, Bud

BUD: I don't know

CARL: Didn't I distinctly tell you about the pile of junked lamps and radios around back of the shed, didn't I distinctly tell you to take it from there and throw it into the lake afterward

BUD: I was...I was busy that night and...

GEORGE: You took it from a working lamp?

BUD: I...I don't know where I took it from...I...who says I did, I...

CARL: The man calling me at dinner time says, that's who says...

BUD: But I replaced it

CARL: Not in time

(Pause.)

CARL: But like you said, George, I got no interest in this

GEORGE: You're up there

CARL: I'm up there, but I got no interest. But listen, a kid like you, Bud, a big tough kid, you could do a little time, I mean if it came down to it

BUD: I'm not doing time

CARL: I mean if it doesn't all blow over, a little time at one of the minimum security farms, there'll probably be no time at all, but even if

BUD: It was your idea, I told them about you, I'll tell them about you again

CARL: And then afterward, there's the job, probably be promoted to admiral of the fleet. But if we aren't here, if there's no job, it's back to setting up the milk bottles and hope somebody doesn't hit you with the baseball bat

(Pause.)

BUD: They know I couldn't do it alone, I'm just a stablehand

GEORGE: You're not telling them about anybody

CARL: You see what you let into your house, George, he'll turn on you

GEORGE: Him, it was you, Carl, you're the one who brought him in

CARL: But you'll deal with him, won't you George

BUD: George...

(Pause.)

GEORGE: I'll take care of it

BUD: He will, I do a good job for him

GEORGE: He does

CARL: Sure he does

BUD: George will take care of me

GEORGE: I will

(Pause.)

GEORGE: As soon as you get out

BUD: What

GEORGE: It'll all be waiting for you

BUD: No way I'm...

GEORGE: We weren't there, we were nowhere near the barn

BUD: But...

GEORGE: I was in Miami, and Carl...

CARL: I was in town

BUD: You're not leaving me out there

GEORGE: I'll get you the best lawyer, I've already got one in mind

BUD: I'll take you all down

GEORGE: You won't take anybody down. There was only one person in the barn

BUD: No there wasn't

(Pause.)

BUD: Junior saw me. Junior saw me go into the barn

CARL: So, you coulda been going to shovel shit. Besides, he didn't see us

(Pause.)

BUD: It was quiet, real quiet. Walking through that barn it was like I was swimming underwater. Why is that

CARL: Why is what

BUD: Why is it that a sleeping horse quiets down a barn. An empty barn spooks you, you want to run right out, but a sleeping horse calms it right down, he makes you so calm you can almost kill him

CARL: Almost?

BUD: I went right up to him, I plugged in the cord, I attached one clip under his tail, just like you told me, I walked along him up to his face and reached with the other clip up toward his ear, my hand was shaking, it was shaking so hard, I thought all I have to do is get it close enough and the shaking will bring it right to him...but it wouldn't

GEORGE: You killed the horse, I know you killed the horse

(Pause.)

BUD: I ran out of the barn, I was just going to keep running the hell away from there, I didn't care about spring training or the guys from Daytona or...but Junior saw me

CARL: He saw you

BUD: He was waiting for me. He looked right at me still holding the cord and he pointed toward the barn. At first I thought he was going to start howling and bring the others, but then I saw he wasn't. So I went up to Junior and wheeled him back into the barn, past all the other stalls, right up to the horse

CARL: Junior spooks horses

BUD: I know. Junior plugged in the cord

CARL: Junior has no business with horses

BUD: I had to stroke the horse to calm him down...so that Junior could get close to him. I started stroking him and he started calming down
(Pause.)

BUD: I always thought that horses hated me but I think they like me. And when I'd got him calmed down...

GEORGE: Junior, don't tell me Junior...

BUD: He clipped the wire under his tail and then wheeled himself up the length of him, pulling himself hand over hand along his side, until he was in front with me, and when I stroked the two-year old, he bowed his head, like he does, and that's when Junior reached up quick as lightning and clipped it to his ear. And that horse just fell straight down out of the sky
(Pause.)

CARL: Look at that, Georgie, still the old man. He only lost once
(Pause.)

CARL: She came by the bunkhouse that night on her way out
(Pause.)

CARL: I knew she would, I had my gear packed, I was ready
(Pause.)

CARL: But she wanted to take you

GEORGE: Take me?

CARL: She wanted to leave with me and take you. I came out in the yard...the wind was blowing, the moon was out...she was wearing a scarf, we talked...we were calm as stones, but the trees were going out of their mind

GEORGE: What did you say

CARL: I said I couldn't let her leave Junior alone
(Pause.)

GEORGE: Why didn't you just go with her yourself

CARL: I couldn't leave you alone with Junior
(Pause.)

CARL: Bud

BUD: Yeah...

CARL: Which horse was it

BUD: What

CARL: Which horse did Junior clip the wire to

BUD: You know which horse. The two-year old
  (Pause.)

CARL: The two-year old. What did I tell you. Junior had you wheel him straight up to the two-year old. I always knew the two-year old was the one
  (Pause.)

CARL: I always knew how to pick a horse

(Lights down.)

END OF PLAY

Misreadings
by Neena Beber

BIOGRAPHY

Neena Beber's plays include *A Common Vision, Tomorrowland, The Brief But Exemplary Life of the Living Goddess, Failure to Thrive* and *The Course of It.* Theatres that have produced her work include The Magic Theatre, Watermark, New Georges, Workhouse Theatre, Padua Hills Playwrights Festival and En Garde Arts. Her plays have been workshopped and developed at Midwest PlayLabs, Audrey Skirball-Kenis Theatre, New York Theatre Workshop, the Public Theater's New Works Project, Circle Rep Lab, South Coast Rep, MCC and GeVa Theatre among others. Her short film, *Bad Dates*, was based on her one-act, *Food* (included in Broadway Play Publishing's anthology *Facing Forward*). She has received commissions from Amblin Entertainment/Playwrights Horizons and Sundance Children's Theatre and a MacDowell Colony Fellowship.

HUMANA FESTIVAL PRODUCTION

Misreadings was first performed at the Humana Festival of New American Plays, March, 1997. It was directed by Jennifer Hubbard with the following cast:

Ruth . . . . Maryann Urbano
Simone . . . . Jennifer London

and the following production staff:

Scenic Designer . . . . Paul Owen
Costume Designer . . . . Kevin R. MacLeod
Lighting Designer . . . . Ed McCarthy
Sound Designer . . . . Martin R. Desjardins
Properties Designer . . . . Ron Riall
Stage Manager . . . . Julie A. Richardson
Assistant Stage Manager . . . . Andrew Scheer
Dramaturg . . . . Liz Engelman
Casting . . . . Laura Richin Casting

CHARACTERS

RUTH: a teacher
SIMONE: a student

PLACE

A college professor's office, minimally represented: just a desk with a tall stack of blue exam composition books on it.

MISREADINGS

Lights up on Simone.

SIMONE: It's important to dress right. I want to look slick. To look sleek. To look like a fresh thing. I've got a message. I'm the message. Study me, baby, because in ten minutes, I'm outta here.
(Simone lights a cigarette. Lights up on Ruth.)

RUTH: What are the issues for which you would kill? I like to ask my students this on their first day of class. I assign novels where the hero or heroine kills, or is killed. I try to bring it home. They tell me they would kill to defend their family. They'd kill to defend their friends. I ask them if they would kill for their country...for their freedom...what would it take?

SIMONE: I'd kill for a pair of Prada velvet platforms in deep plum. *Those* are to die for.

RUTH: Simone. I didn't know what she was doing in my class. Neither did she, apparently. *(To Simone.)* Nice segue, Simone; would we be willing to die for the same things we'd kill for? *(Out.)* I wanted her to participate. She usually sat in the back, never spoke, wore too much lipstick and some costume straight out of, what, *Vogue*. When she did speak, it was always—disruptive.

SIMONE: I'd die for love except there ain't no Romeos, not that I've seen; I'd take a bullet for my daddy but he's already dead; I'd die of boredom if it were lethal, but I guess it isn't.

RUTH: If I couldn't inspire her, I wanted her gone. I asked her to come to my office hours. I asked her several times. She was failing, obviously. I would have let her drop the class, but it was too late for that. She never bothered to come see me. Not until the day before the final exam. She wanted me to give her a passing grade. *(Ruth turns to Simone.)* How can I do that, Simone? You haven't even read the material. Have you read *any* of the material?

SIMONE: I don't find it relevant.

RUTH: If you haven't read it, how do you know? You may find yourself surprised. *Anna Karenina* is wonderful.

SIMONE: It's long.

RUTH: Why not give it a shot?

SIMONE: The books you assign are depressing. I don't want to be depressed. Why read stuff that brings you down? Kafka, Jesus Christ—I started it, OK? The guy was fucked up.

RUTH: So you were moved at least.

SIMONE: Moved to shut the book and find something more interesting to do.

RUTH: That's too bad; you might find one of these books getting under your skin, if you stick with it. Haven't you ever read something that's really moved you?

SIMONE: Nothing moves me, Dr. Ruth.

RUTH: I'm going to have to ask you to put out that cigarette.

SIMONE: OK, ask. *(She puts it out.)* See art or be art. I choose the latter.

RUTH: Somebody must be paying for this education of yours. I imagine they expect a certain return for their money.

SIMONE: How do you know I'm not the one paying for it?

RUTH: I don't believe someone who was spending their own money would waste it so flagrantly.

SIMONE: OK, Dad chips in.

RUTH: Would that be the same father you said was dead?

SIMONE: That was a joke or a lie, take your pick.

RUTH: You're frustrating the hell out of me, Simone.

SIMONE: I don't consider it a waste, you know. I like the socialization part.

RUTH: If you fail out of this school, you won't be doing any more "socialization."

SIMONE: You assume that I'm failing the others.

RUTH: So it's just this class, then? That you have a problem with?

SIMONE: Dangling. *(Referring to her grammar.)* Do you enjoy being a teacher?

RUTH: Yes, I do.

SIMONE: So I'm paying for your enjoyment.

RUTH: It's not a sin to enjoy one's work, Simone.

SIMONE: I just don't think you should charge me, if it's more for your pleasure than for mine.

RUTH: I didn't say that.

SIMONE: Did you ever want to teach at a real school, not some second-rate institution like this?

RUTH: I like my job. You're not going to convince me otherwise.

SIMONE: Four thousand two hundred and ninety-eight.

RUTH: That is—?

SIMONE: Dollars. That's a lot of money. Do you think you're worth it? Do you think *this class* is worth it? Because I figured it out: this is a four credit class, I broke it down. Four thousand two hundred and ninety-eight. Big ones. Well, do you think that what you have to teach me is worth that? Come on, start talking and we'll amortize for each word.

RUTH: You're clearly a bright girl. You can't expect an education to be broken down into monetary terms.

SIMONE: You just did. That's a lot of money, right? It's, like, food for a starving family in a fifth-world country for a year at least. It's a car. Well, a used one, anyway. Minus the insurance. Suddenly this number doesn't sound so huge. It's a couple of Armani suits at most. I don't even like Armani. So hey, come on, can't you even say, "Yes, Simone, I am worth two Armani suits. I have that to offer you..."

RUTH: I can't say that, no.

SIMONE: No useful skills to be had here.

RUTH: The money doesn't go into my pocket, by the way.

SIMONE: I think it should. It would be more direct that way; you'd feel more of a responsibility. To me. Personally. Don't you think, Dr. Ruth?

RUTH: I'd prefer that you not call me that.

SIMONE: But your name is Ruth, and...you do have a Ph.D., don't you?

RUTH: OK, Simone.

SIMONE: Wrong kind of doctor, man. All you're interested in is a bunch of books written a hundred years ago, and the books written about those books; you're probably writing a book about a book written about a book right now, am I right?

RUTH: If you don't see the connection of books to life, you aren't reading very well. I want you to try. Can you do that? Books might even show you a way to live.

SIMONE: I'm already living, Dr. Ruth. Are you? Because it looks like you haven't changed your hairstyle in twenty-five years.

RUTH: *(Insulted but covering.)* Well, that's before you were born, Simone.

SIMONE: Stuck in your best year? Because I see you in a close-cropped, spiky thing.

RUTH: That's enough.

SIMONE: And you might want to do something about the way you dress.

RUTH: Have you been in therapy?

SIMONE: Don't think that's an original suggestion.

RUTH: I'm not suggesting anything. I simply want to point out that this is not therapy. I am a teacher, not your therapist. You can't just waltz into my office and say whatever hateful thing you please.

SIMONE: I don't know how to waltz.

RUTH: I'm giving up here, Simone. You don't like my class, you don't like me, you want to fail out, I can't stop you. *(Ruth goes back to her work. Simone does not budge. Ruth finally looks up.)* What?

SIMONE: Drew Barrymore would move me.

RUTH: Who?

SIMONE: I think Drew would do it. Getting to meet Drew.

RUTH: Who's Drew Barrymore?

SIMONE: Damn, you really should know these things. She's extremely famous. She's been famous since she was, like, born. I saw her on TV yesterday and she was so real. She connected. You know? You really might relate to your students better if you got a little more up to date.

RUTH: You might be right. But you might not be so behind in class if you spent a little less time watching television.

SIMONE: Drew is a *film* star, she's in *films*. Don't you even go to the movies? Probably only the ones that are totally L-Seven. And I know you don't know what that means. *(She makes an 'L' and a '7' with her fingers.)* Square? Anyway, Drew was on TV because she was being interviewed. They have these daytime talk shows nowadays?

RUTH: I've heard of them.

SIMONE: And this chick was in the audience and she started to cry. Because she couldn't believe she was there in the same room with Drew, who's been famous forever, right? She was just, like, sitting there sobbing. And this chick, she had her bleached blond hair pasted down real flat, and she was wearing a rhinestone barrette just like Drew used to, but that whole look is so old Drew, so ten-minutes-ago Drew. The new Drew is sleek and sophisticated and coifed and this girl, this girl who wanted to be Drew so bad, she wasn't even *current.*

RUTH: I don't think we're getting anywhere.

SIMONE: And that is so sad. Because the thing about Drew is, she is always changing. It's a constant thing with her, the change. And that is, like, what you've got to do...keep moving or you die. Drew knows that. How to invent yourself again and again so you can keep being someone that you like, the someone that you want to be. And once you're it, you've got to move on. Now where was it you were hoping we'd get to?

RUTH: The exam is tomorrow morning at 9 AM. If you read the material, any of the material, I might actually be able to give you a passing grade. But right now I don't think we need to waste any more of each other's time.

SIMONE: *(Starts to go.)* You might have said that I go to the movies the way you read books. I would have pointed that out, Dr. Ruth.

RUTH: Yes. Well. I suspect we don't think very much alike.

SIMONE: A wall between our souls? *(Ruth looks at her, about to say something.)* I'm sorry if I've been rude. I'm sure a lot of people like your class. Maybe I wasn't raised well. I'm sure somebody's to blame. *(Simone goes to write in a blue exam book.)*

RUTH: The next day she showed up at nine on the dot. I felt a certain pride that I had somehow managed to reach her, that she was finally going to make a real effort, but she handed in her blue book after a matter of minutes. I was rather disgusted and let it sit there, until a pile formed on top of it, a pile of blue books filled with the scrawling, down-to-the-last-second pages of my other more eager, or at least more dutiful, students. Later I began to read them straight through from the top, in the order they were stacked in. I wasn't looking forward to Simone's.

In answering my essay question about how the novel *Anna Karenina* moves inevitably toward Anna's final tragic act, my students were, for the most part, thorough and precise. They cited the events that led to Anna's throwing herself in front of the train, touching on the parallel plots and the broader social context. I was satisfied. I felt I had taught well this last semester. My students had learned.

In the blue book she had written "All happy people resemble one another, but each unhappy person is unhappy in their own way." So I guess she had read *Anna K;* the opening sentence, at least. My first instinct was to correct the grammar of her little variation. There was nothing else on the page. I flipped through the book; she'd written one more line on the last page: "Any world that I'm welcome to is better than the one that I come from." I'm told it's a rock lyric. Something from the seventies. *Anna* was written in the seventies, too, funnily enough, a century earlier.

I would have given Simone an F, but I noticed she had already marked down the failing grade herself, on the back of the book. Or maybe the grade was for me.

By the time I came to it, days had passed. I didn't leap to conclusions. Come to think of it, Anna's suicide always takes me by surprise as well, though I've read the novel many times and can map its inexorable progression.

(Simone, just as before...)

SIMONE: That's a lot of money. Do you think you're worth it? Do you think this class is worth it? *(Ruth turns to her, wanting to reach out.)*

RUTH: I live in worlds made by words. Worlds where the dead can speak, and conversations can be replayed, altered past the moment of regret, held over and over until they are bent into new possibilities.

SIMONE: Do you think I'm worth it? Am I? Am I? Am I?

RUTH: I live there, where death is as impermanent as an anesthesia, and the moment of obliteration is only...a blackout. *(Simone lights a cigarette as lights blackout.)*

SIMONE: Ten minutes, time's up—told you I'd be gone by now, baby.

(The flame illuminates her for a moment, darkness again.)

END OF PLAY

Private Eyes

a comedy of suspicion

by Steven Dietz

I will eat you slowly with kisses
even though the killer in you
has gotten out.

—Anne Sexton

BIOGRAPHY

Steven Dietz's award-winning play, *God's Country* (Humana Festival, 1989), has been widely produced across the United States, as well as in Johannesburg and Pretoria, South Africa. *Lonely Planet* (PEN USA Award in Drama, Outer Critic's Circle Nomination, Drama-Logue Award) has been seen off-Broadway, at numerous regional theatres and internationally. Other plays include *Handing Down the Names, Trust, Halcyon Days, Ten November, Foolin' Around with Infinity* and *More Fun than Bowling*. His adaptations include Shusaku Endo's *Silence* (Yomuiri Shinbun Award, Japan); Joyce Cheeka's *The Rememberer* (Lila Wallace/Reader's Digest Award); and Bram Stoker's *Dracula*. Mr. Dietz has directed world premieres of John Olive's *The Voice of the Prairie*, Kevin Kling's *21-A* and Jon Klein's *T Bone N Weasel* (Humana Festival, 1987), among others. His most recent plays are *Still Life with Iris* (Kennedy Center Fund for New American Plays Award) and *The Nina Variations*.

HUMANA FESTIVAL PRODUCTION

Private Eyes was produced at the Humana Festival of New American Plays, March 1997. It was directed by Steven Dietz with the following cast:

Matthew	Lee Sellars
Lisa	Kate Goehring
Adrian	V Craig Heidenreich
Cory	Twyla Hafermann
Frank	Adale O'Brien

and the following production staff:

Scenic Designer	Paul Owen
Costume Designer	David Zinn
Lighting Designer	Ed McCarthy
Properties Designer	Mark J. Bissonnette
Stage Manager	Juliet Horn
Assistant Stage Manager	Andrew Scheer
Dramaturg	Liz Engelman
Casting	Sandra Grand

FIRST PRODUCTION

Private Eyes received its world premiere at the Arizona Theater Company in May, 1996. It was directed by David Ira Goldstein with the following cast:

Matthew . . . . R. Hamilton Wright
Lisa. . . . . Sally Wingert
Adrian. . . . . David Pichette
Cory. . . . . Katie Forgette
Frank . . . . Jeff Steitzer

and the following production staff:

Scenic Designer . . . . Scott Weldin
Costume Designer . . . . Rose Pederson
Lighting Designer. . . . . Rick Paulsen
Sound Designer . . . . Steven M. Klein
Dramaturg . . . . Rebecca Million
Stage Manager . . . . Dawn Fenton

CHARACTERS

MATTHEW: a man in his thirties.
LISA: a woman in her thirties.
ADRIAN: a British man in his early thirties.
CORY: a woman in her late twenties.
FRANK: a man *or* woman, fifty.

TIME AND PLACE

The present. Various rooms in an American city.

SETTING

A rehearsal studio that can be transformed, quickly and simply, into a variety of other locales. This is a play predicated on surprise and misdirection, therefore the scenic elements of any given scene should convince us that what we are seeing is real, is "the truth"—until the story of the play reveals it to be otherwise.

PLAYWRIGHT'S NOTE

Private Eyes began as a lie.

Years ago I was sitting in a hotel room in Louisville, Kentucky, writing a scene in which two lovers fail to speak the truth. And, like a lie, the play grew. It began to go to greater and greater lengths to keep its own deceit afloat. It took my sense of structure for a ride and built a web of such complexity that clarity (aka "truth") was rendered virtually impossible. And even now, years later, sitting in a hotel room in Tucson, I think back to that first scene and say to myself: it started so simply. Doesn't it always.

I have a friend who assures me that he is incapable of jealousy. He has convinced his wife of this fact. I admire him for this. I envy him this. And I don't—in my heart's heart—believe him for a minute. Jealousy is part of love's arsenal, with suspicion as its fuse. And though I agree with Camus' adage that "no man has ever dared describe himself as he is"—I have tried to write about my own fascination with the high-wire act known as "an affair": the insidious power of suspicion, the delicious fever of deception…and the accompanying sobriety of truth. For beneath the headlines of our heartache lies something quieter, simpler: the fear of loss. The failure of love to answer its own promise. The low-level panic of two people, alone, looking in each other's eyes, with nowhere to run. Nothing between them but distance. Nothing awaiting them but time.

A play about lies must be a comedy, because only laughter can make us recognize truths that we're not fond of. Only laughter is generous enough to hear us out, to listen to our foibles and our familiar debacles…and let us think that next time, *next time*, it will be different.

Thanks for taking the ride.

Steven Dietz
5 April 96
Tucson

PRIVATE EYES

ACT ONE
Music: Joe Jackson's rendition of "Is You Is or Is You Ain't My Baby?"
—intro only.

As the Intro to the song ends, lights reveal—

A Rehearsal Studio. In the middle of the room, a small round table and two chairs. At one end of the room, a long table cluttered with resumés, scripts in red folders, pencils and coffee cups. A small trash can is next to the table.

Matthew sits behind the table.

MATTHEW: Next. *(Lisa enters, carrying a shoulder bag.)* Hello.
LISA: Hi.
MATTHEW: *(Rifling through the resumés.)* You are—
LISA: Lisa. *(She hands him her resumé.)* Lisa Foster.
MATTHEW: Have I seen you before?
LISA: I don't think so.
MATTHEW: Your face is awful.
LISA: Umm, well—
MATTHEW: *(Looking at her photo.)* Get a photo that does you justice. *(She stares at him.)* Well. Let's get started. *(She moves to the center of the room. He sits behind the table.)* You're reading Carol, yes?
LISA: Yes.
MATTHEW: Did you have a chance to look at the scene?
LISA: Yes.
MATTHEW: Good.
LISA: From the entrance?
MATTHEW: Yes.
    (Lisa moves to a corner of the room. Looks back to Matthew.)
LISA: Is there something you're looking for?
MATTHEW: Yes. Whenever you're ready.

(Pause. Then, using her script as a tray, Lisa enters the scene. She speaks to the [unseen] customer in the chair.)

LISA: Hi. What can I get you to drink?

(Pause.)

Can I start you off with something from the bar?

(Pause.)

Wine.

(Pause.)

Beer.

(Pause.)

HELLO.

(Silence.)

Look. Why don't I give you a little more time? I have other customers who actually take their sunglasses OFF to read the menu and actually acknowledge my questions when I ask them—

(Starts off, stops.)

Oh, god. You're Derek Savage—no, right, that's okay, you don't have to answer. I understand. They'd mob you in here. Oh, god, Mr. Savage. I've seen all your—oh, god, I'm saying it. I always thought that if I met you I'd have something more original to say than "I've seen all your films and I'm a big—" Wow. What?

(Looks at her script, nods "Yes".)

Uh-huh.

(Looks at her script, shakes her head "No".)

Huh-uh.

(She stares at him and then…blushes …looks away.) Thank you. Really. Well…why don't I give you a little more time with the menu and then I'll—

(Looks at her script, shakes her head "No".)

Huh-uh.

(Turning the page in her script, nods "Yes".)

Uh-huh.

(She stares at him and then…slowly covers her mouth with her hand..)

My, uh, food is up. I need to go and do some, uh, waitressing, so—

(She starts to go, but—Something he has said stops her. She stares at him. She looks over her shoulder, around the room. Then she sits in the chair at his table, across from him. She extends her hand, and "shakes" with the air in front of her.)

Carol. Carol Davis.

(A pause, then Lisa lowers her hand and looks up at Matthew, expectant. He stares at her.)

MATTHEW: Okay. Good. Thank you, Lisa.

(He makes some notes on a pad in front of him. She waits, hopeful for him to say something more—but he does not look up. She gathers up her things and starts off.)

Are you in a hurry?

LISA: I thought you were done with me.

MATTHEW: I'm not done with you. Have you ever waited tables?

LISA: *(Setting her bag down.)* Umm...

MATTHEW: *Umm?* There's no umm here. This is a simple question. Have you waited tables or not?

LISA: Well, I—

MATTHEW: People think there are things I want to hear. I don't know where they get that notion. I ask direct questions and then watch *glaciers* form on the faces of people that would eat me alive anywhere else. If we were at a bar and I introduced myself and asked if you'd ever waited tables, you wouldn't hesitate. You wouldn't try to read me for the proper response. You would say yes or no, wouldn't you?

LISA: Yes.

MATTHEW: And why do we think that is?

LISA: Here you have power. Anywhere else you'd have none.

(Silence.)

MATTHEW: Let me try this one more time. Have you ever—

LISA: No.

MATTHEW: Good. Thank you for your honesty.

LISA: You're welcome.

MATTHEW: Truth is air. And air is precious around here.

LISA: Do you want me to do it again?

MATTHEW: Oh, yes. And this time I'm looking for a little something more. A stronger relationship between you and Derek Savage. A bit more *impact*. Don't you think that is needed?

LISA: Absolutely.

MATTHEW: That's lacking, isn't it?

LISA: Yes.

MATTHEW: And why do we think that is?

LISA: We think maybe because right now he's a chair.

(He stares at her.)

MATTHEW: People think I have no sense of humor, but I actually—are you married?

LISA: Yes.

MATTHEW: But I actually do have a sense of humor. I think humor is vital, life-giving. I think humor is air.

LISA: I thought truth was air.

MATTHEW: Let's begin.

LISA: With the chair again?

MATTHEW: Don't you believe you can play a love scene with a chair?

LISA: *(Setting her script down.)* I should just go—

MATTHEW: Don't you believe we project our loved ones? Don't you believe we form a picture in our head and then cast that picture like a shadow onto the person we're with? Don't you think the lover we imagine is actually more real than the one that stands before us?

LISA: *(Turning to go.)* You're not going to want me in your play—

MATTHEW: I want to know this.

(Pause.)

Really.

LISA: I don't think you're describing love. You're describing vanity. If you'd like me to play the scene as though it were about myself and my image of another person's love for myself, I can do that. But I think that's cheap. And hollow. And utterly insignificant.

MATTHEW: But, perhaps that is acting.

(She looks at him, hard. Then she walks up very close to him.)

LISA: Acting is the cold hard fact that someone is standing in front of you and you look into their eyes and they want something from you—and you from them—and through some combination of bloodshed and eloquence you find your place with each other. That is acting. What you're describing is one person's ability to manipulate events around them and keep their hands clean in the process.

MATTHEW: Doesn't that happen? Haven't you seen that happen?

LISA: Yes, I have.

MATTHEW: And what would you call that?

LISA: Directing.

(He stares at her.)

MATTHEW: I'll read with you.

(He grabs a script and sits in the chair. He takes sunglasses from his pocket and puts them on.)

Whenever you're ready.

LISA: *(Entering.)* Hi. What can I get you to drink?

(Pause.)

Can I start you off with something from the bar?

(Pause.)

Wine.

(Pause.)

Beer.

(Pause.)

HELLO.

(Beat.)

Look. Why don't I give you a little more time? I have other customers who actually take their sunglasses OFF to read the menu and actually acknowledge my questions when I ask them—

(She starts off as he removes his sunglasses, and looks up at her. She stops.)

Oh, god. You're Derek Savage—no, right, that's okay, you don't have to answer. I understand. They'd mob you in here. Oh, god, Mr. Savage. I've seen all your—oh, god, I'm saying it. I always thought that if I met you I'd have something more original to say than "I've seen all your films and I'm a big—" Wow.

MATTHEW: *(A British accent.)* Welsh.

LISA: What?

MATTHEW: Your family. Welsh, a little Scottish, a dash of Brit. Close?

LISA: *(Nodding "Yes.")* Uh-huh.

MATTHEW: And maybe, way back, some German.

LISA: *(Shaking her head "No.")* Huh-uh.

MATTHEW: Well, your ancestors did you proud. You are drop-dead gorgeous.

LISA: Thank you. Really.

(Pause.)

Well, why don't I give you a little time with the menu and then I'll—

MATTHEW: Are you married?

LISA: *(Shaking her head "No.")* Huh-uh.

MATTHEW: Boyfriend?

LISA: *(Nodding "Yes.")* Uh-huh.

MATTHEW: See that he worships you. Settle for nothing less.

(She stares at him, caught in his gaze.)

LISA: My, uh, food is up. I need to go and do some, uh, waitressing, so—

MATTHEW: Why don't you join me?

(She stares at him, glances around the room.)

Let people talk. They can't touch us.

(He pulls back her chair from the table and she sits. He sits across from her. Extends his hand.)

Derek. Derek Savage.

(She shakes it, saying—)

LISA: Carol. Carol Davis.

(They hold hands for a moment, then Matthew pulls away.)

MATTHEW: Now, I believe you.

LISA: What's that?

MATTHEW: Now I believe you've never waitressed.

(He quickly returns to his table, shuffles papers.)

LISA: So, that wasn't what you were looking for?

MATTHEW: People don't know what they're looking for. They just know they're looking. Well, thanks for coming in—

(Reading the name off her resumé.)

Lisa.

(He tosses her resumé into the trash can. He speaks, brightly.)

We've done our work. It's lunchtime.

(Music: "Is You Is or Is You Ain't My Baby?"—instrumental break. Lights shift to—

A Restaurant. A small table with two chairs. Matthew sits, alone. He lifts a menu from the table, looks at it, checks his watch, waits.

Lisa enters, now wearing a waitress apron. She stops for a moment when she sees him—then approaches the table. She stands near him, pen at the ready.

Music fades out.)

LISA: Hi. What can I get you to drink?

(He looks up, sees her.)

MATTHEW: Wait a minute. You said you—

LISA: I lied. Something from the bar?

MATTHEW: You work here?

LISA: Not according to my manager. Do you need a little more time?

MATTHEW: I—uh—no, I'm in a hurry.

LISA: Okay, shoot.

(He stares at her, disbelieving. Then he turns to his menu.)

MATTHEW: How's the salmon?

LISA: Very good.

MATTHEW: And the linguine?

LISA: Very good.

MATTHEW: I see. What about the veal?

LISA: Very good.

MATTHEW: I suppose the entire menu is very good.

LISA: Yes. Very good.

MATTHEW: And would you tell me if something wasn't?

LISA: No, I would not.

MATTHEW: A good waitress would tell me.

LISA: Exactly. Now, what do you want?

MATTHEW: Why did you lie to me?

LISA: That bugs you.

MATTHEW: Of course it does.

LISA: Why should it matter if a stranger lies to you?

MATTHEW: You're not a stranger.

LISA: We've seen each other twice.

MATTHEW: In ten minutes.

LISA: Let's pick a china pattern.

(She leaves.)

MATTHEW: Hey. I need to order—

(He looks around. Looks at his watch. Lisa arrives with a glass of red wine. Sets it in front of Matthew.)

What's this?

LISA: Our best Merlot.

MATTHEW: *(Lifting his menu.)* I'm ready to or—

LISA: *(Taking his menu from him.)* You're in a hurry. I ordered for you.

MATTHEW: You can't do that.

LISA: Sure I can.

MATTHEW: Why?

LISA: I have power here. Get used to it.

(She stares at him.)

MATTHEW: I'm not in a hurry.

LISA: You lied.

MATTHEW: I changed my mind.

LISA: There's a difference?

MATTHEW: Yes.

LISA: Do tell.

MATTHEW: So, you're married?

LISA: Ten minutes ago I was.

MATTHEW: And are you still?

LISA: *More so.*

MATTHEW: Let me ask you something—

LISA: Your food is up.

(*She leaves. Matthew sips his wine. Stares front. Looks around. Looks at his wine. Pause. He picks up the small box of matches that is on the table. He shakes it and hears nothing, fearing it is empty. He opens it and happily discovers that there is one match left. He lights it and lets it burn, staring at it. Blows it out. Then, using his knife, he scrapes some of the charred black match into his wine. He quickly hides the burnt match and wipes his knife clean, as—*

Lisa arrives with a covered food plate. Before she can unveil it, Matthew lifts his wine glass.)

MATTHEW: I have a problem.

LISA: That's obvious.

MATTHEW: My wine. It has specks in it. Black specks. I'll need to send it back.

LISA: That's our best Merlot.

MATTHEW: Specks.

LISA: Interesting. Why do we think that is?

MATTHEW: I'm Matthew—

LISA: I know who you are.

MATTHEW: I just wanted to say hello, officially.

LISA: *Officially?*

MATTHEW: Out of the context of work.

LISA: Work?

MATTHEW: The audition.

LISA: You call that work? You sit there and get paid for having opinions and you call that *work*?

MATTHEW: It's what I do.

LISA: Believe me, I'd really love to sit here and get paid to tell people whether *I like the way they eat.* Don't have to make the food, don't have to serve it, and don't have to eat it—I just speak my mind and, miraculously, day after day, everyone mistakes my *criticism for accomplishment.*

MATTHEW: I think you've made your—

LISA: *(Sitting in the chair across from him.)* "Frankly, your eating just doesn't work for me. I'm looking for something more. A stronger relationship between you and your breaded chicken. A bit more *impact.* Don't you think that's lacking?"

MATTHEW: I'd like to be alone now.

LISA: Believe me, *you are. (Referring to the covered plate.)* Careful, that's hot.

(Lisa leaves, taking the wine with her. Matthew watches her go. He uncovers the plate in front of him. The only thing on the plate is a new box of matches.

He smiles a bit. He lifts the box and shakes it. It is full. Pause. Then, he dumps the matches onto the plate. He takes a pen out of his pocket. He writes something inside the empty matchbox. He replaces the cover on the plate, and sets the matchbox on the table in front of him.

Lisa arrives, carrying a new glass of red wine. She sets the wine front of him.)

LISA: Here we are. Is everything all right?

(They stare at each other. No shift in tone.)

Say it.

MATTHEW: No.

(They stare at each other.)

LISA: I'm still married.

MATTHEW: I know that.

LISA: Are you?

(Matthew slides the matchbox across the table, toward her. She looks at him, looks at the matchbox, then lifts it. She shakes the box and discovers its empty. She opens the box. She reads the writing in the box. She stares at him. Then, she drops the matchbox on the table, turns and leaves, quickly, as— Music plays: "I Want You" by Tom Waits.)

MATTHEW: Lisa, wait—

(She is gone. Matthew stares front. Then he stands, throws a few bills on the table, and prepares to go, as—

Lisa reappears. She is wearing her coat and carrying her bag. They stand, facing each other.

Music continues, under.)
Are we leaving?
(Lisa nods.)
Where are we going?

LISA: It doesn't matter. We're strangers. Wherever we go, we'll be alone.

MATTHEW: Lisa, I don't know what I'm looking for here—

LISA: But you know you're looking. Aren't you?
(She walks up very close to him. Looks in his eyes.)
Do this.

MATTHEW: What?

LISA: Lie to everyone but me.

(They stare at each other. Then, they prepare to kiss. As their lips are about to come together—Adrian's voice is heard from the audience.)

ADRIAN: Okay, great, let's take five.

(Music snaps out, as lights expand immediately to reveal—A Rehearsal Studio. Adrian walks to the stage.)

MATTHEW: Can't we finish it?

ADRIAN: What, the kiss?

MATTHEW: Well, yes, of course the kiss. But the rest of it. The rest of the scene.

ADRIAN: I thought we could use a break.

MATTHEW: But, Adrian, how was that? Was that more of what you were looking for?

ADRIAN: Well, as I've said, Matthew, I don't know exactly what I'm—

LISA: He just knows he's looking.
(Matthew stares at Adrian, exasperated.)

MATTHEW: I need coffee. Lisa, you want anything?
(She shakes her head, saying nothing. Matthew goes. Adrian sits, working, at the rehearsal table. Lisa stands alone in the center of the room.)

LISA: That was a little obvious, don't you think?

ADRIAN: What?

LISA: Before the kiss. Just before the kiss.

ADRIAN: There are some things I still have control over.

(*A long silence.*)

LISA: There was a time we'd have prayed for this.

ADRIAN: For what?

LISA: A room of our own. Without hiding, without keeping up appearances.

(*Pause.*)

Five unexpected minutes.

(*Pause.*)

What would we have done?

ADRIAN: With these minutes?

LISA: Yes.

ADRIAN: Taken advantage, I suppose. Used them up.

LISA: How?

ADRIAN: Lisa—

LISA: I want to know this. What would we have done?

ADRIAN: (*Pause, simply.*) We would have devoured each other.

LISA: Yes.

(*Pause.*)

And what will we do now?

ADRIAN: This.

(*Silence.*)

LISA: He's never asked, you know. It amazes me. He's never just come out and asked.

ADRIAN: It's a plan of his.

LISA: It's a what?

ADRIAN: It is a quiet torture.

(*Pause.*)

Sorry.

LISA: Perhaps you'd rather he asked.

ADRIAN: I said I'm sorry. Let it be.

LISA: Perhaps every time I came home late, or every time he walked in the room and we changed the subject, or every time he answered the phone and you quickly hung up—all those times, maybe he should have *asked*. "Are you seeing Adrian behind my back? Are you doing something as passé as having an affair with your director? Don't you have more *imagination* than that?"

ADRIAN: Lisa, I'm not saying—

LISA: No, this is good. This is very good. You're actually *disappointed* that he never found out. Why? Did it rob you of a good scene? An eloquent defense of your actions?

ADRIAN: And your actions.

LISA: That's understood.

ADRIAN: Meaning?

LISA: In this equation, when I say you I mean *us*. We are tethered to this mess.

ADRIAN: So, it's a mess now, is it?

LISA: Yes.

> *(Pause.)*

I'm sorry, but...yes.

> *(Matthew's voice is heard from off—or—he opens the rehearsal studio door quickly. Lisa and Adrian jump a bit.)*

MATTHEW'S VOICE: HOW 'BOUT JUICE? YOU WANT SOME JUICE?

LISA: NO, THANKS.

ADRIAN: I keep imagining him finding out now. Asking you about it *now*. It would just be too ironic to get away with it for the better part of six weeks—and then have him discover us now that we're over.

> *(Pause.)*

To find what we've been hiding after there's nothing left to hide.

> *(She stares at him.)*

LISA: You don't think there's anything left to hide?

ADRIAN: No.

LISA: Really?

ADRIAN: Really.

LISA: You think we can be an open book now?

ADRIAN: Lisa—

LISA: You think we're a *clean slate?*

ADRIAN: I just think we're on the other side of it.

LISA: Well, of course you do. Because after you tell us where to stand and how loud to talk, you hop on a plane and plop into bed in another city.

ADRIAN: Lisa, let's not—

LISA: Let's not what? You're gone, I'm here. That's not fantasy. That's fact. I wake up next to my husband, who I love and who I've chosen to be with—but we are still here. You and I. We are everywhere I turn.

ADRIAN: What can I do about that?

LISA: I don't know. I don't. But there was a time when I thought you could affect everything.

(A quiet realization.)

God, I really did. I thought that through sheer force of will you could bring order to us. I want that back.

ADRIAN: It's over, Lisa. We decided it's over.

(Pause.)

Didn't we?

LISA: *(Soft.)* Yes.

(He moves in close to her.)

ADRIAN: So, we must act on that. We must move on.

(Pause, a bit uncertain himself.)

Musn't we?

LISA: *(Soft.)* Yes.

(Pause.)

Let's move on.

(Pause, still soft.)

Do you really think we can we do that?

(Adrian holds her, speaks softly.)

ADRIAN: Yes.

LISA: Okay.

(Pause.)

Let's tell him.

(Silence. He stares at her.)

Well?

ADRIAN: *("Leese.")* Lis—

LISA: Let's do it. As soon as he comes through that door. Let's tell him.

ADRIAN: *(Moving away.)* Lisa, you're not making any sense—

LISA: We have nothing to hide. You've taught me this.

(She puts two chairs side by side, facing the door/exit which Matthew will enter from.)

C'mon. Sit with me. We'll do this together.

ADRIAN: You'd better think about this, Lisa. You'd better think about the consequences of this—

LISA: No more thinking. Life is not what we think, it's what we *do*—and it's time we did *this*.

ADRIAN: But you don't just come out and tell someone the *truth*.

LISA: You don't?

ADRIAN: Not if you've *gotten away with something*, no. You don't then turn around and *confess*.

LISA: *(Challenging him.)* Why?

ADRIAN: Because—

LISA: Yes—?

ADRIAN: Because it's *disruptive!* Imagine a world in which people *needlessly con-fessed*—it would be BARBARIC. Believe me, honesty should not be an *afterthought*.

LISA: What then?!

ADRIAN: It should be a *last resort*.

(Lisa stares at him, hard. Then, she starts for one of the chairs—)

LISA: I'll do it myself.

ADRIAN: Lis—

(Lisa sits. Adrian stares at her. Then, he moves to the chair next to her, hesi-tates, and finally sits—then immediately jumps to his feet.)

ADRIAN: Enough. All right? ENOUGH. I know you're trying to make a point of some kind, but—

LISA: A point?

ADRIAN: Yes.

LISA: A *point?*

ADRIAN: Forget it.

LISA: Adrian?

ADRIAN: What?

LISA: You're sweating.

ADRIAN: I'm—well, of course I am, I'm—

LISA: You know why, don't you?

ADRIAN: Lisa—

LISA: Because this is the *fever* we were always looking for. Stolen moments, secret phone calls—all of them gave us that FEVER, that heightened and frightened pitch that we were aching for. And Matthew was always near-by.

(Yells offstage—or—throws open the door, briefly.)

WEREN'T YOU, MATTHEW?

MATTHEW'S VOICE: JUST A MINUTE.

LISA: *(To Adrian.)* That was crucial to the equation. If he'd been in South America we might have bored each other to tears. But, he was always in the other room, or waiting in the car, or just out to get a paper—and the

finite time we had made every moment *burn.* But it was never as good as *now.* This, Adrian, is the *thing itself.*
(Pause.)
So, *sit.* We signed on for this, let's end it in style.
(Adrian slowly sits in the chair, once again. Lisa sits again, also. They wait in silence.)

ADRIAN: Lis?

LISA: What?

ADRIAN: I love you.

LISA: *(Tenderly.)* It was sweet, wasn't it?
(Matthew enters.)

MATTHEW: Okay, so I've been in the dark. I've been in the dark about this entire thing. And you've let me. You've let me stumble through darkness like an oaf in a cave. And perhaps you've said this to yourselves over time: "It's for his *own good.* Nothing good would come of him knowing more at this time. Let's do this for *him.* Let's keep a little *darkness* around him." And I thank you for that. For thinking of me with such regard. Because, it seems you've needed to get together quite often—sometimes even outside rehearsal, sometimes till very late at night—to make sure you were doing the *right thing* when it came to me. I'm in your debt for that. I truly hope that somehow, someday I can repay the both of you.
(Adrian and Lisa look quickly to each other, then say —)

| ADRIAN: | LISA: |
| Matthew— | Why don't— |

MATTHEW: Now, you are at a crossroads. You must take the next step. I'm aware of this and I don't envy your situation. At this moment, it must be said, that, for the first time in my life, I am completely thrilled to be *me.* Because my position is the simple one here. I lie in wait for you to enact your plan and then, holding cards you have no idea about, I play my hand. It's almost too easy. It's virtual baby candy. But, it's here and let's just accept it, shall we? Say: "Yes."

LISA and ADRIAN: Yes.

MATTHEW: Good. One thing I ask of you. There is this *myth.* I'd like us to talk about it. The myth of which I speak is that of Telling the Truth Slowly Over Time. Now, this myth does have its proponents. They believe that the cold hard truth can, if rationed out slowly over time like, say, *cod liver oil,* be made more palatable. Perhaps even made attractive. Therapists do this. They are reluctant to come right out and say to a couple: "Tom,

Jeanine, thanks for coming by today and here's my assessment of your relationship: It's fucked. Let it go. Say goodbye, divide up your stuff, and run for your lives." Why are they reluctant to do this? It would make them *obsolete*. Their jobs *depend* on giving out the truth at a *slower rate than it is actually needed*. They claim, of course (and are never challenged, since it is our fate to bow to anyone holding a weapon or a Ph.D.), that they are doing this for the couple's "own good"—that they are giving them the truth at a pace they can *"handle."* But, push has come to SHOUT and here we are:

(He moves closer to them.)

I urge you to take whatever truth is at your disposal and *divest it*. Cut it loose. All of it. Tell it fast and tell it now. It is not more *palatable,* it is not a *gift* to tell someone you love the Slow Truth, unless you happen to know they have a fondness for Slow Disease like, say, *cancer*.

LISA: Matthew—

MATTHEW: Our collisions with others are not measured events. They are *radical*. Our love and lust and all our aching wonder is radical. Affairs don't accrue methodically, they spring up like lightning—like lost tourists with cash in hand. They are *feverish*. They are *fast*. And if we try to come clean by Telling the Truth about them Slowly Over Time, we give birth to a *mutant truth*. A truth that bears no relation to the fierce hearts that we possess. *The truth we tell, and the way we tell it, must be as radical as our actions.*

(Pause.)

And so . . . Carol, Derek, what have you got to say for yourselves?

(Silence. Adrian and Lisa lean forward in their chairs—)

ADRIAN: Who?

MATTHEW: *(A big smile.)* It's delicious, isn't it?

LISA: What is?

ADRIAN: Derek and Carol?

(Matthew happily pulls some folded script pages from his pocket.)

MATTHEW: I'm sure I paraphrased it terribly. But you get the gist of it. It enables Michael to really nail Derek and Carol for the affair they're having behind his back.

ADRIAN: It's a *new page?*

MATTHEW: Yes, came in the mail today. Bonnie is copying them.

(Pause.)

What's wrong? What did I miss?

(Lisa and Adrian look at each other, then jump to their feet and congratulate Matthew.)

LISA: Nothing!

ADRIAN: Right! That's great. Wonderful. We'll work it in after lunch. In fact, let's take lunch *now*. I'm starved.

LISA: I'll just grab my bag.

(Lisa bolts from the room. Matthew approaches Adrian.)

MATTHEW: Adrian?

ADRIAN: Hmm?

MATTHEW: Are you okay?

ADRIAN: Sure fine great. Why?

MATTHEW: You look pale. Peaked.

(Pause.)

Ashen, I guess it is.

ADRIAN: You really did that from memory?

MATTHEW: I took a stab at it. It's good, isn't it? It's what the play needs.

ADRIAN: Yes, I think it will work nicely.

MATTHEW: It will shut the two of them up. It will force them to just sit there and confront their lies.

ADRIAN: Yes.

MATTHEW: Their deceit.

ADRIAN: Yes.

MATTHEW: Their arrogant belief that things can actually be hidden.

ADRIAN: Yes.

MATTHEW: Because they can't, really. Do you know what I'm saying, Adrian?

ADRIAN: I think I do.

MATTHEW: And you agree with me?

ADRIAN: I think I do.

MATTHEW: I think you'd better.

(Silence.)

ADRIAN: Well, I should get a copy of the new pages from Bonnie.

(Matthew opens the folded script pages and holds them up—showing them to Adrian. They are completely blank.)

MATTHEW: Adrian.

ADRIAN: Yes?

MATTHEW: There are no new pages. You know that.

(He crumbles the pages and tosses them to Adrian, saying, brightly—)

Well. We've done our work. Let's eat.

(Music: "Is You Is or Is You Ain't My Baby—final chorus to end. Lights shift to—

A Restaurant. The same table and chairs are used, with perhaps a few added elements to distinguish this from the rehearsal studio "restaurant."

Matthew sits between Lisa and Adrian. They sip their wine. They each are strangely aware of how they all seem to be bringing their glasses to their mouths at the same moment. They each work, subtly, to remedy this. Song ends.)

LISA: It's good.
   (Silence.)
ADRIAN: What's good?
LISA: The Merlot. It's quite good.
   (Pause.)
   It's a little...smoky. Sort of. It has a kind of—
MATTHEW: Lisa.
LISA: Hmm?
MATTHEW: Don't explain the wine.
   (Cory, their waitress, enters. She has long black hair.)
CORY: How's the wine?
   (Lisa stares at Matthew.)
MATTHEW: It's fine.
CORY: Good. What are you eating?
LISA: Maybe we should get three different things and share.
   (The men both lower their menus and look at Lisa.)
CORY: I'll check back.
   (She starts to go—)
MATTHEW: No, I think we're ready. Go ahead, Adrian.
ADRIAN: I'll have the special.
LISA: Two.
MATTHEW: Three.
CORY: Well, that was easy. Salads with those?
LISA, MATTHEW and ADRIAN: Sure.
CORY: Great.
ADRIAN: Dressing on the side.
CORY: Got it.

(Cory goes. Silence.)

ADRIAN: I think it's going very well.

MATTHEW: You do?

ADRIAN: Yes.

MATTHEW: Good.

ADRIAN: I really do.

LISA: What?

ADRIAN: Hmm?

LISA: What's going very well?

ADRIAN: The play.

LISA: Oh, yes, right.

ADRIAN: Don't you?

LISA: Absolutely.

ADRIAN: Yes.

LISA: Very well. Don't you, Matthew?

MATTHEW: It's a *disaster*.

ADRIAN: Well, Matthew, if you—

MATTHEW: At the core of the play (I'm just realizing this now, as we're about to open) at the core of the play is her search for disaster.

(To Lisa.)

Right, Lis?

(Lisa stares at him, blankly.)

In actuality, her affair is a rather *pedestrian* event that will have *dire* repercussions. But, the folly (and I love this, I do), the folly of her life is that she believes just the *opposite*. She believes her affair is an extraordinary event which will offer *danger without consequence*. She is searching for *disaster with immunity*.

(Looks at the two of them.)

Wouldn't you agree?

(Adrian and Lisa stare at him, as Cory returns.)

CORY: Good news and bad news. Which would you like first?

ADRIAN:	LISA:	MATTHEW:
The good.	Whatever.	The bad.

CORY: Well. The bad news is that we just ran out of the special. The good news is that the owner is buying your lunch.

MATTHEW: Why?

CORY: Apparently you're his one millionth table.

(Cory blows a plastic noisemaker. She walks around the table and places

paper party hats on their heads during the following. She also sets three noise-makers in the center of the table. Matthew, Lisa and Adrian put their hats on and wear them until noted.)

ADRIAN: What do you know.

CORY: So, eat and drink till you drop. There'll be a photo later.

LISA: A *photo?*

CORY: For some piece in the *Times.* Congratulations.

ADRIAN: Thanks.

CORY: Now, what are you eating?

LISA: I'll need to look at the menu again.

ADRIAN: As will I.

CORY: *(Nods.)* I'll start you with your salads.

> *(She goes. Silence. Then, Adrian blows his noisemaker.)*

ADRIAN: One in a million.

MATTHEW: *(Also blows his noisemaker, looking at Adrian.)* What do you know.

LISA: Matthew, I wonder if—

MATTHEW: I'm going to the restroom. Excuse me.

> *(Matthew goes. They watch him go, unable to turn and look at each other. Finally...)*

ADRIAN: He knows.

LISA: I know he knows.

ADRIAN: *How?* Were we careless?

LISA: Worse. We were smug. No one gets away with smug.

> *(Silence. At the same time, they both reach for their wine. They stop. They take each other's hands. Adrian moves to the chair closest to Lisa. They look into each other's eyes.)*

> What is it?

ADRIAN: *(Softly, urgently.)* Lisa. It needn't be over between us.

LISA: Adrian...

ADRIAN: There are things I haven't told you. Things that—if they come to pass—could change *everything.* Our lives could begin anew.

LISA: What are you saying?

ADRIAN: I can't tell you more, just now. I'm sorry. But, in time—

> *(Suddenly, the amplified sound of clicking cameras, as—*
> *Several Photographers [played by the crew] enter and circle Adrian and Lisa, snapping numerous photos. Adrian and Lisa stand and hold each other—trying to hide, to bury their faces, as they yell at the Photographers—)*

ADRIAN: No—get out of here—I said no—do you hear me—not now—

LISA: *(Overlapping.)* Could you please not—stop it—I don't want my—stop it—

(The Photographers are gone as quickly as they appeared. Lisa and Adrian, realizing they're holding each other in public, quickly let go of each other and step back, away. Then they remember the party hats on their heads—and quickly remove them. Lisa speaks simply, resigned.)

We have amnesia. We forget what we know.

(Adrian returns to the table and sits. Lisa stands, alone.)

This time, we think, unlike all the previous anguish and innuendo, *this time* the goodbyes will have a grace to them. They don't. They never will.

(Lights shift to another area of the Restaurant—
A Wait Station. Cory is there, busily putting three salads and three sides of dressing on a tray. Matthew approaches her, still wearing his party hat.)

MATTHEW: Hi.

CORY: Hi.

MATTHEW: You're a very good waitress.

CORY: I can die happy.

MATTHEW: Restrooms this way?

CORY: Right through there.

MATTHEW: Thanks.

(Matthew takes a few steps and then stops, turns back. He watches Cory.)

CORY: You need something?

MATTHEW: What? Oh, no. I'm just...waiting.

CORY: Okay.

(Her tray is ready. She starts to go.)

See you.

MATTHEW: Cory.

CORY: *(Stops.)* How do you know my name?

MATTHEW: I asked the owner. Cory, can I ask you something?

CORY: Be quick. I'm busy.

MATTHEW: Have you been following me?

CORY: *What?*

MATTHEW: *(Smiles.)* I know that sounds weird. But wherever I go lately, I keep seeing you. It's weird.

CORY: Why haven't I seen you?

MATTHEW: I don't know. I was there.

(Removes his party hat, extends his hand.)
Matthew.

CORY: *(Shakes his hand, still holding her tray.)* Rest easy, Matthew. I'm not following you.

(Pause.)

I should go—or was there something else?

MATTHEW: What do you mean?

CORY: You didn't come back here to use the restroom.

MATTHEW: I didn't?

CORY: I see it a lot. This is a very good place to escape from one's tablemates. Are they married?

MATTHEW: No.

CORY: Oh. They look married.

MATTHEW: How do you mean?

CORY: They—you know—share a look. They match up.

MATTHEW: I hadn't noticed.

CORY: Well, it's hardest to see in our close friends.

MATTHEW: She's my wife.

(Silence. Cory smiles a bit.)

So, what do you do when you're not waitressing?

CORY: Don't be clumsy. Really.

MATTHEW: I'm not being—

CORY: Don't do this here. If this is a come-on, don't do it here. Really.

MATTHEW: It was an innocent question.

CORY: Wow. An innocent question. Wouldn't that be something?

MATTHEW: *(Simply.)* Set the tray down, Cory.

(They stare at each other. Standoff.)

CORY: One condition. Don't be stupid about this. Not here. Not anywhere. Okay?

MATTHEW: Okay.

(Cory sets the tray down.)

CORY: I'm not really a waitress. I'm a writer.

MATTHEW: What are you working on?

CORY: Actually, I'm working on a book about the Depression.

MATTHEW: So, you have an interest in historical material?

CORY: My Depression. I'm writing a book about *my* Depression.

MATTHEW: I see.

CORY: It's an *epic*.

(She drinks from a glass of water on the Wait Station. Matthew smiles.)

MATTHEW: So you don't like it here?

CORY: Put it this way: we have an owner whose "initiation ritual" for new waitresses involves the *walk-in freezer* and the *mint vinaigrette*. But, I dealt with it.

MATTHEW: *(Curious.)* What did you do?

CORY: *(Deliciously.)* What would anyone do? I became friends with his wife. I told her everything and she threw him out on his ass. If he fires me, I sue him. Game, set, match.

MATTHEW: I believe in that sort of revenge. What's the dressing?

CORY: Creamy garlic and dill.

(He dabs one of the sides of salad dressing with his finger. He tastes it.)

MATTHEW: Strong.

CORY: We like it that way.

MATTHEW: I like the adventure of revenge, don't you? The fever of it.

CORY: Say more.

MATTHEW: You are suddenly in power in a situation where you've previously been powerless.

(He reaches in his pocket and removes a small, glass vial which is filled with yellow powder.)

Do you have a fork?

(She stares at him. Then she hands him a fork.)

Thank you.

(As Matthew speaks, he does the following:

He takes one of the sides of dressing off the tray. He sprinkles some of the yellow powder onto the dressing. He mixes the powder into the dressing with the fork. He repeats this with the second side of dressing, as well.)

This is what you must know about my wife:

My wife loves her wedding ring.

Sometimes I wake in the morning and catch her lying in bed next to me, holding her hand in the air, admiring her ring in the sunlight.

My wife never removes her wedding ring, with one exception: to wash the dishes. She places it carefully on a ledge above the sink. Then, when the dishes are done, she weds the ring to her finger once again.

I imagine she may also take it off to have her affair.

Therefore, this is my picture of her infidelity:

My wife is at the sink, holding a big yellow sponge.

She is doing the dishes.

There is a man *directly behind her*.

He is *not* doing the dishes.

Water gushes into the sink.

Steam glazes the windows.

My wife's hair has fallen across her face.

Her hands are red and wet.

Her fingers furrowed from this prolonged immersion.

With this man directly behind her, my wife washes every… last … dish …in…our…home.

Later, when I walk through the door, she looks up from her chair and smiles. "How was your day?" she asks, rubbing the lotion into her hands.

(Silence. Cory stares at him. He places the second side of dressing back in its place on the tray.)

Have you nothing to say?

(Cory lifts the third side of dressing.)

CORY: And the third one?

MATTHEW: That one's mine. Please, don't mix them up.

(She stares at the dressing, at Matthew.)

I like you, Cory. I hope our paths continue to cross.

(He puts the vial in his pocket. He puts his party hat back on—and leaves. Cory watches him go, as lights shift back to—

The Restaurant Table. Matthew arrives and sits.)

MATTHEW: No food yet?

LISA:	ADRIAN:
She must be busy.	I'm starving.

(Silence.)

LISA: Took you a while.

MATTHEW: Sorry. I stopped and used the phone. Checked our machine.

LISA: Any messages?

MATTHEW: Just Adrian. Saying he'd see you at rehearsal.

(Looks at Adrian, smiles.)

And he did.

(Adrian returns the smile. Silence.)

LISA: Matthew, I—we—have something we'd like to talk to you about.

MATTHEW: Really?

LISA: Yes.

MATTHEW: About the play?

ADRIAN: Not the play, per sé. Not the play *directly*.

MATTHEW: I see.

LISA: Something the play has nurtured. Something it has birthed.

MATTHEW: Something good or bad?

LISA: Something—

ADRIAN: Complicated. Something—

LISA: Rash.

MATTHEW: I see.

(Matthew removes his hat, leans in, concerned. Cory appears at some distance behind the table. During the following, she stands there, with the tray that holds the salads and dressings. The others do not see her.)

It sounds *serious*. Are the two of you in any danger?

LISA: I don't think so.

ADRIAN: I hope not.

MATTHEW: Well, if there's anything I can do, I hope you'll let me know. But, please, if you don't mind, fill me in a little. Even if it's uncomfortable, please try. I feel at this point the three of us are close enough to deal with nearly anything. Don't you agree?

(Cory approaches the table.)

CORY: Here we are. Sorry about the wait. It's odd—but all the phones have gone out. It's total chaos back there. Reservations are all messed up. It's quite a scene. I hope no one needed to use the phone—

MATTHEW: *(Smiles.)* Already did, thanks.

(Cory serves the salads. First to Lisa, then Matthew, then Adrian.)

CORY: Three salads. Three sides of dressing. It's our creamy garlic and dill. We get a lot of comments on it.

LISA: Thank you.

ADRIAN: Looks great. I am *starved*.

(Cory looks down at the three dressings. Stops. Uncertain. Then, she quickly —inexplicably—switches Matthew's dressing with Lisa's. Satisfied, she carries on, as Matthew looks up at her, concerned—)

CORY: *(Brightly, to Lisa.)* Fresh ground pepper?

LISA: Please.

CORY: Say when.

(Cory grinds pepper onto Lisa's salad.)

LISA: When.

   (Cory stops, turns to Matthew.)

CORY: Fresh ground pepper?

MATTHEW: *Please.*

CORY: Say when.

   (Cory grinds pepper onto his salad.)

MATTHEW: When.

   (Cory stops. Before she can turn to Adrian, he says—)

ADRIAN: You bet.

   (Adrian smiles, flirting with her.)

   Shall I say *when?*

CORY: Just tell me when you can't take it anymore.

   (Adrian laughs. Cory grinds pepper onto his salad. At first, he smiles—)

ADRIAN: When when when when—

   (She keeps grinding.)

CORY: You know what to say.

ADRIAN: That's plenty, it's perfect, thank you—

   (She keeps grinding. He's not smiling now.)

CORY: Can you not take *direction?*

ADRIAN: That's enough—

CORY: *Say it.*

ADRIAN: I CAN'T TAKE IT ANYMORE.

   (She stops and smiles, pleasantly.)

CORY: Can I bring you anything else?

MATTHEW: I think this will do nicely.

   (Cory goes. Adrian shakes the pepper off some of his salad.)

LISA: She looks familiar.

ADRIAN: Our waitress?

LISA: Yes.

MATTHEW: I thought so, too.

   (A frozen moment—the three of them looking off in the direction Cory left. Then, they each grab their sides of dressing and—using their forks—noisily cover their salads with dressing. Adrian stabs his fork into a huge piece of lettuce covered with dressing and is about to put it in his mouth—)

LISA: Adrian?

ADRIAN: What?

LISA: Wait. We're in the midst of something. Let's finish it.

ADRIAN: Lisa—

LISA: Let's get it said.

(He looks at her, then lowers his fork.)

Matthew?

MATTHEW: Yes?

LISA: *Something happened.* Something between Adrian and me.

MATTHEW: Yes, so I gather. *What was it?* I'm dying to know.

LISA: Well, it's—

ADRIAN: Enough. I'll do this.

(He sits up straight, looks Matthew in the eye.)

Matthew, your wife and I—

MATTHEW: Adrian.

ADRIAN: Yes.

MATTHEW: Before you go on, I must tell you one thing.

ADRIAN: *(After a glance at Lisa.)* All right.

MATTHEW: You look *famished.* We can't afford you to get sick. Not this far into rehearsal. Let's, please, eat while we talk. Let's, please, chat and chew. *(Adrian and Lisa look at each other. Matthew takes a huge bite of his salad. Adrian and Lisa then take huge bites of their salads. Cory is seen once again, watching from a distance.)*

Mm mmm. There. I feel better already. Now, Adrian, what were you saying?

ADRIAN: Well, Matthew, in plain terms, your wife and I—

(He stops, choking a bit. Distant, eerie music is heard, under.)

Your wife and—

(He chokes more.)

I can't seem to—

(More choking, coughing.)

OH GOD—

(Choking violently.)

OH GOD, HELP ME—

(Lisa stands and steps toward Adrian, trying to help.)

LISA: Adrian, what is it? Adrian! Here, drink something—

(Now, Lisa, too, coughs. She quickly grabs her own throat, choking to death—)

Oh...my...god—

ADRIAN: *(Desperately, to Cory.)* CALL FOR HELP—CALL 911—

CORY: *(Smiling, holding the severed end of a pay phone.)* Phones are dead! Sorry!

LISA: MATTHEW—

MATTHEW: *(Happily.)* Your face is blue, honey. And you know what? It's a very good color on you!

LISA: MATTHEW, DO SOMETHING—

MATTHEW: Okay!

(Matthew stands atop the table and snaps his fingers as—

Loud music suddenly plays: "Tell the Truth" by Ray Charles—beginning with the vocal.

The stage is suddenly flooded with pulsating green and red light. A mirror ball [perhaps] spins, above. Spotlights [perhaps] hit Matthew atop the table and Cory, standing now atop the Wait Station counter—

Matthew and Cory watch and laugh and dance to the music, as—

Adrian and Lisa scream in pain, cough, choke and throw themselves around the room. Lisa reaches up, desperately, for Matthew—just as he jumps down from the table. She pulls the tablecloth from the table and salad flies everywhere. Total chaos—

The Photographers—now wearing Party Hats—rush on and quickly take photos of Adrian and Lisa clinging to each other's necks as they choke and die—

Matthew climbs atop the Wait Station, as Cory puts a long red rose between her teeth. Matthew dips her dramatically, and—as she takes the rose from her teeth—he kisses her, passionately, as—

The Photographers capture the kiss on film, then rush off, as—

Lisa and Adrian die, hideously, as—Matthew stands over them, laughing wildly, and—Cory blows kisses and waves goodbye to them—

The entire sequence, from Matthew snapping his fingers, takes no more than about thirty seconds—

Then suddenly—

Abrupt light shift. Music snaps out. All action freezes.

A person stands at the edge of the stage in a shaft of light, holding a clipboard, looking at Matthew. This is Frank.

A similar shaft of light isolates Matthew.)

FRANK: *(Dryly.)* Matthew?

MATTHEW: Yes?

FRANK: Did that really happen? Is that really what you did?
(Silence.)

MATTHEW: It's what I wanted to do.

FRANK: There's a *difference*, Matthew. We've been over this.

MATTHEW: *(Pause.)* I'm sorry, Frank.

FRANK: You owe me no apologies, Matthew. You only owe me the *truth*. That's the only way I can help you.
(Frank makes a note on the clipboard.)
I think we should add a second session each week. And I think we need to go back, Matthew. Back to the very beginning. Is that clear?

MATTHEW: *(Soft.)* Yes, Frank.

FRANK: Good. *(Brightly.)* Well, we've done our work. It's lunchtime.

(Fast blackout. Music: "Can I Steal a Little Love?" sung by Frank Sinatra.)

END OF ACT ONE

ACT TWO

Music: "Fever"—sung by Peggy Lee.

Music snaps out as lights bump up on Matthew and Frank in positions identical to the end of Act One. The rest of the stage remains in darkness.

FRANK: And I think we need to go back, Matthew. Back to the very beginning. Is that clear?

MATTHEW: *(Soft.)* Yes, Frank.

FRANK: But first, Matthew, let's remind ourselves of our first meeting. Can we do that?

(Matthew nods. Lights expand to reveal—Frank's Office. Two comfortable chairs. Framed degrees and plaques on the wall. Matthew and Frank move to the office and sit.)

FRANK: Splendid. Now. When we first met, what did you say?

MATTHEW: I said: "Hello."

FRANK: Good. And what did I say?

MATTHEW: You said: "I'm Frank. I hope *you'll* be."

FRANK: Well, Matthew, that's my question: *have you been?* Or have I been the only one in the room being Frank?
(Matthew stands.)

MATTHEW: Watch. I'll show you how it started.

(The Rehearsal Studio. Two scripts in red folders neatly stacked on the table. [Note: These are identical to the scripts used throughout Act One.] Freshly sharpened pencils. A coffee mug. Adrian enters, briskly, carrying his script. Frank watches from the office, taking occasional notes.)

ADRIAN: You're early.

MATTHEW: Yes, we had a—

ADRIAN: *(Shaking his hand.)* Welcome aboard, Matthew! I'm greatly looking forward to the next six weeks. I think we're in for a splendid adventure. The company I run in London has often tackled projects of this magnitude and I quite fancy the chance to bring my aesthetic to America—to the provinces, if you will. As soon as Lisa gets here, we'll make a start.

MATTHEW: She's here.

ADRIAN: Really?

MATTHEW: She came with me.

ADRIAN: Really?

MATTHEW: She's my wife.

(Adrian smiles.)

Really.

ADRIAN: I must say I didn't know that.

(Pause.)

Well, congratulations.

(Before Matthew can respond.)

Don't say it. Don't say "thank you." I withdraw my comment of congratulations. Please forgive me, would you? I entreat you—

MATTHEW: Forgive you?

ADRIAN: That's trophyism, don't you think? "Congratulations on your wife"—that's trophyism, it's caveman talk. It shouldn't be thought of as an *accomplishment* that someone landed a strikingly beautiful woman as his wife.

MATTHEW: What should it be thought of as?

ADRIAN: What it more accurately *is.*

MATTHEW: And that is?

ADRIAN: Envy. *(Pause, brightly.)* Well, I've broken a few Commandments and I haven't even had my tea. Excuse me.

(Adrian goes, taking his coffee mug with him.)

FRANK: *Matthew?*

MATTHEW: It happened, Frank. I swear it. You said you wanted to go back to the beginning. Well, here we are.

FRANK: Very well. Keep going.

(Lisa enters, then stops—staring back at the door/entrance she came from. Frank continues to watch.)

MATTHEW: Lis.

LISA: Hmm?

MATTHEW: Are you okay?

(Lisa turns to Matthew. She goes to him and puts her arms around him, tightly.)

LISA: He just said the strangest thing to me.

MATTHEW: Who?

LISA: Adrian. Just now, we passed in the hallway, and he said hello, and then he said the strangest thing.

MATTHEW: What was it?

LISA: *(Pause.)* I can't tell you.

MATTHEW: Sure you can.

LISA: No.

MATTHEW: *(With a laugh.)* Lisa, I'm your husband, I'm your friend, you can tell—

LISA: No. He told me not to. He told me not to tell you.

(Adrian enters, carrying his still-empty mug.)

ADRIAN: Let's jump!

MATTHEW: What?

ADRIAN: Let's jump to the end.

MATTHEW: To the—

ADRIAN: As a way of starting, I'd like to jump to the end.

FRANK: *(Making a note.)* Interesting.

ADRIAN: It's something I do with my company in London (where, of course, one can get a CUP OF TEA before rehearsal begins—but no such luck HERE, is there?). In any case, let's give the play's final scene a "once-over" and see where this thing *ends*. Are you game?

(Matthew and Lisa stare at him, then say...)

MATTHEW and LISA: Sure.

(Adrian sets a wooden chair in the center of the room. After placing it, he looks at it...then changes the angle of the chair ever-so-slightly. Then he steps away from it and looks to Matthew and Lisa, expectant.)

ADRIAN: Would you like to use the chair?

LISA: Do you want us to use the chair?

ADRIAN: That's not my question. My question is—

MATTHEW: No. I don't want to use the chair.

(Adrian nods for a really long time, then says...)

ADRIAN: *Interesting.*

LISA: What is?

ADRIAN: That you don't feel a need to use the chair. That's *very* telling.

LISA: It doesn't really matter to me whether we—

(Matthew grabs the chair and sets it in the center of the room once again. Smiles.)

MATTHEW: We're using it, all right? We're using the fucking chair.

ADRIAN: Your choice.

(*Adrian again adjusts the chair ever-so-slightly. Then he lifts the scripts from the rehearsal table and hands them to Matthew and Lisa.*)

And one thing more: Please use your *real names.*

LISA: When?

ADRIAN: In the scene.

MATTHEW: Not the character's names? Not the names in the *script?*

ADRIAN: No. Your own.

MATTHEW: But—

ADRIAN: Matthew. This is how I work.

(*Matthew stares at him, then nods, sits. Adrian gestures for Lisa to start on the opposite side of the stage.*)

The final scene. At your leisure.

MATTHEW: Are you going to tell us anything? Is there something you're looking for?

ADRIAN: Of course there is. Now: the final scene.

(*Prompted by a gesture from Adrian, Lisa walks slowly past Matthew who sits, reading. Lisa stops...turns...looks back at him...their eyes meet. The scene is quiet...lovely...simple.*)

LISA: Oh, my god.

MATTHEW: Lisa. (*Stands.*) It's been—

LISA: Years.

MATTHEW: Yes.

(*Pause.*)

Four years. And you're still—

LISA: Finishing your sentences.

(*Matthew smiles a bit. Silence.*)

MATTHEW: So, it worked out. Your marriage?

LISA: (*Pause, gently.*) Yes.

MATTHEW: I'm glad for you.

(*Pause, quietly.*)

Really.

LISA: And you?

MATTHEW: Nothing to report.

LISA: (*Tenderly.*) Four years?

(*Matthew nods.*)

And there's been no—

MATTHEW: Only you.

LISA: Matthew—

MATTHEW: This is what happens, Lis. Someone always wakes up first.

(They look into each other's eyes—then, simultaneously, turn the pages of their scripts.)

LISA: I should go. My husband is picking me up.

MATTHEW: Just like old times.

(She nods.)

Something I've wondered.

LISA: What?

MATTHEW: Did he ever—did you ever—

LISA: No. Never.

(Pause.)

It's still our secret.

(Pause.)

Goodbye, Matthew.

(Lisa goes, exiting to the side of the stage. Then, Lisa and Matthew turn and look at Adrian. Adrian is staring intently at the chair, nodding his head, slowly and repeatedly, for a really long time. Finally, Lisa says...)

Well?

(He looks up at her. Speaks, softly.)

ADRIAN: That is what happens, isn't it? I've never known that as fully as I do now. Someone must, of course, wake up first. And the shock is that we mistakenly believe we will recognize the END as mutually as we recognized the BEGINNING. But we are offered no such elegance. *(From his heart.)* Because...when, in a marriage...when, in a life...*(Stops.)* No. No more.

(Adrian has settled into the chair, his head in his hands. Lisa and Matthew look at each other. Then, Matthew tentatively approaches Adrian.)

MATTHEW: So...what we did was okay?

ADRIAN: *(Standing with a flourish.)* It was a revelation. It gave me a clarity of purpose about my own life—well, need I say more, you're married, you know what a circus of neurosis it can be, of course you do—but let's dispense with confession and attend to business at hand.

MATTHEW: But, just so I'm clear: That's what you want—you want us to do the scene that way?

ADRIAN: Matthew, it's not the scene that matters—it's the *art*. And, in the end, what is art, what is LIFE, but this? A bit of love...a few laughs...and then...*death*.

(Pause. Then, brightly.)
Take ten, please.

(Matthew goes directly to Frank, as lights expand to include—Frank's Office.

During the following, Adrian goes through his script, making notations. Lisa sits, across the room from Adrian. She removes a thermos from her bag. Pours herself some tea.)

MATTHEW: *That*, Frank, is how it began.

FRANK: May I see your script, Matthew?

MATTHEW: My—?

FRANK: It may provide a clue to our work. *(Hand extended.)* May I?
   (Matthew hands Frank his script. Frank pages through it during the following—)
   Now, what happened next?

MATTHEW: I went outside to smoke.

FRANK: You don't smoke, Matthew.

MATTHEW: So, I came right back in. And that's when I heard her say:

LISA: Adrian?
   (Adrian looks up at Lisa.)
   Would you like some tea? Everyone around here is a coffee drinker, but not me.
   (She lifts the thermos, offers it.)
   English breakfast. Will you have a cup?
   (Adrian nods. She walks to him and pours him some tea. Frank puts the script aside.)

FRANK: And then?

MATTHEW: And then it began.

FRANK: What did?

MATTHEW: *Them.* The two of them.

FRANK: But how do you know? Did you *observe something?*

MATTHEW: Not right then—no—we were on a break, so I turned and left—

FRANK: She did nothing but offer him a cup of tea. That's all you know for sure, Matthew, and I don't think—

MATTHEW: You know, I thought I was paying you to believe what I say. Do you now want *proof?* Do you now want hair fibers? Surveillance photos? An affidavit from a private detective?

FRANK: Do you have one?

MATTHEW: Forget it—I'm going for a smoke.

FRANK: But, Matthew, you don't—

MATTHEW: It's a FIGURE OF SPEECH, Frank. I'll see you Friday.

(Matthew leaves. Frank watches him go, then turns back to—
The Rehearsal Studio. Lisa and Adrian are sitting across the room from each
other. They sip their tea. Lisa reads a newspaper. Adrian makes the occasional
note in his script.)

FRANK: Odd. How brutal things begin so sweetly. How our greatest regrets take root, at first, as hope.

(Frank turns and addresses the audience.)

Pardon me for addressing you directly, but it seems I'm the only one who can be trusted with this story.

It's possible, of course, that what Matthew said is true. That it began between them on that day, at that moment.

But, *why?* I am asked that often. And, frankly, I've come to believe that each reason is as plausible as the next. One client assured me her affair was caused by the curvature of the earth. What could I say? Did I know otherwise?

So, tonight, I ask it of you. *Why?*

You've all seen that person who caught you off-guard. Who stopped your breath, if only for a moment. That person you walked a little faster just to get a glimpse of. Or slowed your car ever so slightly to observe. And why? Just to see. Just to *take it in.*

Perhaps this was years ago when you were young and hopeful and reckless. Perhaps this was at intermission.

But, however brief, that glance registered.

And you put it somewhere in your mind.

And that...may have been that.

LISA: There's a hurricane coming.

ADRIAN: *(Looking up from his work.)* What's that?

LISA: Oh, I'm sorry. It's a terrible habit. I do it at home all the time and it drives Matthew crazy. I'm a blurter. Sorry.

ADRIAN: You're the person who ruins the newspaper for everyone in the room.

LISA: That's me. Sorry.

(The tea.)

Is your—?

ADRIAN: *(Lifting his cup.)* It's lovely.

(Lisa goes back to her paper. Adrian keeps looking at her.)

What are they calling it?

(She looks up at him.)

The hurricane.

LISA: Cory.

ADRIAN: *(With a laugh.)* Say again?

LISA: Hurricane Cory. Is that a man or a woman, do you suppose?

ADRIAN: Woman. Definitely a woman.

LISA: How can you be sure?

(Adrian just smiles and goes back to his script. Silence, as Lisa stares at him.)

Thank you for casting me in this.

ADRIAN: *(Head in script.)* My pleasure. You were my first choice.

LISA: Really?

ADRIAN: *(Not looking up.)* Mm hmm.

(Silence. Lisa watches Adrian as he makes some marks in his script.)

LISA: *(Simply.)* You're sort of a prick, you know.

(He looks up at her.)

Have people told you that? It's not that you're British—it's not that at all, in fact, that's a large part of your charm—no, it's—I think it's just your—well, just your style. Your manner. You come off as, well—as a sort of—

ADRIAN: Prick.

LISA: Okay, that may have been too harsh. I didn't—

ADRIAN: No, you said "Prick" and in my experience "Prick" is not a word that people just pick out of the air *casually*. It's a word that one *reserves*; an arrow kept in one's quiver till the proper target is found.

LISA: Adrian—

ADRIAN: No. Don't you dare. Don't you dare back down from this.

LISA: I'm not planning on backing down from it, I just—

ADRIAN: *(Approaching her.)* What then? What are you planning?

LISA: Look. This didn't go well, why don't we—

ADRIAN: What makes you think it didn't go well? We've done something *amazing here*, can't you see that?

LISA: What are you—

ADRIAN: We've jumped. It's delicious, isn't it? To not wade in. To not build a rapport slowly and predictably—brick by brick, anecdote and response—

but, instead, to leap past the introductions, leap past the formalities and into—

(He stops.)

LISA: What? Into what?

ADRIAN: We've only six weeks together. We must move with dispatch.

LISA: Translate:

ADRIAN: Quickly.

(He stares at her.)

LISA: Adrian—

ADRIAN: When you auditioned for me, I didn't hear a word you said. Forgive me, but I was looking at your neck, your body—and my mind took off to a time and place I'd long forgotten.

LISA: *(Looking in the direction Matthew exited.)* He's just outside, you know. He'll be back in a—

ADRIAN: It's a chance I'll take.

I was fifteen years old. In the summers, I worked at a market—cleaning and gutting fish all day, packing them in ice. The stink of fish on my hands, in my hair, all summer. The stray cats everywhere.

At lunch, I'd sit outside and look across the street. And there, nearly every day, was a young woman hanging clothes on a line to dry. A light summer dress. Short, red hair. And each day, I'd watch her. Her body. Her neck—the way it held up her head like an offering. The breeze rippling her dress. I'd sit and watch the way she moved (like God's own dream), the cats licking at my fingers.

(Silence. Lisa stares at him.)

LISA: You're not a prick, Adrian. If you were, you wouldn't be dangerous.

ADRIAN: You think I'm dangerous?

LISA: Oh, yeah.

ADRIAN: To whom?

LISA: To no one but me. And that's the point, really, isn't it?

(She stands and approaches him.)

So, no, I won't back down. Even though I should. Even if you ask me to.

(Pause. Close to him.)

What's your middle name? We're strangers till I know that.

ADRIAN: *(Quietly.)* Ross.

LISA: *(Quietly.)* Thank you.

(Matthew enters, holding his script.)

MATTHEW: Well, what now?

LISA: *(Moving away.)* "Adrian Ross." I like that.

MATTHEW: Which scene are we working next?

ADRIAN: *(Paying no attention to Matthew.)* When do they expect her?

MATTHEW: Who?

ADRIAN: The hurricane.

LISA: Oh, not for a while. She's still at sea.

MATTHEW: Are we going back, or what?

ADRIAN: Actually, Matthew, I'd like to work on Lisa's monologues now—

MATTHEW: Fine.

ADRIAN: —So, why don't you go ahead and take lunch.

MATTHEW: I'll wait.

ADRIAN: You needn't.

MATTHEW: I'll wait for Lisa.

ADRIAN: That's not necessary.

MATTHEW: It's no problem. We'd rather have our lunch together, right Lis?

ADRIAN: *(Before Lisa can respond.)* It's a private moment, Matthew. I must insist that you leave us alone. Nothing personal, but...this is how I work.
(Matthew looks at Lisa, then back to Adrian.)

MATTHEW: Yes. I'm beginning to see that.
(Pause.)
Lis?

LISA: I'll meet you at the restaurant when I'm done.
(Matthew looks at her. Nods. Then, leaves. Frank enters the rehearsal room, speaking to the audience, as before.)

FRANK: Most affairs, you see, are over within minutes.
A daring glance, a brazen word—and it's done.
We come to count on that.

ADRIAN: You'll need your script.
(Lisa picks up her script. She stands, waiting. Adrian remains across the room.)

FRANK: A delicious part of living in the world is the number of lives we *brush past* but never *enter*. The bonds we've created, the institutions we've built—not to mention the rigorous logistics of even the most banal infidelity—all these things serve to keep us on the straight and narrow.

ADRIAN: Do you know which scene we're doing?

LISA: Yes.

FRANK: *(Standing close to Lisa, looking at her.)* Every now and again, though, we let ourselves think... *"What if?"*

But, thankfully, the question itself can be counted on to stop us in our tracks.

ADRIAN: Do you know what I'm looking for?

LISA: Yes.

FRANK: Unless, of course, that question leads to another question…"How?" And if we make it to "How?", well, we're only a stone's throw from "When?"

(During the following, lights isolate down to a pool of light on Lisa and a shaft of light on Frank. Adrian circles Lisa, slowly, then approaches her from behind. He stands directly behind her, very close. He does not touch her. She continues to stare front, taking a deep breath…with Adrian's face very near the back of her neck.)

And at that moment, as we stand at the precipice of deceit…we are grateful for the privacy of our fantasies. We revel in our ability to carry out sin *within the confines of our own mind*—leaving our life protected and our spouse unaware.

And having stood at that precipice…our common sense returns. And we put aside our foolish notions. And that is that.

ADRIAN: Any questions before we begin?

LISA: *(Soft, still staring front.)* No.

FRANK: *Usually.*

(Lisa slowly closes her script…turns…and kisses Adrian on the mouth.

Music: "Don't Explain" by Dexter Gordon.)

Unless the earth curves.

(Music continues, as lights shift to—The Restaurant.

Matthew enters and stands near the table. He looks around for someone to seat him or wait on him—but, there's no one in sight.

Cory enters, following Matthew at a distance. She now has short, red hair. She is wearing a black leather jacket and dark sunglasses. She appears to be a different woman than we saw in Act One.

Matthew decides to leave. As he turns, Cory coolly ducks out of sight. Matthew stops, changes his mind, and returns to the table. Sits.

Cory approaches him.)

CORY: Excuse me—is anyone working here today?

MATTHEW: Not that I can tell.

CORY: None of the tables are bussed, and there's not a waitress in sight.

MATTHEW: I grabbed the only clean table I could find.

CORY: I see that.

(Music fades out.)

MATTHEW: This place is usually packed. I've been coming here for two weeks.

CORY: You work nearby?

MATTHEW: I'm an actor. I'm in rehearsal down the street.

CORY: With Adrian Poynter?

MATTHEW: Yes. You know him?

CORY: I've followed his career.

MATTHEW: Really? I didn't know he was well-known.

CORY: It's relative, I suppose.

MATTHEW: I suppose.

(Pause. Stands, looks around.)

Well, this is ridiculous. I think I'll see if there's another—

CORY: Would you like some wine?

MATTHEW: You have wine?

CORY: I was on a plane this morning. They left the cart near my row.

(From her jacket, she brings out two small airplane-size bottles of red wine.)

Join me?

(Matthew stares at her, then nods.)

MATTHEW: Sure.

(Cory sits at the table, across from him. She lifts her bottle, toasting—)

CORY: Here's to it.

MATTHEW: To what?

CORY: *(Removing her sunglasses.)* To truth at all cost.

(They clink bottles and drink. They sit in silence for a moment. Matthew smiles.)

MATTHEW: You know, I don't meet people. It's not that I don't get out— my wife and I do, we do get out—but I don't often, you know, as a general rule, just *meet people.*

CORY: It's what I do for a living.

MATTHEW: Really?

CORY: Or, more specifically, *follow* people.

MATTHEW: *(With a laugh.)* Follow them—why?

CORY: It's my job. Deadbeat dads, cheating wives, runaway kids. I meet a lot of people—

(Extending her hand to him.)

MATTHEW: Matthew.

CORY: *(Shaking his hand.)* An awful lot of people. And it's nice to meet you. How's the play going?

MATTHEW: You're like a private investigator?

CORY: I prefer "dick"—but it's a word that's out of favor.

MATTHEW: That's really wild. I've never—it must be—I don't know—I think I'd like to do something like that.

CORY: You want to chase after misery day and night?

MATTHEW: Well, it can't be all that bad—I mean you get to travel and—

CORY: And I get to act, pretend to be things I'm not, just like you—

MATTHEW: Well, yeah, right—

CORY: But the bullets are real and the deaths are final.

MATTHEW: Wait. You said you followed people, you didn't say anything about—

CORY: I follow them. And if I'm asked to do *more* than follow them...I do what I'm asked.

MATTHEW: You carry a gun?

CORY: Don't you?

(She looks at Matthew gravely for a moment, then breaks into a large, warm smile.)

I like you, Matthew.

MATTHEW: *(Smiling with her.)* You know, you had me going there for a minute—

CORY: How is it, working with Adrian?

MATTHEW: It's—well, it's funny (not like laughing funny, more like maddening funny). We've been in rehearsal for a two weeks now. And nearly every day, just before lunch, he sends me out of the room. He closes the door. And he works on the scenes featuring my wife, Lisa.

CORY: Do you think they're going to run away together?

MATTHEW: *(With a laugh.)* Run away?

CORY: Yes.

MATTHEW: You mean like the Dish and the Spoon?

CORY: So, while they do that, you come here?

MATTHEW: Yes. But, usually there are waiters and food.

CORY: Why don't you stay and watch?

MATTHEW: He sends me away. He's the director and he can—

CORY: Why don't you stay and watch?

MATTHEW: You just said that.

CORY: Through a parted window blind. A door left ajar. Why don't you leave your coat behind with a tape recorder running?

(Pause.)

Don't you wonder what they're doing?

MATTHEW: They're rehearsing the play, I assume. I hope. What kind of question is—

CORY: Don't you wonder what they're doing?

(Matthew stares at her, then takes a very long swig of his wine.)

It's odd. We think our lives will be changed in front of us—that we'll be present when it happens. But, we never are.

Our lives are changed in distant rooms. Without our knowledge or consent. Some word or glance, some quiet decision across town or across country is often the very thing which comes back and does us in.

Ignorance, Matthew, is not bliss.

It simply postpones the inevitable.

MATTHEW: You're gorgeous.

(A delicious pause between them.)

God, that felt good. Do you have more wine?

CORY: Sure.

(She hands him another small bottle of wine from her jacket.)

MATTHEW: The thing about loving someone—this might turn into a speech, is that okay?

CORY: It's fine.

MATTHEW: —The thing about loving someone, over time, is that you start to feel the only way you can truly surprise them is to hurt them. That's terrible, I know, and avoidable, I suppose—but it hovers there, nevertheless. After some years together, you've spent all your compliments, dished out all your praise, used up a thousand "I love you's" and "I love you" variations, you've got a history of kind words and houseful of pet names—but you've lost the ability to *shock*.

(Leaning in to her.)

I don't know your name.

CORY: Cory.

MATTHEW: Cory...you're gorgeous. (God, that rings when it's new.) But what could I say to Lisa, after all these years, that would carry the same weight? I want out.

I'm leaving you.

I'm having an affair.

Surely there must be more options than that.

CORY: Are you having an affair?

MATTHEW: I don't know. Am I?

(He looks in her eyes. She stares at him. Then, she leans in very close to him...reaches her hand toward his chest...and removes a pen from his shirt pocket. She lifts a matchbox from the table and shakes it—it's empty.)

CORY: They're even out of of matches.

(Using Matthew's pen, she writes something inside the box of matches.)

What's Lisa's last name, Matthew?

MATTHEW: Foster. Same as mine. Why?

(Cory closes the matchbook. She slides it across the table to Matthew.)

CORY: Now, you have my number.

(Stands, touching his cheek gently.)

As things develop, give a call.

(Cory puts on her sunglasses and leaves. Matthew watches her go, as lights shift to—Adrian's Hotel Room. Adrian and Lisa are sitting on the bed, drinking red wine. Clothes loose, spirits high. Music under: "Please Be Kind" sung by Ella Fitzgerald.)

LISA: I don't know. Am I?

ADRIAN: Not pissed, exactly. Not pissed, per sé. But, perhaps on the verge of pissed.

LISA: It's an awful word you people use—"pissed." I much prefer "drunk." It sounds more like what it feels like.

ADRIAN: American common sense strikes again.

LISA: I've no sense.

(She kisses him.)

No sense at all.

(She kisses him again.)

Did you see the paper this morning?

ADRIAN: No.

LISA: The hurricane is picking up speed.

ADRIAN: A new one, you mean?

LISA: Yes. It's headed straight for shore. Evacuations have been ordered.

ADRIAN: And what are they calling this one?

LISA: Adrian.

(Kiss.)

Adrian Ross.

(They hold each other. Music has faded out.)

Why did you divorce your wife?

(He stares at her, pulls away a bit.)

What? I'm sorry—is that a nerve?

(He continues to look away.)

Adrian, I—

ADRIAN: We divorced because I was a mediocre husband. And though my wife could tolerate that, I could not. I've been mediocre at many things in my life—my work as a director included—yes, you needn't say it, you needn't coddle me, I'm fully aware that I'm only half the director I wish to be. Thankfully it's a job in which one is encouraged to be an asshole, so I've done quite well for myself—but, in the case of my marriage, I couldn't bear the weight of my own *commonness*. The harder I looked at my life, the more I discovered how very *ordinary* I was. A tepid man slogging through his days, hauling around the albatross of my own minutiae.

(Pause. Then, a laugh at his own expense—)

I'm sorry. I think it's the wine talking. Maybe we should—

LISA: Shut up and let the wine talk.

(She pours him some more wine.)

Where is she now? Your ex?

ADRIAN: I've no idea. She spent the greater part of our marriage trying to change into the woman she thought I wanted her to be. But, since I didn't know, really, who that woman *was*—she just...kept on changing. So by the time I finally left her, I barely recognized her.

(She looks at him. Then she removes her gold wedding ring from her finger.)

What are you doing?

LISA: We've only four weeks left. We must move with dispatch.

ADRIAN: And then?

(Lisa holds her ring up to the light, looking at it.)

When that time is over...what then?

(She looks at him. Music: "Am I Wrong?" by Keb Mo—first verse, as lights

shift quickly to—Frank's Office. Frank is making notes on the clipboard, as—Matthew enters, buoyantly, carrying a white paper sack from a deli. Music out.)

MATTHEW: Hello, Frank. Sorry I'm late.

FRANK: No problem. Were you out having a smoke?

MATTHEW: No, Frank. I've turned over a new leaf.

(Matthew removes two small salads in plastic containers from the sack. He hands one to Frank.)

Salad? I didn't know what kind of dressing you like, so I grabbed a bunch.

(Matthew drops a handful of packets of dressing into Frank's lap.)

FRANK: Matthew, to what do we owe—

MATTHEW: I'm having an affair, Frank!

FRANK: Say again?

MATTHEW: An affair. A torrid affair. More about that later. And you know what else: I got a tattoo. A huge RED HEART—it covers my entire back. Hurt like hell. I'll show you in a minute—

FRANK: Matthew, what in the world—

MATTHEW: And furthermore, Frank: Yesterday a guy cut me off on the free-way. So I followed him. And I pulled him over. And I *shot him* to *death*. He bled like a leaky garbage bag.

You've hardly touched your salad.

FRANK: Matthew, I think we need to go back.

MATTHEW: We went back.

FRANK: *(Firm.)* No. Back to the beginning of this session. I want you to stand up and get your thoughts in order and come through that door again.

MATTHEW: For you, Frank, anything.

(Matthew stands and leaves. He immediately returns, saying—)

Hello, Frank.

FRANK: Hello, Matthew. What's new?

MATTHEW: *(Happily.)* I've been making things up! (But you probably could tell—you're a professional, you've got plaques on the wall.) I've been pre-tending to have an affair, get a tattoo, kill people who don't use their turn signal—things like that. And, in doing so, Frank, I've had a break-through.

FRANK: Of what sort?

MATTHEW: I was walking to the deli just now and it hit me: "Matthew, *maybe you're wrong.*" Amazing, isn't it? All these weeks you've been asking me: "Are you *sure*, Matthew? Are you *certain* that your wife is having an affair?" But, now I know that's not my true fear, Frank.

FRANK: It's not?

MATTHEW: No, my true fear is this: that Lisa has stopped loving me.

(*Pause. More quietly.*)

That is my true fear—

FRANK: (*Making a note.*) Good, Matthew—

MATTHEW: And now, having named that, I see that all my other fears are ILLUSIONS. *She is not sleeping with Adrian* —I invented it!

FRANK: Matthew—

MATTHEW: I made it up!

FRANK: Matthew, I applaud your realization, but that doesn't mean your *suspicions* are necessarily *untrue*—

MATTHEW: ALL IN MY MIND, Frank. I've misconstrued EVERYTHING because I fear our love is gone. And, perhaps it is. And that will break my heart and I'll spend years with you in this stupid room. But, for now, this much I'm certain of: there is no affair.

FRANK: Matthew—

MATTHEW: (*Definitively.*) None at all.

(*Frank stares at him, as lights shift quickly to—*

A brief silhouette of Cory, looking in the direction of—

Adrian's Hotel Room. A moonlit night. Adrian and Lisa are in bed, covered by a sheet. Lisa's head rests on Adrian's chest. Her shoulders are bare and exposed.

The light on Cory vanishes.

Music under: "Moon Love" by Chet Baker.)

LISA: Do you remember?

ADRIAN: Hmm?

LISA: When I met you—that first day—you passed me in the hallway. And you said hello. And then you said something else. Do you remember?

ADRIAN: Tell me.

LISA: You said: "Yes." And I looked at you—not knowing what you meant. And you said: "Yes is the answer." To what? I asked.
"To whatever you'd like to do with me."
(A wry smile.)
You were such a prick.
ADRIAN: Yes. So you said.
(They kiss. They hold each other.)
LISA: We've got to tell him, you know.
ADRIAN: How?
LISA: We'll sit him down. We'll look him in the eye. And we'll say—
(Adrian sits up in bed, saying—)
ADRIAN: That's what I'm looking for.

(The Rehearsal Studio. Bright lights once again. Music out, abruptly. Matthew sits at a distance, watching.)

ADRIAN: Do you see now, Matthew? *That's* the quality the scene desperately needs.
(Adrian throws off the covers and gets out of bed. With the exception of his shirt, he is fully clothed. He pulls his shirt back on, as—Matthew glares at him. Lisa pulls her shirt or sweater back up over her shoulders.)
Try it yourself this time. And, please, keep in mind—
MATTHEW: Adrian. May I ask you something?
ADRIAN: Certainly.
MATTHEW: Just how STUPID do you think I am?
(Quick beat.)
Let me rephrase that: Have you no SHAME? Do you think I'll just stand blindly to the side as you BED MY WIFE?!
LISA: Maybe we should take ten—
ADRIAN: Yes, let's do that—
(Calling to the Stage Crew.)
Let's strike the bed, please—
(The Crew strikes the bed during the following.)
MATTHEW: *Say it.* Both of you. Just *look me in the eye and SAY IT.*
LISA: Matthew, what are you—
MATTHEW: *(Sharp.)* You know perfectly well.
(Matthew quickly sets two chairs, side by side—identical to Act One.)
Let's do this. I'll go out and have a smoke. And when I return, you'll be

sitting here, side by side. And you'll *tell me all of it.* Is that too much to ask?

LISA: ADRIAN:

This is not the—   Matthew, listen—

MATTHEW: Just SAY THE WORDS.

(They stare at him, saying nothing.)

Was it *good*? Is it *still* good? Will it be good *tonight*? Or maybe at *lunch* if you can give me the slip and steal an hour? Or *half an hour*? Or maybe just a *few minutes*—a few, protected moments alone to look in each other's eyes. To kiss. To bury your faces in each other's clothing. To put your tongues in each other's mouths. To *plot*. To whisper.

(Silence. Then, Lisa goes and sits in the chair, facing Matthew. Adrian does not move.)

Thank you, Lisa. Adrian?

ADRIAN: *(A firm resolve.)* We are here to talk about the play. The play and nothing more. Do you understand?

LISA: Adrian, please, there's no point in—

MATTHEW: The *play*?

ADRIAN: Yes.

MATTHEW: And nothing more?

ADRIAN: Yes.

MATTHEW: You know, *I quite agree*! Let's work on the PLAY, shall we?!

LISA: Matthew—

MATTHEW: *(Taking her script from her.)* Could I look at your script, Lis? Thank you so much. I think I left mine at the office of my SHRINK during one of my INNUMERABLE SESSIONS to REHABILITATE my sense of DISAPPEARING SELF WORTH.

(Quickly, to Lisa, anticipating her question.)

Yes, I'm in therapy. WhoopDeeDoo.

(Opening the script.)

NOW: Let's begin. Please, Mr. Director, advise us. Which scene shall we be undertaking today?

ADRIAN: The final scene.

MATTHEW: How fitting. C'mon, Lis. "This is how he works"—you know that.

(To Adrian.)

I'm, of course, happy to *use the chair* or *not*. Whatever you think.

ADRIAN: Now, as we've discussed, the affair between them is long over. The *entire thing* is in the past—

LISA: *Well* in the past—

ADRIAN: It's been *four years*—

MATTHEW: Yes. But, I wonder from, say, her HUSBAND'S point of view, if it really is over? Do the two of them really think he's been blind to EVERY-THING?

ADRIAN: I think they're operating under that premise, yes.

MATTHEW: *Interesting.*

LISA: *(Moving away.)* Shall we begin?

MATTHEW: One more thing: In the flashback scene—the one in which her husband first declares his love for her—Lisa's character says: "Be careful what you're getting into. I'm trouble."

(To Lisa.)

Do you know the scene I mean?

LISA: Yes, I do. He should have considered that before he married her. She gave him fair warning.

MATTHEW: But that's just the thing: When a man hears that a woman is "trou-ble"—he doesn't take it as a warning. He takes it as a *dare.*

LISA: That's not her fault.

MATTHEW: It seems *nothing is.*

LISA: She was being truthful with him. Completely truthful. And she expected the same in return.

MATTHEW: *(Laughs.) Complete truth?*

LISA: Yes.

ADRIAN: Matthew, I don't think Lisa is—

MATTHEW: I'm sorry, but that would be brutal. You don't—your CHARAC-TER doesn't want that much truth. No one does. Truth as a RULE—yes. Truth MORE OFTEN THAN NOT—yes. But not ALL THE TIME. Any good mate knows the value of the *comforting little lie.*

LISA: Such as?

MATTHEW: Oh, in the case of her husband: What he really thinks of her FAM-ILY. Her FRIENDS.

LISA: Hey, wait a minute, he LIKES her friends.

MATTHEW: *(To Adrian.)* There's the BEAUTY OF LYING! She really believes it!

ADRIAN: Let's get on with the scene, if we could—

LISA: No, let's *address* this. MY character sees it differently.

MATTHEW: *(Tossing the script at her feet.)* Do enlighten us.

LISA: *(Not picking the script up.)* I think if you look carefully at the TEXT, you'll see that her husband lives in some kind of *dream world*. He can't stand the fact that his LIFE does not match his FANTASIES, his little THOUGHTS—

MATTHEW: What are you—

LISA: And not that she KNOWS his thoughts—not at all—how could she?—when he *won't let her in.* He wouldn't dare trust her with his thoughts—because that might SHOCK HER or SURPRISE HER—

ADRIAN: Lisa, let's move on—

LISA: He'd never PUT HIS HEART ON THE LINE FOR HER, because that requires *courage*—that requires—

ADRIAN: Lisa, please, stop it—

LISA: *(Turning to Adrian.)* And, then there's her lover.

(Pause.)

Or what *passes* for a lover in a *play like this.* His idea of courtship is to talk her ear off and then buy her a bathing suit the size of a bookmark.

ADRIAN: Lisa—

LISA: He thinks he can *chat* his way into her heart—but this man's got nothing to say. He's pure noise. This man is *noon at a clock shop*!

ADRIAN: That's QUITE ENOUGH—

LISA: Look at it, both of you: it's all a *dirty mess* and she's CAUGHT IN THE MIDDLE OF IT.

MATTHEW: *(Simply.)* That explains the showers.

(They both look at him.)

It seemed so *odd* to him that she began to take a shower every night before she climbed in bed. In all the years of their marriage, she'd never done that—until now. What did it *mean?* he wondered. Why this sudden need to be *clean?*

(Lisa stares at Matthew. Then, she picks up the script from the floor. Her voice softens, she moves closer to him—holding the script in front of them both.)

LISA: If you do, though, look at the text...this is what you'll find: That when the affair is over and done, four years later, *she returns to him.*

(From the script, softly.)

"So, it worked out?" he asks her.

MATTHEW: And she says—

LISA: "Yes."

MATTHEW: "Your marriage."

LISA: "Yes."

MATTHEW: "I'm glad for you.
(Pause. Quietly.)
Really."
LISA: *(Also quietly.)* "Thank you."
(Matthew stares at Lisa. Then, he moves the chair out of the way, saying—)
MATTHEW: You know, Adrian, I've always wished that—for the final scene of the play—the stage could be bare. *Completely bare.* Pared down to its essence. Leaving only the fundamental unit of human life: Two people. And time.
(He approaches Lisa.)
I've wished I could walk up very close to her.
And then—as the play ends—the two of us would attempt love's one true act of bravery:
To face each other.
To look into each other's eyes.
And to not run.
(He looks in her eyes. After a moment, Lisa looks away from Matthew, turns and leaves. Matthew watches her go. After she is gone, he turns to Adrian.)
Have you had a nice month with my wife?
(Adrian is silent.)
I don't blame you for loving her. She's a warm, smart, vibrant woman— and you know as well as I that without the likes of her, the known world is a parking lot.
I don't even care if you love her *better* than I do. That's for her to decide. But never...*ever*...think you love her *more* than I. For that, my friend, will be your undoing. I promise you that.
(Matthew leaves. Pause. Then, Lisa steps back into the room, looks at Adrian.)
LISA: What did he say? Adrian?
ADRIAN: It's so odd: I'm jealous of him. That he is your husband. That you go to his bed at night. Think of it—I'm jealous of a man whose wife is deceiving him, whose trusting heart is crumbling to ash.
(She stares at him.)
I'm still married, Lisa. I came to the States to hide, really. My wife had hired a private investigator to track my whereabouts in London. To gain proof of my indiscretions.
(Silence. Lisa speaks softly, reigning in her anger.)
LISA: Indiscretions. You mean, like, lies?

(Pause.)

Like telling me you're divorced? You mean, *little things like THAT?*

ADRIAN: Lisa, listen to me—

LISA: Well, you know something: you can add *us* to the list of things you're mediocre at.

ADRIAN: I'm not alone in this, Lisa. You are—

LISA: *Indiscretions.* Is that us? Is that who I am? Am I *this month's indiscretion?*

ADRIAN: Lisa, please—

(Lights shift instantly to separate shafts of light on—Lisa and Frank. Frank holds the clipboard, pen poised.)

LISA: *(Urgently.)* I had a dream last night—

FRANK: Tell me, Lisa.

LISA: And in my dream I am washing dishes. I have taken off my wedding ring, as I always do. And I reach into the soapy water and pull out a little Tupperware container. And I remove the top. And there is a *heart* inside. A human heart, still beating. And in the dream I remember reading that a heart can live for about five hours outside the body before it dies—

FRANK: Between four and six hours, actually, depending on age, condition—

LISA: And I know that before it dies I have to find out who it belongs to—and return it to him.

So, I seal it up in the Tupperware. And I get in my car. I go to Adrian's hotel room. I open the door. I reach inside his chest...and his heart is there, pounding away. So, I drive home. And I look everywhere for Matthew. I drive to rehearsal. I check the restaurant, the book store, the deli. I can't find him anywhere. I go home and wait for him. I sit on the floor and stare at my watch...holding the little container in my hands...the heart beating...the hours ticking away...

FRANK: And did Matthew ever arrive?

LISA: I woke up.

(Silence.)

FRANK: The waiting is very telling. What are you waiting for, Lisa?

LISA: I'm waiting for—

FRANK: Yes?

LISA: I'm—

FRANK: Yes?

LISA: Let me *finish.*

FRANK: It's been more than a month—

LISA: I'm aware of that—

FRANK: Well?

LISA: I'm waiting for the right time.

FRANK: The right time to break it to him?

LISA: Yes. Is that so bad?

FRANK: Oh, I see. There is a *good day* to devastate someone?! Perhaps you'll wait till he wins the *lottery* and then tell him. Or wait till you're on your *deathbed* and then tell him.

LISA: You've made your point—

FRANK: Lisa: *the perfect time to hurt someone never comes.*

(Lights instantly restore to—The Rehearsal Studio. Lisa and Adrian are exactly where we left them.)

ADRIAN: Lisa, please—

LISA: So I was, what, the person who looks after your feelings when you're on the road, away from home? I was, what, your *heart-sitter*?

ADRIAN: I was going to tell you—

LISA: When?

ADRIAN: When the time was right.

(Silence.)

LISA: You should go.

ADRIAN: Lis—

LISA: Rehearsal is over.

*(Adrian looks at her, then exits. Lisa sits on the ground in the center of the room. She closes her eyes, breathes heavily, as, from behind her—
Cory enters. Her hair is short and red, as before. She wears her leather jacket and sunglasses. She carries a leather shoulder bag.)*

CORY: Pardon me. Sorry to disturb you, but—

(Lisa turns.)

I'm looking for a Lisa Foster.

LISA: That's me.

CORY: *(Removing her sunglasses.)* Really?

(Lisa nods.)

Lisa, I wondered if I could ask you a few questions.

LISA: About...?

CORY: It's a private matter.

(*Cory produces an 8x10 photo of Adrian from her shoulder bag. She holds it out to Lisa.*)

Do you know this man? His name is Derek. Derek Savage. He often directs under an alias: Adrian Poynter.

LISA: I know who he is.

(*Pause.*)

His wife hired you, didn't she? To track him down.

CORY: I'm not at liberty to say.

LISA: Well, you've found him.

CORY: You're working with Adrian currently?

LISA: Yes. I was his first choice.

(*Pause.*)

You can tell his wife it was me. Whatever information she needs, I can give it to you.

(*Pause. Stands.*)

And...stupid as it sounds, and inadequate as it is...you can also tell her I'm sorry. I had no idea he was still married. Will you tell her that for me?

CORY: I will.

(*Cory is staring at Lisa.*)

LISA: Is there anything else?

CORY: I met your husband, Lisa. He seems very nice.

(*Cory turns and goes. Lisa is alone for a moment. Then, Matthew enters. He walks directly up to Lisa and looks in her eyes.*)

MATTHEW: (*Quietly.*) Lis.

(*Pause.*)

You can tell me the truth.

(*Pause.*)

It's all I ask. Just look in my eyes and answer me: Are you having an affair?

(*A pause, then...*)

LISA: (*Honestly, directly.*) Yes.

MATTHEW: (*Pause. Quietly.*) Thank you.

LISA: With Adrian. But it's over now, Matthew. It's over and done.

(*Pause. From her heart.*)

I'm sorry.

(Frank appears in the room, holding Matthew's script—unopened.)

FRANK: *Matthew?!* Is that really what she—

MATTHEW: Okay, NO, that's what I *wanted* her to say, and I know there's a DIFFERENCE—but right now I'm not—

FRANK: *(Firmly.)* Matthew—we've come this far together. Tell me what she *really said.*

MATTHEW: All right.

(Matthew pauses, turns back to Lisa—who has not moved.)

What she really said was:

LISA: *(Honestly, directly.)* No. Don't be silly, Matthew. I'd never do that.

FRANK: *Matthew?!*

MATTHEW: OKAY, SO I NEVER ASKED HER!

(Lisa exits.)

FRANK: Why?

MATTHEW: Because it makes no difference what she says! I'm trapped by my own suspicions: If she says "Yes"—I'm proved right and DEVASTATED. If she says "No"—she's *lying* and I'm VINDICATED. I can't win, Frank!

FRANK: Matthew, for god's sake, stop *fooling yourself.* You've got to face facts, you've got to—

MATTHEW: HOW, Frank? In what way? What is it you want me to tell you?!

FRANK: *(Exasperated, turning away from him.)*

People think there are things I want to hear. I don't know where they get that notion. I ask direct questions—and then watch glaciers form on the faces of—

(Matthew points to the script in Frank's hand—)

MATTHEW: That's from the PLAY. Those are lines from MY SCRIPT. Why would you be saying—

FRANK: *(Opening the script.)* I've had some experience in the theatre *myself,* Matthew, and I think it may serve our purpose here—

MATTHEW: Well, then. You should come to rehearsal with me. I'm sure *Lisa would be thrilled to see you.* Are her SESSIONS with you going well?!

FRANK: Matthew, where did you get the idea that—

MATTHEW: I have a new friend, Frank. She's a dick. She follows people. She followed Lisa to your office.

FRANK: Matthew, the privacy of my clients is—

MATTHEW: Oh, right—that's "*confidential.*" The words "*conflict of interest*" also sort of come to mind, don't they, FRANK?!

ADRIAN'S VOICE: Okay. Great. Let's set up the RESTAURANT.

(Adrian approaches the stage from the audience.

During the following, the Stage Crew enters and changes the stage into the restaurant from Act One.

Eerie music—similar to Act One—underscores this transition.)
MATTHEW: We're not FINISHED HERE!
(Adrian ignores him, and goes about setting up the stage. Frank approaches Matthew.)
FRANK: Do as he says, Matthew.
MATTHEW: Leave me ALONE, FRANK—
FRANK: Go *back to the restaurant.* Back to the *final day of rehearsal*—when it all unraveled.
MATTHEW: Enough, Frank—no more sessions—
FRANK: This is not a session, Matthew—
MATTHEW: *(To Adrian—who does not hear him.)* Can we take ten, please?!
FRANK: And it's not a rehearsal.
MATTHEW: But, Frank—
(Frank ushers Matthew away, saying—)
FRANK: This, Matthew, is the thing itself.

(Lights shift quickly to—

The Restaurant. Lisa and Adrian standing together. The scene is identical to that in Act One—with one exception: no party hats.

Eerie music out.)

LISA: We have amnesia. We forget what we know.
(Adrian returns to the table and sits. Lisa stands, alone.)
This time, we think, unlike all the previous anguish and innuendo, *this time* the goodbyes will have a grace to them. They don't.

They never will.

(Lights shift to another area of the restaurant—

A Wait Station. Again, identical to Act One. As Matthew arrives, Cory is removing her long black wig—revealing her short red hair underneath. During the following, she takes off her waitress apron and puts on her leather jacket.)

MATTHEW: Cory?! What are you doing?

CORY: *(Tossing the wig to him.)* No more illusions, Matthew. No more playing games. Are they still at the table?

MATTHEW: Yes. And, the restaurant is empty again—just like the day I met you. How does that happen?!

CORY: I have an arrangement with the owner.

MATTHEW: You *what*?!

CORY: I like the adventure of revenge, don't you? The fever of it.

MATTHEW: Cory, what are you—

CORY: It's just as you said: the only way to truly surprise someone is to hurt them.

(Matthew stares at her, baffled.)

Let's do it.

(Cory goes, and Matthew follows her, as lights quickly return to—

The Restaurant Table. As Cory approaches, Lisa, not looking up, says—)

LISA: I think we need more wine.

CORY: Check the yellow pages under "Liquor." Hello, Adrian.

(Adrian looks up. He freezes. Cory sits in the chair between them, as she says—)

Mind if I join you?

(Cory looks up at Matthew, standing.)

Matthew?

(Matthew pauses, then brings a fourth chair to the table and sits.)

MATTHEW: Yes. I think I'll use the chair.

(The four of them sit there, looking at each other. Cory smiles.)

CORY: How nice to be together. You remember me, don't you, Lisa?

LISA: Umm—

CORY: There's no umm here. You told me about your affair with Adrian.

(Pause.)

I told you his real name was Derek.

(Pause.)

And you told me to tell his wife that you were sorry.

LISA: I am.

CORY: Well. I accept your apology.

(Lisa and Matthew stare at Cory.)

MATTHEW: *(Softly.)* What?

ADRIAN: *(Simply.)* The hurricane has arrived. Lisa, this is Cory. My wife.

CORY: *(Now an impeccable British accent.)* Hello.

(Cory lifts a glass from the table and drinks.)

I think it's going very well. Don't you, Matthew?

ADRIAN: So, this is who you are now?

(Cory nods.)

I thought you'd hired a private eye.

CORY: Oh, love. Who could possibly track you down better than I? Lisa, dear, I have something of yours.

(Cory holds up Lisa's gold wedding ring. Lisa checks her ring finger, surprised that it's bare.)

LISA: Where did you get—?

CORY: I was going through my husband's hotel room. And there it was under the bed.

(Holding it up to the light.)

It's the simplest thing, you see. A *circle.*

(Giving the ring to Lisa as she looks at Adrian.)

Everything comes round.

(Cory pulls a gun from her leather jacket and points it at Adrian.)

Stand up.

(Matthew and Lisa stand and back away.)

MATTHEW: LISA:

Cory, what are you—   Oh, my god—

ADRIAN: Cory, PLEASE —

CORY: Quiet, love. You don't have lines in this scene. Move away from the table.

(Cory trains the gun on Adrian, who pleads with her—)

ADRIAN: You mustn't do this, Cory—

CORY: Oh, *mustn't* I?

ADRIAN: Listen to me. It needn't be over between us—

CORY: Are you going to lie to me again?

ADRIAN: No, I'm not.

CORY: There! You lied again.

ADRIAN: Our lives could begin anew—

CORY: And again!

ADRIAN: I never intended to hurt you, Cory—

CORY: You *can't stop*, can you?!

> (*Matthew steps in, toward Cory—*)

MATTHEW: CORY, NO—this is not the way I remember it!

CORY: *(Turning to Matthew, with the gun.)* No, Matthew, this is the way it happened.

> (*Matthew backs away. Cory returns the gun to Adrian.*)

ADRIAN: Cory—please—let me explain—

> (*Cory cocks the gun. Adrian kneels and grovels, quaking with fear.*)

CORY: *Just tell me when you can't take it anymore.*

ADRIAN: I can't, Cory! I CAN'T TAKE IT ANYMORE! Please. Don't do this. I beg of you—

> (*Adrian has curled up into a ball on the floor, whimpering, terrified. Cory keeps the gun trained on him—shaking with rage—about to pull the trigger. Then...exhausted...Cory lowers the gun to her side, unable to shoot him. She sighs deeply, turns away from him.*)

CORY: *(Softly.)* Don't be silly, love. I could never hurt you. You know that.

> (*A long pause as Adrian stands, takes a deep breath, collecting himself.*)

ADRIAN: Thank you.

> (*Cory quickly turns and fires, saying—*)

CORY: Goodbye.

> (*A loud gunshot which echoes for a long time through the room, as lights instantly isolate—
>
> Frank, addressing the audience. Frank holds the script—unopened—but does not refer to it.
>
> The sound of a distant siren.*)

FRANK: Why?— you may ask. I am asked that often. In this case, the common casualty was truth and the reason given was love. The bullet—like Cory herself—merely grazed Adrian's heart. No charges were filed. The wounds healed. And they returned, on separate flights, to London.

(The siren fades away.)

As for Matthew and Lisa: They stood side by side as the ambulance took Adrian away. Then they parted, saying nothing—and haven't seen each other in *years*.

Passion and suspicion—they are twin fevers. Each blinds us to this, the most obvious of facts: in time, everything gets known. Everything. And, in the end—

MATTHEW'S VOICE: Okay, great, thank you.

(Lights immediately expand to reveal—

The Rehearsal Studio. Identical to the beginning of the play.

Matthew sits behind the table—wearing a change of clothes, to indicate passage of time. Frank opens up the script, pleading —)

FRANK: But, I'm not *finished*—

MATTHEW: I've seen all I need. Thanks for coming in—

FRANK: But, please, if you'd just let me—

MATTHEW: We'll call you when we know. Now, if you'd—

FRANK: *(Starting off, carrying the script.)* You didn't even give me a *chance*—

MATTHEW: If you'd please leave the script behind, and—

FRANK: But, Matthew, I—

MATTHEW: *Drop it, Frank.*

(Frank stares at him, then drops the script to the ground. Turns and leaves. Matthew enjoys throwing Frank's resumé into the trash, then says—)

MATTHEW: Next.

(Lisa enters. She, too, is wearing a change of clothes. She stands in the room, as Matthew makes a note in front of him—not looking up.)

Name?

(Lisa says nothing. Matthew looks up, saying—)

I said—

(He sees her. Stops. Speaks, quietly.)

Oh, my god. Lisa. It's been—

LISA: Years.

MATTHEW: Yes.

(Pause.)

Four years. And you're still—

LISA: Finishing your sentences.

> *(He smiles a bit. So does she. Silence.)*

So, it worked out? Going off on your own?

MATTHEW: Yes.

LISA: I'm glad for you.

> *(Pause.)*

Really.

MATTHEW: And you?

LISA: Nothing to report.

MATTHEW: Four years?

> *(Lisa nods.)*

And there's been no—

LISA: Only you.

> *(Silence. He stares at her.)*

Something I've wondered. All that time with Adrian, you never—I kept waiting for you to just *come out and ask me*, but you—

MATTHEW: No. Never. It's still your secret.

> *(Silence.)*

LISA: I'm here to audition.

MATTHEW: Lisa—

LISA: Just like old times. I'd like to do the final scene. I'd like to have the ending you always wished for.

> *(Pause.)*

The two of us. And nothing else.

> *(Pause.)*

Can we do that?

> *(Matthew takes a long look at Lisa, then says, simply—)*

MATTHEW: Yes.

(Matthew snaps his fingers. As he does so—

Music: "I Want You" by Tom Waits.
The Stage Crew enters and removes everything from the stage. If possible, all other existing scenery and masking—including the Rehearsal Studio itself is carried and/or flown away—leaving the stage [and theatre] as barren as possible.

Matthew and Lisa watch, surprised, as the set disappears around them. Then, they turn to each other—the entire stage between them.

Music continues, under.)

LISA: *(Quietly.)* What now?

MATTHEW: I want to see your eyes.
  (Lisa steps toward Matthew. He, too, steps forward—until they are facing each other at center stage. They look into each other's eyes.)
  Do this.

LISA: What?

MATTHEW: Lie to everyone but me.

(Matthew and Lisa remain, face to face, looking into each other's eyes, as—

The song concludes, and—

The lights fade slowly to black.)

END OF PLAY

Gun-shy
by Richard Dresser

BIOGRAPHY

Richard Dresser's plays include *Below the Belt*, which premiered in the Humana Festival in 1995 and was subsequently produced off-Broadway and at a number of regional theatres. Also *Alone at the Beach* (Humana Festival 1988), *The Downside, Better Days, Bait & Switch, The Road to Ruin, Bed & Breakfast, At Home* and *Splitsville*, all of which are published by Samuel French. He has twice attended the O'Neill National Playwrights Conference, is a former member of New Dramatists and a current member of the HB Playwrights Unit. For television he wrote HBO's *Vietnam War Stories* and has served as writer/producer on such shows as *The Days and Nights of Molly Dodd, Bakersfield P.D., Public Morals* and *Smoldering Lust*. He currently resides in Los Angeles.

HUMANA FESTIVAL PRODUCTION

Gun-shy was first performed at the Humana Festival of New American Plays, March, 1997. It was directed by Gloria Muzio with the following cast:

Evie	Maryann Urbano
Carter	V Craig Heidenreich
Duncan	William McNulty
Caitlin	Twyla Hafermann
Other People	Lee Sellars

and the following production staff:

Scenic Designer	Paul Owen
Costume Designer	David Zinn
Lighting Designer	Ed McCarthy
Sound Designer	Martin R. Desjardins
Properties Designer	Ron Riall
Stage Manager	Julie A. Richardson
Assistant Stage Manager	Andrew Scheer
Dramaturg	Liz Engelman
New York Casting	Eve Battaglia

CHARACTERS

EVIE: a woman about forty
CARTER: a man about forty
DUNCAN: a man in his mid-forties
CAITLIN: a woman in her twenties

The other characters are to be played by one actor:
WAITER
RAMON
NEIL
NURSE
PARAMEDIC

SETTING

Act I takes place in various locations in the Pacific northwest, New England, and Washington, D.C.

Act II takes place in Duncan's house outside Boston.

GUN-SHY

ACT ONE
SCENE 1

Lights up on a revolving restaurant. Evie and Carter are at a table by the window eating clams and sipping champagne.

EVIE: You don't know what pain is.

CARTER: I know what pain is.

EVIE: You don't know what pain is.

CARTER: I know what pain is.

EVIE: You don't know what pain is.

CARTER: I know what pain is. Pain is talking to you when you're like this.

EVIE: Like what? This is me.

CARTER: No it isn't. It's not the real you. The real you is fun and wild and spontaneous.

EVIE: Except when the real me wants to talk. *(Opens her purse.)* What do you see?

CARTER: Is that...

EVIE: Yes, my underwear. I took it off in the ladies room.

CARTER: Bravo! *(Pouring more champagne.)* This is why I love you.

EVIE: Shut up. I am somebody's mother. There's a boy who calls me mom. I swear I'd strip for you, right here, right now, just watch me.
(Evie starts to unbutton her dress.)

CARTER: Please wait. You're welcome to strip in the car.

EVIE: I don't know what we're doing. I don't know where we're headed. We're going a hundred and twenty miles an hour and who, pray tell, is at the wheel?

CARTER: I swear to God I have never been so happy in my entire life.

EVIE: Yes, because you've had a largely pathetic and unrewarding life. But I have been happy, and I want to be happy again. No, I *demand* to be happy again.

CARTER: You're not happy?

EVIE: This isn't happiness. This is sickness, this is fever, this is delirium.
> (*Downs her champagne.*)
> We have to hold hands and leap into the void or I'll retreat. I'll go back to some small safe place. I've spent nearly two hundred thousand dollars to learn this about myself. Is this a fling? It's fine if it's a fling, I've flung with the best.

CARTER: How could what we share be just a fling?

EVIE: Then what is it?

CARTER: It has...significant implications for the future.

EVIE: Why don't I just kill myself?

CARTER: We could be good together. Long-term.

EVIE: How can we be good for each other? There are so many things wrong with you.

CARTER: More than normal?

EVIE: But still, I want you. Is there reason to hope? Tell me I can hope. Can I hope? Please?

CARTER: *(Glances out window.)* No.

EVIE: No? Did I hear the word "no"?

CARTER: No! *Look*! Somebody's breaking into my car!

EVIE: No, Carter, *you* look! Look at me! Talk to me!

CARTER: I should *never* drive that car! Never! *(Carter strains to see, but the car is lost to view as the restaurant turns.)* Why did we come to a revolving restaurant, anyway?

EVIE: Well, how convenient.

CARTER: Don't you understand? It's my car!

EVIE: It's always something, isn't it? I am opening my heart to you and you won't even look at me.

CARTER: Waiter!

EVIE: What do you think a waiter is going to do?

CARTER: Somebody's got to save my car.

EVIE: But a waiter? Even a good one...

CARTER: I'm going down there myself. If my time is up, then so be it.

EVIE: You'd face death on the street before you'd deal with me honestly, wouldn't you? You'd rather go out in a hail of gunfire than answer the hard questions. Sniveling bastard!
> (*A waiter comes over.*)

WAITER: How are we doing?

CARTER: You have to stop the restaurant.

WAITER: I can't stop the restaurant.

CARTER: Who can?

WAITER: No one.

CARTER: It can't go on forever!

WAITER: In seven years I've never known it to stop.

CARTER: Disadvantaged peoples are attacking my car!

WAITER: This is why we encourage valet parking.

CARTER: Dear God. Please bring me a phone.

(The waiter leaves.)

CARTER: *(Continuing.)* If they mess with my car-phone I'll get a gun and blow their brains out and teach them a lesson they'll never forget.

EVIE: Carter, you've never shown this much passion for *me*, even in bed, even drunk in bed. I'll be damned if I'll compete with a car, not at my age.

(The waiter brings them more drinks.)

CARTER: *(Staring at the drinks.)* That isn't a telephone.

WAITER: All the phones are in use. These drinks are on the house.

CARTER: Do we look like we need more drinks?

EVIE: We need therapy.

CARTER: We need to rescue my car. Here it comes! *(Looks out.)* Oh, God, they're burning it.

EVIE: Please, Carter, if you love me you've got to look at me and listen to me because I feel like I'm disappearing.

CARTER: I need to get to a phone.

EVIE: Don't leave me. Please!

CARTER: I'll be right back.

EVIE: Stop!

(As Carter starts to leave, Evie plunges her clam fork into his hand.)

EVIE: *(Continuing.)* Oh my God, oh, Carter. Look what's happened to you.

CARTER: It didn't just happen. You did it.

EVIE: Let's not quibble, not now. I am not a violent person and here you've got me putting clam forks through your hand. I honestly don't know how you did this.

(A moan from Carter as lights fade.)

SCENE 2

Lights up on Duncan's house. Caitlin is at the table wearing her coat. Duncan sets down two plates.

CAITLIN: Oh, Duncan, it looks almost good enough to eat.

DUNCAN: But?

CAITLIN: I'm only allowed to smell it. They told me to imagine each bite as a large, glistening eye, staring at me with contempt. Wine?

DUNCAN: You know I can't drink.

CAITLIN: Oh, right. Sorry.

(Caitlin pours herself wine. Duncan eats, Caitlin drinks.)

DUNCAN: You aren't cold, are you? I could splurge and turn up the furnace.

CAITLIN: Oh, no, I've got mittens if it gets colder.

DUNCAN: Eating would warm you up. You have to eat sometime. I learned that before I dropped out of med school.

CAITLIN: Seven more pounds, and why are you being so judgmental? If I choose to stop eating I'd like encouragement, not criticism.

DUNCAN: I get concerned. I finally found the love of my life, it would be such a disappointment if you died.

CAITLIN: You're tense. What's going on?

DUNCAN: Evie was supposed to call. I wanted her to call before you got here.

CAITLIN: You oughta cut her some slack. She just needs to live a little.

DUNCAN: You mean after being married to me for fourteen years?

CAITLIN: She needs to kick up her heels, sleep with a whole bunch of guys and maybe two or three women, experience everything she's missed, then maybe she'll come back.

DUNCAN: I don't want her to come back. Do *you* want her to come back?

CAITLIN: Duncan, you have to admit our relationship was so much better when you were married. It was sexy and dangerous, sneaking around Evie.

DUNCAN: But this is what I've wanted for so long. The two of us spending the whole night together *without* sneaking around.

CAITLIN: Don't you feel like something's missing?

DUNCAN: Yes. What's missing is deceit.

CAITLIN: Maybe when you take that away from us, there just isn't much left.

DUNCAN: Caitlin, what's wrong with letting the world know about us?

CAITLIN: It's all so easy for you. You get a divorce and you're free and clear, but for me it's just a whole lot of pressure. I have to be everything to you because Evie isn't around to pick up the slack. I've never even met Evie and yet I miss her.

DUNCAN: I want to tell her about us. She told me as soon as she met that jerk Carter she's sleazing around with.

CAITLIN: Don't you dare tell her! It will make it so much harder for the two of you to get back together.

DUNCAN: You honestly believe the key to our relationship is me getting back with my wife?

CAITLIN: I certainly wouldn't rule it out. And I plan to fight for what we have. That's why I sent her flowers.

DUNCAN: You sent Evie flowers? From me?

CAITLIN: But we've *both* got to work at this, honey. Which means you keep lying to Evie. Don't you trust me?

DUNCAN: Of course I trust you, Caitlin. We'll sneak around as long as we can.

(Duncan embraces her and they snuggle as lights fade.)

SCENE 3

Lights up on a spa. Evie is on the phone while getting a massage from Ramon. Carter enters in a robe. His hand is bandaged.

EVIE: How are you feeling, Carter?

CARTER: Look, I don't need that kind of pressure right now. I thought we were here to relax.

EVIE: And we will, if Duncan ever picks up. I can't believe it. He isn't home.

CARTER: Know what happens when somebody lets *me* down? They become a colorless, odorless vapor drifting over the ocean, about a thousand miles out. They never get a chance to let me down a second time.

EVIE: I don't have the vapor option with Duncan.
   (Lights hold on Evie as she waits on the phone and lights up on Duncan's house. Duncan and Caitlin are snuggling under a blanket. Duncan answers the phone.)

DUNCAN: Hello?

EVIE: Were you asleep?

DUNCAN: We said eight o'clock.

EVIE: It *is* eight o'clock.

DUNCAN: Not here. It's eleven o'clock.

EVIE: I'm the one doing the calling, Duncan, I assumed it was *my* eight o'clock.

DUNCAN: Of course, why would you give a hoo-hah about anyone else's eight o'clock?

EVIE: Why should it be *your* eight o'clock?

DUNCAN: This is *our* eight o'clock. You're the one who left it for another eight o'clock. *(Hears Evie moan at the massage.)* What's going on? You appear to be moaning.

EVIE: My moaning is officially outside your bailiwick, Duncan. To say nothing of your time zone. Did Jack tell you the trouble he's in?

DUNCAN: It sounds like harmless fun to me.

EVIE: It may be "harmless fun" to you, but the state of New Hampshire considers it a crime. Luckily, the school's protecting him.

(Carter is doing stretching exercises.)

CARTER: He needs discipline.

EVIE: *(On phone.)* Carter thinks he needs discipline.

DUNCAN: *(On phone.)* What the hell does Carter know about it?

EVIE: *(To Carter.)* Duncan wants to know what the hell you know about it.

CARTER: Tell Duncan I am the living product of a whole shitload of discipline.

EVIE: *(On phone.)* Duncan, I'm concerned that I go away for a little vacation and Jack gets in trouble.

DUNCAN: *(On phone.)* Like it's my fault, Evie?

(Caitlin starts to get dressed. Duncan motions for her to stop.)

CAITLIN: *(Whispers.)* I have to go.

DUNCAN: No! Stay! Sit!

EVIE: *(On phone.)* Did you get a dog, Duncan?

DUNCAN: *(On phone.)* No, although it's not a bad idea.

EVIE: *(On phone.)* Who's there?

DUNCAN: *(On phone.)* A friend dropped by.

CAITLIN: Duncan! Don't tell her! You promised!

EVIE: *(On phone.)* What kind of friend, a girlfriend? It's alright, you're entitled. Is it serious? Or just some cheap, slutty one-night stand? It doesn't matter, what matters is I'm happy for you.

(Duncan is trapped between Evie on the phone and Caitlin getting dressed.)

DUNCAN: *(On phone.)* Can you hold on, Evie? *(Covering phone.)* Caitlin, I thought you were going to spend the night.

CAITLIN: You shouldn't make assumptions like that. *(Kisses him.)* Call me?

DUNCAN: *(Covering phone.)* Let me get rid of Evie and we'll talk.

CAITLIN: I don't want you to get rid of Evie!

DUNCAN: *(On phone.)* Honey—I mean Evie—I have to go.

(Caitlin finishes getting dressed and goes to the door.)

EVIE: *(On phone.)* Look, I'm more involved with Carter than you are with your little tramp du jour, but I'm making time to talk about our son!

DUNCAN: *(On phone.)* Evie, just give me a goddam second here!

(Rushes to door, yells...)

Caitlin! Don't leave !

(Goes back to phone, defeated.)

Fire away, Evie, I've got all night.

EVIE: Well *I don't* have all night. I'm practically naked.

(Evie puts away her phone. Lights fade on Duncan, alone.)

EVIE: *(Continuing.)* I don't know how I stood it so long. All yours, Carter.

(Evie gets up, leaving the massage table for Carter.)

CARTER: Where's Iris?

EVIE: Unavailable. Ramon is nice enough to pinch hit.

CARTER: They promised me Iris.

EVIE: You don't even know Iris. Do you?

CARTER: I just think for the money we're spending we should get a little goddam follow-through.

(Carter anxiously knots the cord around his robe.)

EVIE: Oh, boy, money money money money money. Ramon, do you know what's wrong with Iris?

RAMON: Iris took a header in the Eucalyptus Room. Ruptured her spleen, dislocated her shoulder. It made her irritable.

CARTER: Jesus, this place scares me. I'll skip the massage.

EVIE: Carter, this is my treat and you are very tense.

CARTER: I'm not going to get promised Iris and settle for Ramon. Nothing personal, Ramon.

EVIE: Does Ramon disgust you? Nothing personal, Ramon.

CARTER: No!

EVIE: Do you find him attractive?

CARTER: "Attractive"? Am I *attracted* to Ramon? Jesus Christ, Evie.

EVIE: Then you're simply afraid to be touched by a man, is that it?

CARTER: No, that is not it.

EVIE: Why are you cowering?

CARTER: I'm not "cowering."

EVIE: Believe me, I've seen men cower and you, my friend, are a textbook case. Ramon does men all the time, don't you, Ramon?

RAMON: Yes, sure, I do many men.

EVIE: And *they* don't have a problem with it. Look, you've tied the most amazing knot in your robe. Are you *that* afraid of your own sexuality?

CARTER: Ramon, you can leave.

EVIE: Don't you *dare* leave, Ramon. This is my gift to Carter and he *will* accept it.

CARTER: Get out of here, Ramon! Nothing personal.

(Ramon starts out.)

EVIE: Ramon, please don't abandon this man. He's lost faith in the world because of the evil way he was treated by his wife.

(Ramon hesitates.)

CARTER: I just don't want this guy touching me, okay?

EVIE: Nothing personal, Ramon. *(To Carter.)* It's fear, sweetie, and it's holding you back. Which means it's holding *me* back. How can you do that to someone you say you love?

CARTER: Alright. I'll have the goddam massage to shut you up.

(Carter maneuvers his way to a face down position on the table.)

EVIE: I'm proud of you, honey. Sometimes the first step of the journey is the hardest.

CARTER: Well let's get this sick little journey over with.

(Ramon starts the massage and Carter tenses.)

RAMON: Let me do the work and you relax.

EVIE: You might as well ask him to fly.

CARTER: I can relax. I can relax as well as the next guy.

EVIE: See? He even makes relaxing a competition.

CARTER: I'm not going to keep fighting you, Evie.

(Music is softly playing as Ramon massages Carter.)

EVIE: I just think your fears about homosexuality are a roadblock that's sending you on a long, bumpy detour away from yourself.

CARTER: *(Deadly calm.)* I don't have any fears about homosexuality.

EVIE: Uh-oh. The Daddy voice. You are really defended in this area.

CARTER: I wish you wouldn't ambush me at every turn, darling.

EVIE: It's a door you're afraid to open but once you discover what's on the other side, you realize there's nothing to be scared of. My first job out of college my boss had us all over to his house for a barbecue and after many beers we were all sitting around the pool in this happy, silly glow. I went inside to get another beer and I heard this voice from the laundry room, "Evie." It was kind of dark and my boss's laundry was hanging everywhere and I saw this girl, Cara, from the art department, and I said, "What?" And she just smiled and kissed me and I was so stunned I kissed her right back, and my God, it felt so good and so natural to be kissing her and holding her. We could hear the voices and the laughter just outside the window but we might as well have been on a different planet. This kiss went on forever and ever and it was one of the top four or five kisses in my whole life.

CARTER: Yeah, so what happened?

EVIE: We were lost in this absolutely delicious place when we heard someone coming in for more beer.

CARTER: Couldn't the drunken bastards wait?

EVIE: There we were in the laundry room, our shirts half-off and we started to laugh but we couldn't make any noise so we just held onto each other, our hands with a mind of their own, starting to—

RAMON: Could you turn over?

CARTER: Actually, at this moment, I couldn't.

RAMON: The way I usually work—

CARTER: Ramon, I don't give a flying fuck how you usually work! Nothing personal. *(To Evie.)* Okay, you're kissing, you're touching, tell me *everything* that happened.

EVIE: What happened was a whole constellation of fears disappeared. And I'm telling you this not to fuel your demented fantasy life but to show that your own fears are stopping you from a real commitment to me.

CARTER: I was afraid that's where we were headed.

EVIE: It's not where we're headed, it's where we are. And I don't know how much longer I can stand it. Duncan's getting on with his life, why can't I?

CARTER: I would rather talk about this when we're alone.

EVIE: It's always something with you, Carter, either you're shy in front of the masseur or your car is getting torched.

CARTER: My car *was* getting torched! I've got the scars to prove how understanding you were!

EVIE: Are you always going to be throwing that in my face?

CARTER: It still hurts, even though I don't talk about it.

EVIE: It hurts, Carter, boo-hoo, I stabbed you with a clam fork, I'm sorry, but *love* hurts. I hope that isn't a big revelation.

CARTER: No, Evie, you remind me of that in so many ways.

EVIE: And you don't need to worry about holding back in front of Ramon because he isn't even listening, are you, Ramon?

RAMON: Excuse me?

EVIE: See? Aren't you ashamed of the position you've taken, Carter?

CARTER: I haven't taken a "position."

EVIE: *Exactly.* You're there for the good times, the four star restaurants, the wild sex in every resort up and down the Pacific coast, but as you so eloquently put it, you haven't taken a position.

CARTER: My position is I love you. Which is why I don't want to wreck your life.

EVIE: How could you wreck my life?

CARTER: I don't know who I am anymore. How can I commit to you if I don't know who I am?

EVIE: I'll tell you who you are. You're the guy who made a lot of promises to me. You're the guy who wanted to change his life.

CARTER: I'm the guy who got betrayed by his wife. My anger prevented me from mourning the end of my marriage. How can I give you what you deserve if I haven't gotten closure on that?

EVIE: Carter, if we can slip back into English for a moment, what exactly are you saying?

CARTER: What I seem to be saying, is, and don't get upset because this really has nothing to do with you: I don't think I can be in a relationship right now.

EVIE: Interesting. And this has nothing to do with me?

CARTER: Not directly, no. It's more about me.

EVIE: I see. That took a lot of courage to say. Thanks.

CARTER: *(Relieved.)* Thank *you.*

EVIE: You realize, of course, you're already *in* a relationship. So how can you say you can't be in one?

CARTER: I haven't worked out all the wrinkles, but I'm positive I'm saying it out of consideration and love for you. Because goddammit, you deserve the best.

EVIE: What the hell is going on here? Are you breaking up with me? Ramon, is he breaking up?

RAMON: That's not how I break up. I don't know any man who breaks up like that.

CARTER: Oh, so you think I'm breaking up like some kind of pussy? *(Pause.)* Maybe I'm not even breaking up. Maybe I just need some time.

EVIE: Here's the news, Carter. You don't *have* time. By the time you finish mourning the end of your marriage I'll be gone and then you'll have to break up with your next girlfriend so you can mourn me and then you'll have to break up with the one after that to mourn the one after me and you'll always be one woman behind and then you know what will happen?

CARTER: What?

EVIE: You'll fucking die. And you'll have spent your whole stupid pointless life mourning. You want some free advice? Get over it.

CARTER: I'm ready to turn over now, Ramon.

(Carter rolls onto his back. Ramon continues the massage.)

EVIE: Good. Now you look like a corpse. This is how I'm going to remember you, Carter.

CARTER: This is nothing but pain for me.

RAMON: Sorry.

CARTER: Not you. Her.

EVIE: You want to break up with me, fine, do it right now. Pull the trigger, that's the least you owe me.

CARTER: I don't want to lose you, Evie. Everything happens so fast.

EVIE: And then it's over. Look, I'm a lousy party girl. I want something real. I want to have a life with you. And I'm sorry if I drive you insane and make you regret your own existence, but hey, we all have our little quirks, don't we?

CARTER: This is hard to say, especially while looking into Ramon's eyes, but I want you too. I love you. I want to take the plunge.

(Carter is looking into Ramon's eyes as lights fade.)

SCENE 4

Lights up on the safe deposit area of a bank. Caitlin is in a gown trying on jewelry from her safe deposit box. Duncan, wearing a clunky sport coat, looks on.

DUNCAN: I can't understand why the school is making such a big deal. Jack just went along with the other kids.

CAITLIN: I bet the other parents are saying exactly the same thing.

DUNCAN: Hey, whose side are you on?

CAITLIN: I'm on the side of making things safe again. Which is why I'm devoting my life to getting guns off the street.

DUNCAN: Jack's a good kid. He didn't have a gun.

CAITLIN: We want to think criminals are *them*, we don't want to think it's us, we're raising a whole generation that doesn't care.

DUNCAN: Easy for you to say, you don't know Jack.

CAITLIN: Right, I haven't been given that opportunity.

DUNCAN: I know in my heart he's a good kid.

CAITLIN: Every criminal is somebody's kid, and by your logic, nobody's really guilty.

DUNCAN: Alright, it's not logical. It's hopeless, insane, scary, everlasting love, which you'll understand when you have a kid.

CAITLIN: I'm not going to have a kid.

DUNCAN: Why?

CAITLIN: I just don't want to.

DUNCAN: You say that now. Wait a few years.

CAITLIN: I'm very clear on this subject.

DUNCAN: You'd make a wonderful mom.

CAITLIN: You're not listening to me, Duncan. I happen to like my life the way it is.

DUNCAN: I felt exactly the same way. And now I can't imagine my life without Jack. When the time is right you'll see what I mean.

CAITLIN: Why do you think you know what's best for me?

DUNCAN: Because with all the circles of hell I endured with Evie, the most magical time was when Jack was young.

CAITLIN: I'm not Evie.

DUNCAN: Which is one of the things I love the most about you.

CAITLIN: Look. I don't want to lead you on. This isn't a stage I'm going through. This is who I am.

DUNCAN: Well, I think that's...sad.

CAITLIN: Spare me your fucking pity. I think people passing misery on to their kids is pretty sad, too.

(Caitlin starts returning her jewelry to the safe deposit box.)

DUNCAN: What, we aren't going now?

CAITLIN: I never wear my jewelry outside the vault. Too dangerous. I just try it on and look fabulous and then lock it up again. We'd better go back so you can change.

DUNCAN: This is as good as it gets.

CAITLIN: *That's* what you're wearing? Duncan, this is my job, it's a fund-raiser, it's very important.

DUNCAN: You're afraid the gun control lobby is going to collapse because of my jacket?

CAITLIN: It's not just the jacket, it's the shirt, the pants...

DUNCAN: You like the tie?

CAITLIN: And the tie.

DUNCAN: Back home you thought this visit was a good idea.

CAITLIN: Yes. I remember.

DUNCAN: And now you're wondering what you're doing with a schlumpy ex-drunk who runs a tired little moving company.

CAITLIN: Please don't do this now. There isn't time.

DUNCAN: Oh, I think we have time to split up.

CAITLIN: This is hard. This is the first time you've seen me on my home turf and it's obvious we're different.

DUNCAN: How do you think we're different?

CAITLIN: Well...I have a good job and an exciting future and lots of friends.

DUNCAN: And I—

CAITLIN: —don't, but together, we have something special.

DUNCAN: What do we have?

CAITLIN: We have each other.

DUNCAN: A litter of kittens has each other, too. What do *we* have?

CAITLIN: *(Looks at her watch.)* Jesus, Duncan. Okay, we love each other.

DUNCAN: Why do you love me?

CAITLIN: You want me to tell you why I love you?

DUNCAN: Just one thing you love. Besides the tie.

CAITLIN: I could never find a man who loves me as much as you do.

DUNCAN: So what you really love about me is how much I love you?

CAITLIN: I'm sorry. I'm nervous. I don't want you to be embarrassed tonight.

DUNCAN: You don't want *me* to be embarrassed?

CAITLIN: You don't know this crowd. They're vultures, they're sick, they're cruel, they're my friends.

DUNCAN: You don't have to be nervous. I won't embarrass you. Take care of yourself, okay?

CAITLIN: You're leaving?

DUNCAN: It's been a helluva ride, but I'm getting off.

CAITLIN: Shit. This is an extreme overreaction to a fund-raiser. Fine. Leave. See if I care.

DUNCAN: If I thought you cared I'd stay.

CAITLIN: I *do* care!

DUNCAN: Not enough to convince me to stay.

CAITLIN: I can't convince you to stay if you want to go.

DUNCAN: You could tell me there's some kind of future here.

CAITLIN: Look, I don't need all this heat about the future. And to tell you the truth, I really resent that you're suddenly putting me first in your life.

DUNCAN: You've been first in my life for a long time. Do you have any idea of the love and devotion it took to cheat on my wife?

CAITLIN: The cheating was magnificent, Duncan, and I truly appreciate it, but now you seem to want more.

DUNCAN: Yes. Now that Evie's met someone, it means the marriage is really over. I have to get on with my life. And it's a little disturbing to find out there isn't much here.

CAITLIN: There's plenty here, it just isn't what you want. I usually like to take more time when I break up, but I have to fly if I'm going to make cocktails.

DUNCAN: At least I know where I rank. Come on, I'll walk you out, make sure you're safe. I've had bad luck with people getting mugged.

CAITLIN: Duncan? If things ever work out with you and Evie, I'd really like to see you again.

(Lights fade on Duncan and Caitlin.)

SCENE 5

Lights up on Carter's condo. Evie and Carter are drinking wine. Flowers are on the table.

EVIE: We were so lost we tried to celebrate our anniversary during the darkest days of our marriage. The whole dinner he only spoke to the waiter, ordering one drink after another. I couldn't just watch the marriage go up in flames, so I left. I'm waiting for a bus when suddenly there's a gun jammed in my ribs and a voice telling me to give it up, bitch. I screamed and fought him for my bag...it seemed as if my whole life was in that big dumb bag. And he got it. I ran after him, crying and screaming and when I finally stopped it was absolutely cold and silent up and down the street and I knew I was really all alone, I couldn't pretend there was anyone else. And I knew I'd better grab whatever I wanted out of this life because it was all going to end in the smallest, safest moments, buying groceries, walking the dog, watching my son play baseball. Jack had been a surprise, we never even talked about having a baby, and then, later, we always talked about having another. Standing on that desolate street, I knew the baby thing was just part of this dream I was living. I moved out so I could stop dreaming.

CARTER: Just like that.

EVIE: All it took was a little urban crime.

CARTER: Look at those flowers. He still loves you.

EVIE: Those flowers mean "bon voyage." Now that Duncan's met someone, it means our marriage is really over. I have to get on with my life.

CARTER: This baby thing is really important to you, right?

EVIE: I guess it is.

CARTER: You probably think I'm one of the toughest, most masculine guys you ever met. *(Beat.)* Right?

EVIE: Oh, right, of course. Where are we going with this, Carter?

CARTER: This is hard for me to say. A lot of guys would *never* be able to say it.

EVIE: What?

CARTER: I shoot blanks.

EVIE: Blanks?

CARTER: Blanks.

EVIE: Oh. Blanks.

CARTER: Yes. Blanks. The truth is, I'm a few soldiers short of an army. Hard to believe, isn't it?

EVIE: Not really.

CARTER: You mean you already suspected? How?

EVIE: Carter, it just isn't that important.

CARTER: You just said it *was* important.

EVIE: As long as we love each other, there aren't problems, just solutions.

CARTER: You see a solution to this?

EVIE: I see a whole lot of medical alternatives that weren't out there a few years ago. Maybe we can get you some reinforcements for your army.

(Carter assumes a martial arts stance.)

CARTER: Duncan let that guy mug you. I'd never let anyone mug you. Come after me, I'll prove it.

EVIE: Excuse me?

CARTER: Attack me! I'll show you what I'd do to him!

EVIE: I don't want to attack you, I want to comfort you.

CARTER: I don't need comfort. I need to be attacked!

EVIE: Oh, honey...

CARTER: I do everything for you and you won't do this one thing for me? Why won't you attack me?

EVIE: Why would I want to hurt you?

CARTER: Oh, like you ever could, sweetheart. *(Advances on her.)* If you won't attack me then I'll attack *you*!

EVIE: Alright. I'll attack you.

CARTER: I'm going to prove I won't let anyone hurt you.

(Evie and Carter circle each other. Evie makes a move, Carter tries to stop it. His back goes out. He collapses to the floor in agony.)

EVIE: Oh, God, Carter, I am so sorry.

CARTER: You didn't do anything! If my back hadn't gone out I'd have knocked you cold. Right?

EVIE: Yes, Carter, I'd be begging for mercy. Now what can I do?

CARTER: Nothing. Just drink your wine...glance at a magazine. Enjoy.

(Carter is sprawled on the floor as lights fade.)

SCENE 6

A chopping sound. Then lights up on Duncan's house where he's chopping meat. Caitlin enters.

CAITLIN: Duncan?
(Duncan turns, revealing his bloody apron. Caitlin screams and starts to leave.)
DUNCAN: Caitlin! Come back!
(Caitlin warily comes in.)
CAITLIN: You haven't snapped? I saw you and my first thought was, Jesus, it finally happened.
DUNCAN: The last moving job, the guy didn't have any money so he paid with a pig.
CAITLIN: I'm not supposed to smell meat anymore.
DUNCAN: How are you staying alive?
CAITLIN: *(Pulls a baby food jar from her purse.)* Seventy-five bucks a jar. Gotta lose four more pounds. The perfect weight for me is when I get dizzy standing up and the walls kind of flutter around me.
DUNCAN: Then let's sit down. It feels like it's been forever.
CAITLIN: I was meeting with these Handgun Control people in Boston and I was going to call you but then I decided I'd surprise you.
DUNCAN: Consider me surprised. I was just thinking about you.
CAITLIN: While you were hacking up a pig?
DUNCAN: They were kind thoughts. Can I get you something? Food? Shelter?
CAITLIN: I can't stay. I just came for the day. I'm taking the shuttle and I have to turn in my car and Fridays are crazy.
DUNCAN: Take a later shuttle. Like Sunday.
CAITLIN: I don't even know why I'm here. I was headed for Logan and then I just drove out here without thinking. Have you really been okay, Duncan?
DUNCAN: Does "paralyzed by existential despair" count as "okay?"
CAITLIN: To be honest, I thought you'd call.
DUNCAN: I didn't think you'd want me to call.
CAITLIN: I thought you wouldn't be able to stop yourself.
DUNCAN: I was too despondent to dial. I'd do about five digits and then run out of steam.
CAITLIN: I guess I've been kind of miserable myself.

DUNCAN: *(Brightening.)* Really?

CAITLIN: Every time I'd be out with another guy I'd start to think about you. Isn't that silly? Not one of them did it for me. Not even two of them.

DUNCAN: It's only been a couple of weeks, Caitlin, how many guys could there be? *(Quickly.)* I don't want to know. *(Beat.)* A lot? *(Beat.)* Forget it. *(Hopefully.)* Maybe just a few? *(Beat.)* It's none of my business.

CAITLIN: Oh, God, this was stupid, wasn't it? I just couldn't bear the way it ended. I should have called, the telephone isn't as dangerous as this. *(Caitlin rises. Duncan stops her.)*

DUNCAN: Wait. I'll build a fire, get you a glass of wine. What the hell, I'll even turn on the furnace. *(They're close. They kiss.)*

CAITLIN: God, I've missed you. Which is weird, because you're really not my type. I'm usually attracted to successful guys. And of course, there's the age difference.

DUNCAN: What's a few decades between friends?

CAITLIN: You'll probably die first. On the plane I was thinking how great it is that I can speak straight from the heart at your memorial service. Usually when my friends and stuff die, I have to fake it a little when I make the speech.

DUNCAN: What would you say about me?

CAITLIN: It's pretty touching, but maybe a little long.

DUNCAN: You mean it's already written?

CAITLIN: I had time on the plane and you know me, I'm not one to procrastinate. You can read it later.

DUNCAN: "Later." I like the sound of that. Like maybe you'll stay.

CAITLIN: *(Slips him her car keys.)* Would you get my suitcase out of my car, Duncan?

DUNCAN: *(Starts for the door.)* Caitlin? Why did you bring your suitcase if you were just coming up for the day?

(Lights fade on Caitlin and Duncan.)

SCENE 7

Lights up on Neil at a desk. He's meeting with Evie and Carter, who's lying on the floor to rest his back.

EVIE: So much of my life has been spent standing on the sidelines waving a little pennant and cheering people on. At some point I have to roll up the pennant and say, "When is it *my* turn?"

NEIL: Your son is thirteen? I'd say it's your turn in another five years.

EVIE: Five years? Do you have any idea how old I'll be in five years?

NEIL: No I don't. How old?

EVIE: Well, I'll be—I'll be five years older than I am now, which is just not acceptable. And I'd like to do something with my life besides get older. Frankly, I'm tired of waiting for my fish to come in.

CARTER: Ship.

EVIE: Whatever. We want a baby. Very much. Both of us.

NEIL: Doesn't a baby mean more time on the sidelines with a little pennant?

EVIE: It's my last chance, and let's be honest, I think I owe it to Carter after his wife betrayed him, having a baby with a policeman and telling Carter it was his.

CARTER: Whore! Bitch! Hooker! Slut! Pig! Nympho!

NEIL: Carter, what do you think?

CARTER: Evie feels strongly about this. I think I owe it to her.

NEIL: So you owe it to each other?

CARTER: If I love Evie—and I do—and if at any point in my life I will want a baby—and I will—then this *must* be exactly what I want to happen.

NEIL: But *is* it what you want?

CARTER: Devil's advocate, if it *isn't* exactly what I want at this moment—and I'm not saying it isn't—then I know I will grow into wanting it, and if I don't act on it now, it will be too late. I believe it is the right thing to want, especially in light of my history.

EVIE: Tell him what you said the other night.

CARTER: What?

EVIE: The only way to end the pain of your wife's having a policeman's baby is by having a baby of your own.

CARTER: You said that.

EVIE: Did I?

CARTER: Driving back from dinner. You said it about me.

EVIE: You agreed.

CARTER: I'm not saying it isn't true.

EVIE: If it's true then it's just nit-picking who actually said it. I mean you *could* have said it.

CARTER: Could have but didn't. You said it.

EVIE: *(To Neil.)* So that's how he feels. I don't mean to pat us on the back, but I think we're brave to go after this.

NEIL: Isn't it kind of sudden?

CARTER: Thousands of years ago Mount Vesuvius erupted without warning and completely buried the city of Pompeii. *That* was sudden.

NEIL: You're losing me here. Carter, you see yourself as the glorious city of Pompeii being smothered and ultimately buried by Evie's molten sea of lava?

EVIE: No, look, something wonderful happened. Carter and I found each other. And my ex-husband met someone, which is the only way I'm free enough to even *think* about this. I know what we both want.

NEIL: And you have to do it right away?

EVIE: The best times in my marriage were when Jack was young. It brought out the best in Duncan.

CARTER: It'll bring out even better stuff in me!

EVIE: I know it will, sweetie.

CARTER: She's my miracle, Neil. She's convinced me that all women aren't necessarily out to destroy me.

NEIL: Carter? Beware of the c-word.

EVIE: Which c-word? Is this some kind of moronic male code?

NEIL: You just seem a little controlling.

EVIE: Carter, do *you* think I'm controlling?

CARTER: My back hurts. I should avoid stress.

EVIE: Just answer. Right now. Am I controlling?

CARTER: When you say controlling, do you mean...what do you mean?

EVIE: *I* think I'm controlling. So what? You want to get on an airplane with a pilot who isn't controlling? You want to have eye surgery with a doctor who isn't controlling? Would someone tell me what the hell is wrong with control? Neil?

NEIL: I'm just here to help. To ask the hard questions.

EVIE: Carter, can we please leave?

CARTER: As soon as I can get up.

NEIL: Where do you intend to live?

EVIE: We haven't worked out all the details yet.

NEIL: You understand Carter cannot leave the area?

EVIE: You're making him sound like a felon.

NEIL: I can assure you it would be professional suicide.

EVIE: He's a salesman. Can't he sell anywhere?

NEIL: Please. Carter is not a "salesman." He's a visionary. When you talk about the proliferation of specialty coffees throughout the Pacific northwest, you're talking about Carter.

EVIE: I'm not belittling his achievements. I'm exploring options.

NEIL: There aren't any options. You barely have an income, you wish to bring a child into the world through an expensive medical procedure, Carter must keep his income up. He can't move.

EVIE: Listen, my divorce just came through, I needed a break, I came out here to visit my sister in Seattle. I sure didn't plan to meet Carter.

CARTER: Sorry, honey—

EVIE: Like I would trade the last forty-two days for *anything*. The point is, my life is on the east coast. I share custody, I'm not going to lose Jack.

NEIL: Why don't you move out here with Jack?

EVIE: Jack would miss his father. And he's going through a difficult time with tattoos and peer pressure.

NEIL: Get his father to move out.

EVIE: His business is there. He's president of a moving company.

NEIL: Big operation?

EVIE: It used to be three men. He recently downsized.

NEIL: Sounds like he could use a fresh start.

EVIE: Why would he leave his new girlfriend to be near his ex-wife?

NEIL: So he could stay in his son's life. Get his girlfriend to move out too.

EVIE: You're an accountant. Do you just sit in here and rule the world?

NEIL: Yes, I do. And I would advise you to relocate your son and the significant adults in his life if you're serious about your relationship with Carter.

EVIE: Carter. We're leaving.

CARTER: I'm doing the best I can, babe.

(Carter lies still. Evie and Neil wait. Lights fade.)

SCENE 8

Gunshots. Lights up on Duncan and Caitlin in the woods.

CAITLIN: Should we be scared?

DUNCAN: No more than usual. It's just our local militia. Preparing to over-throw the government.

(They move behind a rock.)

CAITLIN: Do you realize this is the best weekend we ever had? We got to a whole new place. I'm proud of you, Duncan.

DUNCAN: I have no idea what you're talking about, but I totally agree.

CAITLIN: It meant so much that you came around to my point of view. That we should just enjoy what we have and not make demands because at my age and with my potential it would be a tragedy to get tied down.

DUNCAN: When exactly did I say all this?

CAITLIN: You've said it a million ways ever since I got here.

DUNCAN: I'm glad to make you happy, but I'm drawing a blank on the specifics.

CAITLIN: You're not going to ruin this, are you? I'm complimenting you and we both know that isn't easy for me.

DUNCAN: I just don't remember saying anything remotely like that.

CAITLIN: Okay, maybe not verbally, but I thought that's what this weekend was all about. You accepting the limits on our relationship and being happy about it.

DUNCAN: See, I thought the weekend was about you making a commitment and that's why I've been so happy.

CAITLIN: I never said anything like that!

DUNCAN: The fact that you showed up. I thought that meant you'd come around to what I've been saying.

CAITLIN: I showed up out of concern for your emotional well-being and I was planning to go back on Friday night.

DUNCAN: Then why did you bring a suitcase?

CAITLIN: So I'd be prepared if things evolved.

DUNCAN: Which they did, thank God, and when you stayed, I assumed it was because you wanted to make a commitment.

CAITLIN: How could you assume that without even discussing it?

DUNCAN: How could you assume I'd come around to your point of view with-out discussing it?

CAITLIN: Oh, God. This is hopeless. Nothing's changed. What can we do? Duncan, tell me what we can do.

(Duncan stands up. The gunfire is closer. He crouches next to Caitlin behind the rock as lights fade.)

SCENE 9

Lights up on Evie and Carter in a hospital waiting room. Carter has a cane for his back problem.

EVIE: This isn't the most romantic way to conceive a child.

CARTER: No, but it's pretty expensive. I mean effective.

EVIE: When Jack was conceived we were bumming through Italy, backpacks, Fodors, youth hostels, no money. The one time we splurged on a hotel it was just the two of us and bottle of Chianti and some quaaludes and what a lovely night that was. Where were you when Max was conceived?

CARTER: Chicago. My wife was in Portland.

EVIE: Oh, God, the policeman!

CARTER: Bimbo! Bitch! Pig! Slut! Whore! *(To Evie.)* How long are they going to keep us waiting, honey?

EVIE: I don't know. I wish I still smoked.

CARTER: You could pick it up in no time.

EVIE: I never should have stopped. What a mistake that was.

(A male nurse enters with a clipboard and a specimen jar.)

NURSE: Evie? They'll see you now.

CARTER: Ready for an afternoon of love?

EVIE: Just me and a team of doctors.

(Evie leaves.)

NURSE: Carter? You won't have any trouble, will you?

CARTER: Trouble? What do you mean?

NURSE: Producing a sample.

CARTER: Please. I've had a little practice along the way. *(Quickly.)* No more than anyone else, you understand.

NURSE: We just have to make sure.

CARTER: Other guys really have that problem? It's like getting rejected by yourself. "Sorry to disappoint me, but I've got a headache." What could cause a problem like that?

NURSE: Mainly stress.

CARTER: Stress? Jesus, who *are* these people?

NURSE: The sample has to be produced in a specific period of time based on the retrieval of the eggs or the entire procedure is wasted. Which means the woman has gone through a lot of discomfort for nothing and of course this isn't cheap, as you know. So the time factor can cause performance anxiety.

CARTER: How long does it take these other guys to produce a sample?

NURSE: It varies.

CARTER: Average, median, whatever.

NURSE: It varies a lot.

CARTER: Ballpark.

NURSE: We don't keep those statistics. It's not a competition.

CARTER: How long does it take you?

NURSE: *Me?* You're asking how long it takes *me?*

CARTER: As a point of reference. Or maybe I'm totally out of line. Jesus. Idiot! Me, not you.

NURSE: When it's time, go to the Collection Room down the hall and when you finish, put the jar in the cabinet just outside the door.

CARTER: Excellent. I've had worse jobs, believe me.

NURSE: *(Starting out.)* I'm sure you have.

CARTER: Excuse me? Mister Nurse? As a matter of professional interest...what do you do if someone *is* having a problem?

NURSE: There are magazines and videos in the Collection Room, and other materials can be provided on an "as needed" basis.

CARTER: Hypothetically, what are the "other materials" that are available if— and this is so unbelievably hypothetical—there's not so much a problem as a...delay?

NURSE: Anything within reason to make it easier.

CARTER: Could you—and this is just to be way way on the safe side—could you get the film *The Sands of Iwo Jima?*

NURSE: I think that can be arranged.

(The nurse starts to leave.)

CARTER: Any war movie will do...just as long as there's an army that wins.

(Carter is in solitary misery as lights fade.)

SCENE 10

Lights up on Duncan's house. Caitlin is drinking tea. Duncan has an axe.

CAITLIN: Just because we're breaking up, we can still be friends.

DUNCAN: When I break up with someone I want them to die.

CAITLIN: You don't want me to die.

DUNCAN: I don't want a lot of inane chit-chat with you, either.

CAITLIN: Is that what friendship is to you? Inane chit-chat?

DUNCAN: Usually. Will you be leaving soon?

CAITLIN: Can I finish my tea?

DUNCAN: Take your time. I'll be outside with my axe.

(Duncan starts for the door.)

CAITLIN: Don't trip. You son of a bitch!

DUNCAN: I thought we could be honest with each other.

CAITLIN: No, you thought you could be cruel to me.

DUNCAN: It's a lot crueler to pretend we're just friends.

CAITLIN: We've been through a lot. Doesn't that count for something?

DUNCAN: You want this to be nice. You want me to think highly of you. Well I don't.

CAITLIN: You actually believe this is all my fault, don't you?

DUNCAN: I'd say it's eighty percent you and twenty percent factors outside my control.

CAITLIN: You're such a fraud. You say you want me in your life but you never made the slightest move to put me there.

DUNCAN: Come on, Caitlin, you think it's *my* fault you can't make a commitment?

CAITLIN: "Commitment?" Like that idiotic word means something? You know what would have meant something?

DUNCAN: I'm dying to hear.

CAITLIN: If you'd let me spend some time with Jack.

DUNCAN: What?

CAITLIN: Is it that strange to put the woman you say you love together with the son you obviously adore?

DUNCAN: No. Of course not.

CAITLIN: Then why didn't you ever do it?

DUNCAN: I don't know. He's up at school.

CAITLIN: You run up there all the time and never once invite me to go.

DUNCAN: I guess it's a little awkward. He's going through a confusing time.

CAITLIN: And I couldn't have been a part of it and maybe even helped?

DUNCAN: I didn't think you'd want to.

CAITLIN: You say you're so open and honest and *you're* the one who sneaks around as if you're ashamed of me.

DUNCAN: You've never shown the slightest interest in children, except to say you don't want one.

CAITLIN: We're not talking about children, we're talking about *your child*, who you keep hidden away from me.

DUNCAN: He's not "hidden away." He's in prep school.

CAITLIN: Shut up. You've had this just the way you wanted it. *Me* over here and Jack over there and me feeling guilty *I'm* not giving enough. And now you're blaming me!

DUNCAN: You're always saying you don't want to get tied down.

CAITLIN: I was protecting myself! I wanted you to make a move to change things and you never did! You'd have gone on like this the rest of your life. The main course would be raising your son and I'd be some kind of fabulous dessert with whipped cream. Well, no thanks!

DUNCAN: I am so deeply confused right now. You've been talking about leaving from the time you got here.

CAITLIN: Like I want to go back to a lonely little studio apartment that doesn't even have cable?

DUNCAN: All I hear about is your big job in the big city.

CAITLIN: My big job is entirely dependent on funding. Which, as I recently learned, did not come through.

DUNCAN: When did this happen?

CAITLIN: Friday. That was the meeting in Boston. God, it just sucks how they're treating me after all the time I put in.

DUNCAN: You've known all week-end and you didn't tell me?

CAITLIN: Why would I?

DUNCAN: It might have made a difference.

CAITLIN: My career has to crumble under my feet to give us a chance? I don't think so, Duncan. Thanks for the herbal fucking tea.

(Caitlin starts for the door.)

DUNCAN: Don't go. Please don't go.

CAITLIN: Why?

DUNCAN: Because I want you to stay.

CAITLIN: How much do you want me to stay?

DUNCAN: A lot. A huge enormous amount.

CAITLIN: Do you want me to stay even more than I want to stay?

DUNCAN: Yes. I want you to stay even more than you want to stay. Do you want to stay?

CAITLIN: I don't know. Maybe. I could. I think I might.

(Lights fade on Caitlin and Duncan, who hold their position.)

SCENE 11

Lights up on the hospital. Carter hurries over to Evie's gurney.

CARTER: How did I do?

EVIE: You were great, sweetie.

CARTER: Now I guess all the pressure's on you. How do you feel?

EVIE: Rungout. Happy. They say I can fly in three weeks.

CARTER: *Fly?* What kind of operation was this?

EVIE: In an airplane, silly. We'll be there in time for Jack's birthday.

CARTER: Don't you think it's kind of a risk to travel?

EVIE: The doctor assured me it was okay.

CARTER: No, for *me.* Your ex isn't going to want me around. He'll feel threatened.

EVIE: The sooner you meet him the better. If all goes well he'll be moving out here with us.

CARTER: What am I supposed to do while you're convincing him to move?

EVIE: I couldn't go alone anyway. You have to give me shots. Progesterone to help our baby.

CARTER: Other guys have to do this?

EVIE: And *they* don't have a problem.

CARTER: Then it'll be a slam-dunk. Just like today in the Collection Room. "He shoots, HE SCORES!"

EVIE: It's a miracle, isn't it?

CARTER: You're the miracle in my life, Evie.

(Lights up on Duncan and Caitlin.)

DUNCAN: I want you to stay here. Move your stuff in. This is your home, Caitlin. We'll really be a family. You and me and Jack.

(Lights stay up on Duncan and Caitlin in Duncan's house and Evie and Carter in the hospital.)

EVIE: Oh, honey, I can't wait. We'll really be a family. You and me and Jack.

(Lights fade to black.)

END OF ACT ONE

ACT TWO
SCENE 1

Lights up on Duncan's house. Caitlin is wielding a dust-buster. A large bowl of donuts is on the table. Evie enters.

EVIE: Don't bother. The house will win in the end.

CAITLIN: *(Startled, turns off dust-buster.)* Oh! You scared me.

EVIE: Already? I'm Evie.

CAITLIN: And I'm Caitlin. Duncan promised you'd be late.

EVIE: Sorry. Carter has a thing about getting places on time. Frankly, I don't understand it.

CAITLIN: I was going to improve myself. I never look like this.

EVIE: You look lovely.

CAITLIN: Please. My face is about to erupt.

EVIE: That can be a problem for girls your age.

CAITLIN: I'm a little nervous. This is the first time we've had guests in the house.

EVIE: This is the first time I've ever been a guest in this house.

CAITLIN: I think you'll like it, having been a guest in this house myself.

EVIE: I know all about your role as a guest in this house.

CAITLIN: I think it's easier to be a guest in this house than to have guests in this house.

EVIE: We used to have guests in this house all the time. As I recall, we were happy having guests and they were happy being guests.

CAITLIN: Well, you're our very first. *(Calls out.)* Duncan? Our guests are here! *(Picks up the bowl of donuts.)* Donut?

EVIE: That's just what they are.

(Caitlin puts the bowl down. Duncan enters wearing an apron. He hugs Evie.)

DUNCAN: Is something wrong? You're right on time.

EVIE: Hello, you. It's freezing in here. This house is one small step above camping out.

DUNCAN: A new record, ten seconds to your first complaint.

EVIE: You don't mind us staying here, do you? We only have a few days and I'm dying to see Jack.

DUNCAN: You'll have to wait till tomorrow. He's snowed in.

EVIE: No! I can't stand it!

DUNCAN: And the storm is headed our way.

EVIE: Why do they let this happen year after year? Carter and I could squeeze into my apartment if this is a problem.

DUNCAN: This is fine, Evie. You two met?

EVIE: She's lovely, Duncan. Young young young. Thin thin thin. How nice for you.

DUNCAN: She's quite a remarkable woman.

EVIE: I'm glad. You deserve a remarkable girl.

CAITLIN: Excuse me, could you two please talk about me behind my back? Thank you.

EVIE: And polite. She offered me a donut.

DUNCAN: Is that what you put out?

CAITLIN: I'm sorry. I don't know what older people eat.

(Duncan and Evie exchange a look.)

DUNCAN: *(Leaving.)* I'm going to turn up the furnace for Her Highness.

EVIE: Don't let me interrupt. If you wanted to bust any more dust.

CAITLIN: I think I'm done.

(Evie sits on something hard on the sofa. She reaches into the crevice and pulls out Duncan's axe.)

CAITLIN: *(Continuing.)* Except for that.

(Lights fade on Evie holding the axe.)

SCENE 2

Lights up on the kitchen. Duncan is heating mulled cider. Carter comes in.

DUNCAN: You must be Carter.

CARTER: Either that or some maniac who came here to kill you. I'm kidding. Duncan?

DUNCAN: Welcome.

(They shake hands. Awkward pause.)

CARTER: Evie tells me you're an alcoholic.

DUNCAN: No, I'm a drunk. Non-practicing.

CARTER: Jesus, what an idiot. Not you, me. So you're one of these twelve-step people?

DUNCAN: One step. I stopped.

CARTER: Sorry. I generally don't like to talk after I've been on an airplane. This is why.

DUNCAN: Was the trip okay?

CARTER: Aces. No problem finding the place. Which isn't too surprising, seeing as how Evie lived here for twelve years. Moron! Me, not you. So how long does it usually take you to get here from the airport?

DUNCAN: I don't know, half an hour. Why?

CARTER: I just did it in twenty-four minutes. And that's with Evie having a fit every time I get out in the passing lane.

DUNCAN: She's quite a back seat driver.

CARTER: Tell me about it. So, that's interesting that I would make it six minutes faster than you from the airport. I'd think you would know all the shortcuts.

DUNCAN: I don't know any shortcuts.

(Lights fade on Duncan and Carter.)

SCENE 3

Lights up on Caitlin and Evie.

EVIE: I want you to know how happy I am that you and Duncan found each other.

CAITLIN: Thanks. You have every reason to be a screaming bitch. I would totally understand.

EVIE: The truth is, I felt so guilty about leaving him. If he were here by himself I don't think I could have spread my own personal wings.

CAITLIN: I was feeling guilty myself.

EVIE: What do *you* have to feel guilty about?

CAITLIN: You two go so far back. I mean when you two met, I was—

EVIE: Yes, yes, you were just a tiny little girl.

CAITLIN: And now I'm suddenly in the middle of two big grownups.

EVIE: You'd only be in the middle if Duncan and I were together. As it is, you're...

CAITLIN: Next in line?

EVIE: If it sets your mind at ease, Carter and I are really planning a life together. We're having a baby.

(Carter enters with two glasses of cider.)

EVIE: *(Continuing.)* Carter, Caitlin, Caitlin, Carter.

CAITLIN: Hello, Carter.

CARTER: *(Handing them cider.)* Yeah, hi. Cider?

   (Carter sits on the sofa.)

CAITLIN: Evie says you two are having a baby.

CARTER: Yes, I heard.

CAITLIN: That's great.

CARTER: That's what she tells me.

   (Duncan comes in with two glasses of cider. He gives one to Carter.)

CAITLIN: Honey? Did you know they're having a baby?

DUNCAN: What?

CAITLIN: You know. A baby.

DUNCAN: I heard you.

CAITLIN: Then why did you say "what?"

DUNCAN: It just seems kind of...

EVIE: Kind of what?

DUNCAN: I don't know. You mean you're actually...

EVIE: Yes, Duncan. We're pregnant.

CARTER: "We?"

CAITLIN: Duncan? Is something wrong with that?

DUNCAN: It just seems sudden.

CARTER: That's what *I* thought.

EVIE: Really, Carter? And you've waited till now to tell me?

CARTER: But of course there were mitigating factors.

EVIE: You sound like you're on the witness stand.

DUNCAN: What "mitigating factors"?

CARTER: I don't think we need to get into the problems Evie had getting pregnant.

CAITLIN: It's not unusual with women your age.

EVIE: It wasn't that kind of problem, Caitlin.

   (All eyes turn to Carter.)

CARTER: What are you looking at me for? There were no problems performance-wise.

EVIE: Nobody said there were, honey-bunch, but sperm-wise...

CARTER: We're just a bit on the low side.

EVIE: "We"?

CARTER: Low-average. I bet a lot of guys would kill to have my sperm count. What's your count, Duncan?

DUNCAN: I don't have the slightest idea.

CARTER: Yeah, sure you don't.

EVIE: This is nothing to be ashamed of, it's not a reflection of your masculinity. Carter's a little touchy on this issue because, tell them, Carter.

CARTER: Tell them what?

EVIE: About the evil thing your wife did.

CARTER: I don't think that's relevant.

EVIE: *(To the others.)* His wife had a baby. Carter thought it was his for eight months.

CAITLIN: Whose was it?

EVIE: Some state trooper. He stops her for speeding, smash cut to a motel room containing two very naked bodies, dissolve to the maternity ward nine months later where poor Carter is nervously awaiting the birth of the policeman's baby.

CARTER: Bitch! Slut! Whore! Hooker! Pig! Nympho!

CAITLIN: That has to be the absolute worst nightmare.

EVIE: I don't know how we got through it. Carter was so devastated he almost killed himself three times.

CARTER: Twice!

EVIE: Carter, sweetie, it was three times.

CARTER: You weren't there. I hadn't even met you.

EVIE: The point is, he didn't see the handwriting on the wall because he was so relieved she got pregnant in the first place.

CAITLIN: Given his sperm problem.

CARTER: Situation! And remember, it's low-*average*.

EVIE: Carter, doesn't it feel better to talk about this?

CARTER: I wouldn't know, Evie. You're the one talking about it.

(A bell goes off in the kitchen.)

DUNCAN: Well, there's the end of the first round.

(Duncan exits. Evie follows him.)

CAITLIN: I'm really sorry.

CARTER: Believe me, my life is great. Anyone who feels sorry for me is an idiot.

CAITLIN: But all those months with a little baby and everything you must have felt and all that love just wasted.

CARTER: Why was it wasted? It wasn't wasted.

CAITLIN: Well if the baby wasn't yours and the baby's gone...

CARTER: The baby isn't *gone*, the baby is just someplace else. It happened. It happened to me and the baby and now it's part of our lives so how could it be wasted?

CAITLIN: But it can all be taken away and then you're alone, except it's worse because you're even more alone than you were before.

CARTER: Okay, it's a risk. What the hell *isn't* a risk?

CAITLIN: It's more than a risk, it's opening your life up to tragedy. Isn't it better to find some way to live so you don't *need* anything else? So you don't get smashed into little pieces?

CARTER: It doesn't sound as if you're planning a family anytime soon.

CAITLIN: Just this family. I want to get involved in Jack's life to take the pressure off me having a baby. That's why this birthday party is a big deal. I plan to check in and be wonderful and check out and be myself. I'm pretty excited. We're really going to be a family, Carter.

CARTER: Us?

CAITLIN: No, Duncan, Jack and I.

CARTER: I don't think so. Evie and Jack and *I* are going to be a family.

CAITLIN: *(Disbelieving.)* Shut up!

CARTER: I'm serious.

CAITLIN: We had a long talk. Jack is pretty much ours.

CARTER: Oh, really? Have you ever met him?

CAITLIN: Not yet. Have you?

CARTER: Jack is my son. That's all you need to know.

CAITLIN: That's poppycock. Hurtful poppycock. I don't think I even want you staying in my house.

CARTER: *Your* house? Try *Evie's* house.

CAITLIN: Oh, so you guys get Jack *and* the house? That's fair.

CARTER: That's just the way it is.

CAITLIN: Evie's the one who screwed up the marriage, why should *she* get everything?

CARTER: She didn't screw it up, she left it because Duncan wasn't there for her in any meaningful way. She was emotionally parched.

CAITLIN: Duncan was trying to heal himself and he could have used a little support from Evie.

CARTER: Is it Evie's fault that Duncan was a big fucking baby?

CAITLIN: I think your sperm is just the beginning of your problems, Buster.

(Lights fade on Carter and Caitlin.)

SCENE 4

Lights up on the kitchen. Duncan and Evie frost the birthday cake, which is shaped like a catcher's mitt.

EVIE: I thought you'd be happy I'm happy.

DUNCAN: I *am* happy you're happy. Are you happy *I'm* happy?

EVIE: I'd be happier if she was fifteen years older and thirty pounds heavier.

DUNCAN: She's on a death camp diet. My goal is to get her to eat again. What do you think of her?

EVIE: She's adorable. And you've always been great with children.

DUNCAN: Are you going to be nice, Evie? Or are you going to be yourself?

EVIE: I haven't decided. I actually think she's perfect for you. She's so self-involved she won't ever challenge you. But I'm surprised she's living here.

DUNCAN: I told you it was getting serious.

EVIE: You also said you met her pretty recently.

DUNCAN: And things progressed quickly.

EVIE: Which is odd.

DUNCAN: Look at you and Carter.

EVIE: True, but I'm impetuous and impractical. You're slow and careful.

DUNCAN: Maybe there were things slowing me down.

EVIE: Like me?

DUNCAN: Or too many years of serious balls-out drinking.

EVIE: Oh, that. *(Sizing him up.)* You look annoyingly good. I go through hell so that child can enjoy your prime years.

DUNCAN: Sorry. But I wasn't the one who left.

EVIE: I know, Duncan, I walked out, let me have a few guilt-free moments every once in a while, okay? *(Beat.)* You know, it's really spectacular out where Carter lives. You should give it a chance.

DUNCAN: What kind of chance?

EVIE: You never go anywhere. It would really be wonderful for you and Caitlin to see it.

DUNCAN: I'm so glad you've taken an interest in our vacation plans.

EVIE: Duncan, I just don't want you to make the same mistakes with her that you made with me.

DUNCAN: I don't have enough time left on this planet to make the mistakes I made with you.

EVIE: We always planned to go all these places and we never did.

DUNCAN: *You* always planned.

EVIE: Maybe it isn't too late.

DUNCAN: For a visit?

EVIE: Or, perhaps longer.

DUNCAN: Longer than a visit?

EVIE: I think when all is said and done, the thing we do best is raise our son.

DUNCAN: What are you saying? Are you saying you'd move out there with Jack?

EVIE: Duncan, please, we've had such a lovely divorce, let's not spoil it with something hypothetical.

DUNCAN: You're carrying his baby. That's not hypothetical. Now you think you can take Jack?

EVIE: I'm exploring options.

DUNCAN: Why doesn't Carter move east? That's an option.

EVIE: His work is too important.

DUNCAN: What does he do?

EVIE: He sells coffee.

DUNCAN: I never would have brought it up if I'd known he sold coffee.

EVIE: It's more involved than that. His accountant says he's a visionary.

DUNCAN: And this sounds like a good plan to you? Caitlin and I move three thousand miles so Carter can hold onto his sales route?

EVIE: So our child has both his parents.

DUNCAN: What if I won't go?

EVIE: A thirteen-year-old boy can make up his own mind.

DUNCAN: If he has parents selfish enough to make him choose. *(Pause.)* Say I *did* want to move. How do I explain it to Caitlin?

EVIE: Tell her...*(Moving closer him, softly.)* there are too many memories here, my love. Let's go find our place, a place that will be yours and mine forever and ever. Where our love can grow...

(Evie stares into Duncan's eyes as lights fade.)

SCENE 5

Lights up on a bed. Carter is in his pajamas with a hypodermic.

CARTER: What if they mixed up the sperm and you're carrying someone else's baby? I couldn't go through that again, Evie.
(Evie enters and starts to undress.)

EVIE: There's nothing to worry about.

CARTER: There's always something to worry about.

EVIE: But what good does it do?

CARTER: It gives you an edge. Sometimes you can see what they're trying to do to you and you can stop 'em.

EVIE: Nobody's trying "to do" anything to you.

CARTER: Right. Everybody wishes everybody the best.

EVIE: What's wrong?

CARTER: Nothing's wrong!
(Turning on her.)
Look, some days I work twelve, fourteen hours. I get on a roll and that's when they show me the money. You're saying you won't want me to cut back once we have a baby?

EVIE: Why would I interfere with your job?

CARTER: I start missing those big paydays I'm a wounded man. I *have* to close the deal. The bastards smell that and they walk away. So I get in my car and by the time I get out I'm just one more son of a bitch who's worried about his mortgage. I'm not going to let you do that to me.

EVIE: You think I want to take away your job?

CARTER: My parents split up when I was fourteen and I was on my own at sixteen. I know what it takes to get by.

EVIE: I don't know what you're talking about.

CARTER: You wanted a baby, so you found me. Once you have your baby, what do you need me for?

EVIE: You're afraid I'm going to leave you?

CARTER: I'm not afraid.

EVIE: Carter, I want you in my life.

CARTER: For now.

EVIE: Forever.

CARTER: That word doesn't mean a thing. They should ban it. Maybe it isn't even me you want.

EVIE: What do you think I want?

CARTER: You keep after me for this and that and I get to thinking you're trying to turn me into someone you could spend your life with, but that person isn't me. I'm very good at anticipating things.

EVIE: Which is probably why they happen.

CARTER: Has anyone ever left *you*?

EVIE: Actually, yes, in college.

CARTER: Jesus Christ. College. Your parents are still together. You're on speaking terms with everyone in your family. What the hell do you know?

EVIE: I don't know who you are right now.

CARTER: I'm a survivor, that's who I am.

EVIE: Even survivors run out of time, Carter.

CARTER: See? You even want to take that away from me.

EVIE: I thought I was giving you something.

CARTER: People who take always think they're giving.

(Beat.)

Come on, I'll give you the shot and we can go to bed.

EVIE: I don't think so, Carter.

(Evie leaves. Lights fade on Carter with the hypodermic.)

SCENE 6

Lights up on Duncan and Caitlin getting ready for bed.

DUNCAN: She knows precisely how to get me crazy. It's like microsurgery.

CAITLIN: You don't get that angry with me.

DUNCAN: You oughta be glad.

CAITLIN: Actually, I think it's sad. It means our relationship is incomplete.

DUNCAN: Anger like that doesn't happen overnight. It grows and mutates in the fertile soil of a marriage, through years of arguments and betrayals and disappointments. Give me time I'll go nuts on you, baby.

CAITLIN: Could you slap me?

DUNCAN: Excuse me?

CAITLIN: As a sign of our love. Of the anger you plan to feel for me in the future.

DUNCAN: Hard?

CAITLIN: Pretty hard. Like this.

(She slaps him, hard.)

DUNCAN: Wow. I feel kind of angry.

CAITLIN: Oh, sweetie. Now it's your turn.

DUNCAN: Caitlin.

CAITLIN: Come on! I want everything Evie has.

DUNCAN: Alright. But first you have to do something for me.

CAITLIN: Anything. I've done stuff you wouldn't believe. The wildest, weirdest trip you ever thought of, Duncan, here I am. Just tell me what to do.

DUNCAN: Eat.

CAITLIN: *(Recoiling.)* Food? Ick! That's where I draw the line.

DUNCAN: It has to happen sometime.

CAITLIN: Two more pounds. Please?

DUNCAN: Tomorrow you eat. And I'll get angry.

CAITLIN: The scary way you do with Evie?

DUNCAN: You got it. *(Beat.)* Is it hard for you, having them here?

CAITLIN: It's just a week-end, and I've been through many strange weekends in my life.

DUNCAN: I wonder if it's even fair. Asking you to move in.

CAITLIN: What do you mean? You don't want me here?

DUNCAN: There are just so many memories. What if you and I took a chance someplace else?

CAITLIN: Are you serious? You'd actually move?

DUNCAN: We could find our own place, a place that's yours and mine. Where our love could grow.

CAITLIN: *(Fighting tears.)* Oh, God.

DUNCAN: What?

CAITLIN: I think this is what I've always wanted. I didn't dare dream you'd ever really put me first. Duncan, if you go away with me that's all I could ever ask.

(Lights fade on Duncan and Caitlin locked in an embrace.)

SCENE 7

Lights up on Evie on the phone, looking out an icy window with the sunlight pouring in. Nearby is a little pile of presents.

EVIE: *(On phone.)* It's so beautiful, the whole world is frozen, the driveway is solid ice and the sun is just exploding off it and the trees are shimmering like jewels—honey? Can you hear me? I can't hear you.
(Beat.)
Can you hear him?
(Lights up on Duncan in another room on the phone.)
DUNCAN: *(On phone.)* I lost him.
EVIE: *(On phone.)* Oh, he's back! We can't wait to see you, honey. Daddy and I have some friends over and we're going to have just what you like, hot dogs and pop tarts and Dr Pepper and your father created a rather unusual cake. *(Pause.)* That's *always* been your favorite meal! Hasn't it, Duncan? He always loved it. Not since you were five years old?
DUNCAN: *(On phone.)* I think you're mistaken, Jack, your mother and I are quite certain you still love this stuff. What? You can't come? Did he say he can't come?
EVIE: *(On phone.)* Jack, honey, you have to! Your mother is more important than a blizzard! He's gone again.
DUNCAN: *(On phone.)* He says they're not letting anyone leave.
EVIE: *(On phone.)* What can we do, Duncan? *(To Jack.)* I know, we'll have the hot dogs and pop tarts and cake and we'll sing "Happy Birthday" as if you were here.
DUNCAN: *(On phone, singing.)* "Happy birthday to you..."
EVIE: This is the first birthday we haven't all been together.
DUNCAN AND EVIE: *(Singing on phone.)* "Happy birthday dear Jack, happy birthday to you."
EVIE: *(On phone.)* Now I lost him.
DUNCAN: *(On phone.)* Me too. It's just us, Evie.
(Lights fade on Duncan. Evie hangs up the phone and looks out the window at the snow. Carter enters.)
CARTER: Any sign of breakfast?
EVIE: There's coffee.
CARTER: You know I can't drink coffee with my excitable bowel. *(Pause.)* You should check the insulation in this house.

EVIE: Are you cold?

CARTER: Old insulation can be dangerous. It can release fumes...my sinuses are pretty sensitive and that stuff will go right to your head. I remember saying some pretty crazy things last night.

EVIE: Is this an apology?

CARTER: I don't owe you an apology, but if you think I do then that was it.

EVIE: Whatever happened to "I'm sorry?"

CARTER: You gotta have everything, don't you, Evie? And I can't even get breakfast.

EVIE: Jack isn't coming.

CARTER: So this whole trip was a waste?

(Duncan and Caitlin enter.)

CAITLIN: Morning everyone. Sorry about Jack.

EVIE: It's this damn storm!

CARTER: Is that what he told you?

EVIE: What do you mean?

CARTER: If I was thirteen years old and got in serious trouble I don't think I'd come home either.

DUNCAN: Jack didn't do anything a normal adolescent wouldn't do.

CAITLIN: The letter from the school said he was with a mob of kids.

DUNCAN: He has friends. He's popular. You think that's bad?

CARTER: They were in a cemetery.

EVIE: Oh, you never walked through someone else's property, Mister Perfect?

CAITLIN: They had shovels.

DUNCAN: Shovels. Jesus Christ, call in a SWAT team.

CAITLIN: Why were they in a cemetery in the middle of the night with torches and shovels...chanting?

DUNCAN: They didn't want to disturb anyone.

EVIE: They were considerate young people.

CARTER: They were up to no good. They need punishment.

CAITLIN: They need help. Or they'll be just more people we're scared of. Our own children.

EVIE: *(Siding with Duncan.)* No, *our* own children.

CARTER: *(Siding with Evie.)* That's right, *our* own children.

DUNCAN: *(Siding with Evie against Carter.)* No, *our* own children.

CAITLIN: *(To Duncan.)* I thought they were *our* own children.

DUNCAN: Neither one of you has a child. You couldn't possibly understand this.

CARTER: I understand why he didn't come home.

EVIE: This has nothing to do with those silly cemetery pranks. It's just a storm. Duncan and I were singing "Happy Birthday" when the phone went dead.

CARTER: There's no phone? Goddammit to hell! You promised I could do business here. How can I do business with no phone?

EVIE: There's a blizzard, Carter.

CARTER: A promise is a promise!

EVIE: It's an act of God. He does His thing and I do mine.

CARTER: I have clients counting on a call. And here I am. Trapped, just like I predicted. I'm going into town and find a pay-phone.

EVIE: Take it slow, it's pretty slippery out there.

(Carter leaves. A scream from outside. Evie opens the door.)

EVIE: *(Continuing; calling out.)* Don't try to move! We'll get a rope!

(Lights fade on Evie at the door.)

SCENE 8

Lights up on Duncan writing on the cake. Evie comes in.

DUNCAN: Broken?

EVIE: Bruised. He'll live.

DUNCAN: That's good.

EVIE: Easy for you to say.

DUNCAN: What's he doing?

EVIE: Just lying in bed. He sounds like someone's press secretary. I asked him how he was and he said he was "resting comfortably."

DUNCAN: Give him a break. He's traumatized.

EVIE: That's his normal state. That must be what attracted me.

(Evie helps Duncan put the candles on the cake.)

DUNCAN: It pains me to admit this, but your approach to Caitlin was shockingly successful.

EVIE: Oh, Duncan, that's wonderful.

DUNCAN: It worked so well I'd have a hard time wriggling out of it.

EVIE: Lovely.

DUNCAN: If we actually do this—and I'm not saying we will—it's making things pretty easy for you, isn't it?

EVIE: And that's the worst thing in the world?

DUNCAN: It's right up there.

EVIE: I couldn't imagine living far away from you, Duncan. Ever.

(Lights fade on Evie and Duncan.)

SCENE 9

Lights up on Caitlin setting the table. There's a brightly colored table cloth, paper plates, and decorations for a child's birthday, including noise-makers and party hats. Carter limps in.

CARTER: This is what happens if you try to leave.

CAITLIN: Oh, dear, does it hurt?

CARTER: No, it feels good, taking a spill on sheer ice, bouncing down a fifty foot driveway and smashing into a mailbox. You oughta try it sometime. Where are they, anyway?

CAITLIN: Cooking.

CARTER: That's nice. When I got a divorce I tried to hit my wife with the car. These people "cook."

(Duncan and Evie come in with hot dogs, potato chips, pop tarts, and Dr Pepper.)

CARTER: *(Continuing.)* I'm not going to eat this crap.

EVIE: Oh, yes you are.

CAITLIN: Carter? I'll get you something else.

EVIE: Sit down. This is the birthday meal.

CARTER: What if I don't want "the birthday meal?"

EVIE: Then you won't get any cake.

CARTER: Well boo hoo hoo.

DUNCAN: Caitlin? You'll have the birthday meal?

CAITLIN: Yes, thank you. This is the first time I've eaten in seventy-one days. I'm doing it for you, Duncan.

EVIE: I guess you're on your own, Carter.

CARTER: Oh, like that's something new.

EVIE: But I have to insist you put on your party hat if you sit at this table.

CARTER: Jesus, I hate all these rules.

(They put on their party hats and start in on the food. Carter doesn't eat; Caitlin is in heaven.)

CAITLIN: This is amazing food. I can't remember the last time I was this happy.

DUNCAN: Sorry about the phone, Carter. Evie told me how important your business is.

CARTER: Am I catching some attitude? Like selling coffee isn't good enough? There's only one thing in this country that's gotten better in the last ten years, and that's coffee.

CAITLIN: I know something else that's gotten better. My life, ever since I met Duncan. It was this rainy day in Boston and my hair was defying gravity and Duncan looked like he'd just wandered out of the jungle, he was carrying a gun.

CARTER: Why did he have a gun?

DUNCAN: It doesn't matter, we met each other at our worst, so everything since then has been an improvement.

EVIE: Why did you have a gun, Duncan?

DUNCAN: It's a rough town. Caitlin was able to see beyond the gun.

CAITLIN: To the crazed lunatic who was carrying it.

EVIE: Why did he have a gun, Caitlin?

CAITLIN: I was doing PR for Handgun Control in Boston, and Duncan was turning in his gun for some Reeboks.

EVIE: I remember that gun turn-in very well.

CAITLIN: Thanks. We kicked butt with publicity, not that anyone appreciated my personal contributions.

EVIE: We were still married then.

CAITLIN: Uh-oh.

EVIE: You went right from our therapy session to turn in the gun.

DUNCAN: That's possible.

EVIE: I remember sitting in that office on that awful dreary day and knowing you had a gun in your gym bag and hoping it would stay there till the end of the session.

DUNCAN: Alcohol, anger, and guns. It's a nasty combination.

EVIE: I thought we were trying to solve our problems.

DUNCAN: We were.

EVIE: While you were banging some bimbo on the side?

CAITLIN: I resent that.

EVIE: I resent you sleeping with my husband while we were still married.

CARTER: You're not married now, Evie. It's over. This is like giving somone a physical after they're dead.

EVIE: You couldn't possibly understand this, Carter, because it involves trust.

CARTER: I said I was sorry, what do you want from me? *(Picks up spoon.)* Here, gouge out my eyes, maybe that'll make you feel better.

EVIE: Jesus, Carter.

CAITLIN: Just so you know, Evie, the only reason I got involved is because he said it was over with you two.

DUNCAN: It *was* over.

EVIE: Then why were you coming to therapy, Duncan?

DUNCAN: To find a decent way to end it.

EVIE: You were telling me you wanted it to work.

DUNCAN: I did want it to work. But you didn't.

EVIE: Can't you at least be honest about running around?

DUNCAN: Can't you be honest about leaving?

CAITLIN: *(To Duncan.)* See, honey, this is the kind of anger *I'd* like from you.

DUNCAN: We both knew you wanted out, you didn't even have to say it. You'd already moved on.

CARTER: I have to side with Duncan on this one, babe. It's always pretty clear where you stand.

EVIE: Please, please shut up, Carter. Duncan, I was dying. I needed some kind of peace.

DUNCAN: Which meant you wanted out!

EVIE: I wanted things to change!

DUNCAN: I *didn't* want out. I loved you so much, Evie, I'd have done anything. I never would have gone to that insane, psychopathic therapist nut for anyone but you.

EVIE: She was very good except for the doll and the paddle.

DUNCAN: I needed you and you were slipping away and there were times I couldn't even breathe. Do you know what that's like, to be gasping for breath so you're flopping on the floor like a dying fish because you need another person so you can live? You were that person, Evie, and when you started drifting away I did whatever I had to do to survive and if it hadn't been an affair it would have been a bottle or some pills or just maybe that gun I turned in, okay?

CAITLIN: I was just a bottle of booze to kill your pain?

DUNCAN: Caitlin, you know I was hurting.

CAITLIN: You never told me you were trying to work it out.

DUNCAN: You didn't need to walk through my personal hell.

CAITLIN: Evie, I never would have gotten involved if I'd known you were working it out.

DUNCAN: *(To Caitlin.)* You're the one that got such a thrill out of sneaking around.

EVIE: You two were "sneaking around" on me?

CAITLIN: It was the situation you put me in, Duncan. I'm sorry, Evie.

DUNCAN: If you didn't like that situation then why would you send Evie flowers from me to get us back together again?

EVIE: *You* sent the flowers?

CAITLIN: Oh, God, in a very weak and confused moment.

CARTER: You wanted out, Evie, and I'd say they made it easy on you, as opposed to my wife, for example, who had the entire Portland police department after me.

EVIE: I'm sorry, sweetie, but nobody gives a fuck right now. *(Turning on Duncan.)* Duncan, I wasted all that time feeling guilty and you were out having the time of your life.

DUNCAN: The worst time of my life.

CAITLIN: Everything you're saying makes me feel worse and worse.

DUNCAN: I'm trying to deal with this thing, honey.

CAITLIN: What thing? What is there to deal with? You and I are going to be together. That's why you're moving away with me, right?

DUNCAN: Yes, honey. We're going west to start a new life.

CARTER: That's the plan.

CAITLIN: What plan? *(Looks at the others.)* What is this plan, Duncan? It's not just you and me, is it?

DUNCAN: It's so we can be together, Caitlin.

CARTER: So we can *all* be together.

CAITLIN: I don't understand. *(Pause.)* Would someone tell me what the plan is?

EVIE: Duncan and I need to be there for Jack.

CAITLIN: *(To Duncan.)* You son of a bitch. Nothing you told me was true.

DUNCAN: Caitlin, we're going away, wherever you want.

CAITLIN: *(Starting to leave.)* As long as it's near Evie.

DUNCAN: Caitlin!

CAITLIN: I don't know who I hate more, Duncan, you or me.
(Caitlin leaves.)

EVIE: *(To Duncan.)* This whole divorce is based on a lie.
(Evie leaves. Carter and Duncan are left with the birthday meal.)

DUNCAN: Nice move with your fat stupid mouth, Carter.

CARTER: I thought you already told her.

DUNCAN: I was going to tell her in stages, getting a little more honest each time so finally she'd know the truth. Why'd you have to blurt it out?

CARTER: I'm a little jittery. Evie does these psychic drive-bys so I spend half my time diving for cover. Christ, I can't even go outside because of the ice, my business is dying, I'm trapped, and then no phone, come on, that's like spitting in my face.

DUNCAN: Caitlin has a phone in her car.

CARTER: *(Limping to the door.)* A phone. Thank you, God. I'll never ask for anything again.

DUNCAN: There's a bucket of sand. Toss some on the ice so you don't fall.

CARTER: I wonder why Evie didn't tell me that.

(Carter leaves. Evie comes in with the birthday cake.)

EVIE: What a festive party this turned out to be.

(The sound of three gunshots.)

EVIE: *(Continuing.)* Someone isn't going to be having any cake.

(Lights fade on Evie and Duncan.)

SCENE 10

Lights up on Caitlin, on the bed in pain. Her entire body shudders with terrible sobs. Evie enters.

EVIE: Caitlin, are you alright? Where do you hurt?

CAITLIN: Everywhere. Even my clothes hurt.

EVIE: What happened?

CAITLIN: I just couldn't take any more.

EVIE: What did you do to yourself?

CAITLIN: I was trying to leave and I saw someone breaking into my car and I just snapped. Don't you have to stand up sometime and say, "Stop! Enough! You can't do this anymore!"

EVIE: You shot a burglar?

CAITLIN: My gun control credibility is kaput.

EVIE: Oh, Caitlin. Whose gun?

CAITLIN: Mine, okay? Mine, mine mine! I'm all alone in that city and everyone else has a gun, why can't I?

EVIE: Did this burglar get away?

CAITLIN: I don't know. He was grabbing stuff out of my car so I shot him and came back inside. I can't believe I pulled the trigger. I'm so stressed out. I've never shot anyone before, and believe me, it felt stupendous! I have to leave.

EVIE: No! We'll tell the police exactly what happened.

CAITLIN: Who cares about the police? It's Duncan. He's only with me because he can't have you.

EVIE: He adores you, Caitlin. And he's a wonderful man.

CAITLIN: But he's not *my* wonderful man. I won't live in your shadow.

EVIE: I'm history, Caitlin, I'm the Hundred Years' War.

CAITLIN: It was fine when it was an affair and he was stringing me along, *that* I understand. But it got bigger and bigger and last night when he said he'd go anywhere for me—I knew that's what I wanted all along. Today I found out I couldn't have it.

EVIE: But you can!

CAITLIN: I've made up my mind. I don't think I'd have the strength to leave him if I hadn't started eating again.

EVIE: You're not the only one involved, young lady. Duncan won't move out there without you and if he doesn't then Jack won't and if Jack won't then how can I?

(Lights fade on Evie and Caitlin.)

SCENE 11

Lights up on Carter in bed. Duncan is standing nearby.

CARTER: Nice goddamn neighborhood.

DUNCAN: It's usually pretty safe.

CARTER: "Usually" isn't very reassuring when you get shot.

DUNCAN: It grazed you, Carter.

CARTER: One shit-head with a gun and all bets are off.

DUNCAN: Can I look at it?

CARTER: By "it," you're referring to where the bullet hit me?

DUNCAN: Grazed you, yes, what other "it" would I be referring to?

CARTER: I don't know. It's just, when one guy says to another guy in bed, "can I look at it?" You know.

DUNCAN: Would you rather have me clean the wound or would you rather risk infection?

CARTER: *(Considers.)* Risk infection. How come you got chosen for this, anyway?

DUNCAN: I had a year of med school.

CARTER: Excellent preparation for the moving business.

DUNCAN: If they ever take the blood and needles out of medicine, I'm there.

CARTER: I'll wait for a real doctor, nothing personal.

(Beat.)

Duncan? Did you ever find a way with Evie to...handle it?

DUNCAN: Handle what?

CARTER: The way she is, the relentless attacks that put you in a foxhole and the incredible love that lures you out into the open so you're totally naked for the next attack.

DUNCAN: What do you want, Carter?

CARTER: I want pointers...guidelines, some kind of battle plan for having a relationship with your wife. I think you owe me that.

DUNCAN: The best I came up with was a divorce. Now we get along great. Shall I send her up?

CARTER: I think I'd like to be alone.

(Lights fade on Carter.)

SCENE 12

Lights up on Evie at the table. Duncan enters.

DUNCAN: I think we can be guardedly optimistic.

EVIE: "Guardedly optimistic?" What is with you people?

DUNCAN: What people?

EVIE: Men! A little tension and you get so robotic I could scream.

DUNCAN: Just thought you'd want to know how your boyfriend's doing.

EVIE: Feeling a little guilty?

DUNCAN: For what?

EVIE: Your girlfriend shoots my boyfriend, it's nothing to be proud of.

DUNCAN: It was an accident. It could have happened to anyone.

EVIE: Anyone carrying a gun. I suppose I should go up and see him.

DUNCAN: He'd prefer to be alone. He's pretty shaken up.

EVIE: Of course he is, the little baby.

DUNCAN: Evie, the man has just been shot.

EVIE: It's always something with him. Oh, speaking of shot.

DUNCAN: What?

EVIE: Can you give me mine? Carter isn't up to it tonight.

DUNCAN: Boy, I wish it was painting your house or fixing your car.

EVIE: That's okay. I respect your squeamishness.

DUNCAN: No, I'll do it.

EVIE: Thank you, Duncan.

(Evie gets out the hypodermic and hands it to Duncan .)

DUNCAN: Where?

EVIE: On the sofa is fine.

DUNCAN: No, I meant...

(Evie lies face down on the sofa.)

DUNCAN: *(Continuing.)* Oh. There. You know, if someone offered me a drink about now...

EVIE: You'd go into a spiral of rage and depression that could wipe out the next decade of your life.

DUNCAN: *(Considering.)* Still...

EVIE: You honestly don't have to do this.

DUNCAN: I *want* to do this.

(Evie reaches back and starts to pull down her underwear.)

EVIE: Oh, it's lots of fun.

DUNCAN: Are you ready?

EVIE: I don't have to be ready, you do.

DUNCAN: I'm totally ready.

EVIE: Just a single firm move.

DUNCAN: *(Jabs the air with the needle.)* Like that?

EVIE: I can't see, but yes. Hurry up, Duncan, I mean *Carter* manages to do this, for God sakes.

DUNCAN: Why did you have to bring him up?

EVIE: For inspiration.

DUNCAN: You think it inspires me that I'm helping to make his baby?

EVIE: Duncan, what am I going to do with him?

DUNCAN: Keep trying to mold him into someone you want until one of you has had enough and bolts.

EVIE: That's what he thinks I'm doing. He's really made me miss you. What are you doing?

DUNCAN: Getting ready. I plunge it in, press down on the top, then pull it out. Right?

EVIE: Right.

DUNCAN: *(Ready to plunge.)* Beautiful.

EVIE: The only way to screw it up is if you're hesitant.

DUNCAN: *(Stops.)* I'm not hesitant. Am I?

EVIE: Do *you* think you are?

DUNCAN: Yes and no. But never about something as important as this. Why would you bring up the one thing that could spell disaster?

EVIE: So you'll do it right.

DUNCAN: But now you've got me thinking "hesitant" and I should be thinking "firm." Why did you do that?

EVIE: Please don't judge me by what I do and say.

DUNCAN: What *should* I judge you on?

EVIE: Everything else.

DUNCAN: What else is there besides what you do and say?

EVIE: Just do it, Duncan!

DUNCAN: *(Raising the needle.)* I'm preparing to do it...and now...I'm about to do it...

EVIE: So do it!

DUNCAN: I said I'm about to do it. Don't you trust me?

EVIE: Look at me! Of course I trust you!

DUNCAN: Good.

EVIE: To give me a shot.

DUNCAN: Meaning you don't trust me in other, more significant areas?

EVIE: I don't think we need to get into that now.

DUNCAN: So there's something to "get into." I find that pretty unsettling at a time like this.

EVIE: Can we please talk about this later?

DUNCAN: No. We can't.

EVIE: Duncan, for Chrissakes, you weren't honest with me.

DUNCAN: Okay. The thing with Caitlin started before I told you it started.

EVIE: I don't care about Caitlin!

DUNCAN: Then what wasn't I honest about?

EVIE: Me! What you said tonight!

DUNCAN: What?

EVIE: The fish thing.

DUNCAN: Are you insane? What "fish thing"?

EVIE: You needed me to breathe. Like the fish. You never said that before, you never found a way to tell me how much you loved me.

DUNCAN: *That's* what you're angry about?

EVIE: I had to guess, and I guessed wrong.

DUNCAN: You mean it would have made a difference?

EVIE: To know you couldn't live without me? To know I was needed somewhere in this big stupid world? To know there was a bond between us that all the blackness and horror couldn't break? Yeah, I think that might have made a difference.

DUNCAN: I feel sick.

EVIE: You weren't honest about what was in your heart. You backed away.

DUNCAN: Because you were backing away!

EVIE: If I was backing away then you should have come after me!

DUNCAN: I thought you were backing away from me!

EVIE: I don't know why I was backing away and if I don't know why I was backing away then how could you?

DUNCAN: I assumed you were backing to get away. Why else would you back? Why would anyone back? To get away. And away you got.

EVIE: Away I got.

DUNCAN: I don't know if I can do it now. My hands are shaking.

EVIE: Tell them to stop!

DUNCAN: They won't! They're idiots!

EVIE: You always find reasons to put things off and now you've got to just do it!

DUNCAN: I'm doing it! I'm really really doing it!

(Duncan is in agony with the hypodermic. He starts, stops, starts again, stops, then plunges it into her. Blackout.)

SCENE 13

Lights up on Carter in bed. Caitlin has a bottle of medicine.

CARTER: Haven't you ever heard of a warning shot?

CAITLIN: I forgot. What is it, a crime?

CARTER: Yes, it is.

CAITLIN: Well you were really mean to me yesterday.

CARTER: Fine. Now we're even.

CAITLIN: Let me see where it grazed you.

CARTER: How come everyone acts like this isn't an authentic wound?

CAITLIN: Try to shut up, Carter.

CARTER: *(Exposing his wound.)* Is this going to hurt?

CAITLIN: Quite a lot.

(Caitlin swabs the medicine on Carter, who gasps.)

CAITLIN: *(Continuing.)* Sorry about the bullet. I have this thing about my car. I make people take off their shoes when they get in.

CARTER: You too? I don't care if it's raining or snowing or twenty below, you don't wear shoes in my car.

CAITLIN: So you can imagine when I saw you climbing in the front seat...

CARTER: *(Points with finger.)* Bang bang bang! Hey, I'd have done the same thing. Evie and I were in this restaurant and these punks were outside burning my car and she was yammering about "commitment." It nearly killed me.

CAITLIN: Duncan wouldn't have even noticed, his car is so full of junk. I have very few things that are mine and I don't want anyone messing with them.

CARTER: They don't get it: if you don't protect your stuff, your stuff will be gone.

CAITLIN: All my stuff's in storage. It was going to come here, then it was going to Seattle, now, who knows?

CARTER: Aren't you going to move?

CAITLIN: When I met Duncan I had a nice apartment and a good job and I thought I was happy. Now I have no job and no place to live and I'm very confused.

CARTER: If you don't move then Duncan doesn't move and then Evie won't.

CAITLIN: Look, I can't solve everyone's problems.

CARTER: Yes you can! Refuse to move. I'll be off the hook with Evie.

CAITLIN: That's what you want?

CARTER: I think so.

CAITLIN: Too bad she's pregnant. You're getting screwed out of being a dad all over again.

CARTER: I hope I handle it better this time. But if you were a kid, would you rather live with me and Evie ripping each other to shreds, or the two of them baking cakes or whatever the hell they do all day?

CAITLIN: Are those my only choices?

CARTER: That's how it's starting to look from here.

CAITLIN: Carter? Could I ride in the ambulance with you?

CARTER: *(Hesitates.)* Alright. But let's keep it casual. I don't need a lot of pressure right now.

(Lights fade on Caitlin and Carter.)

SCENE 14

A flashing red light through the window. Lights up on Duncan and Evie .

DUNCAN: All of a sudden I felt so calm, my hands stopped shaking and I knew it was a home run. I should go back to medical school.

EVIE: But first, why don't you put some sand on the driveway?
(Duncan goes outside. A paramedic wheels Carter in on a gurney.)

EVIE: *(Continuing.)* I'll get my coat and go with you.

CARTER: You don't need to.

EVIE: You shouldn't be all alone, Carter.
(Caitlin comes in carrying a suitcase.)

CAITLIN: I shot him, I'll go.

EVIE: Is that what you want, Carter?

CARTER: I just want to live.

CAITLIN: I'd kind of like to atone for my actions, if that's cool. Evie?
(She pulls Evie aside.)
Could you possibly break up with Duncan for me?

EVIE: Caitlin, you have to be a big girl.

CAITLIN: *Please?* You did it once already, what's the big deal?

EVIE: Just tell him on your way out.

CAITLIN: *(Looks out the window.)* He's at the bottom of the driveway. He'll never even see me. *(To Carter.)* If you're not too wounded can we get something to eat on the way?
(Caitlin leaves. Evie steps in front of the gurney, with the paramedic at the other end.)

EVIE: Not so fast, Mister.

CARTER: I'd like to go to the hospital, if that's okay.

EVIE: Why are you acting like everything's my fault?

CARTER: Look at the facts. Since I met you my car got torched, I got stabbed, my back went out, I fractured my ankle, I got shot.

EVIE: Nobody said this would be easy.

CARTER: I love you but I fear for my life.

EVIE: You're not going to come back, are you?

CARTER: I don't know.

PARAMEDIC: You're not the only guy in town who got shot tonight. You're not even the only guy on this street. So could we get this baby rolling?

EVIE: *(Confronting the paramedic.)* You're not breaking up with me. If he's leaving me I want to hear it from him. *(Turning on Carter.)* Say it, Carter! Say it!

(Carter is in turmoil.)

PARAMEDIC: Do what ya gotta do, man. The bodies are piling up out there.

CARTER: Goodbye, Evie.

EVIE: I won't stay in this relationship alone, Carter. As far as I'm concerned, it's over.

(The paramedic wheels the gurney out. Evie sits at the table and starts eating the birthday cake. The flashing light outside leaves. Duncan comes in.)

DUNCAN: I thought I saw you in the ambulance.

EVIE: That was Caitlin.

DUNCAN: She went with Carter?

EVIE: To atone for the shooting.

DUNCAN: And here you are at the table. The awesomely familiar is suddenly brand new.

EVIE: She's left you, Duncan. She didn't want to live in my shadow. She knew you were in love with me and would be forever and ever.

DUNCAN: Our divorce is in a shambles, isn't it? *(Sits down at table.)* Look what we're throwing away. Jack's stopped trying to get us together. We've already made our friends choose whose side they're on. We've found inspired ways of torturing each other.

EVIE: It's been a lovely divorce, Duncan, but it's over.

DUNCAN: Yes. It's all over.

(They eat the birthday cake. Fade to black.)

END OF PLAY

Polaroid Stories

an adaptation of Ovid's Metamorphoses

by Naomi Iizuka

BIOGRAPHY

Naomi Iizuka is a Los Angeles-based playwright. *Polaroid Stories* was originally commissioned by En Garde Arts and workshopped site-specifically. Her other plays include *Scheherazade, Skin, Marlowe's Eye* and *Tattoo Girl*. *Scheherazade* was produced at San Francisco's Magic Theatre in 1996 as part of Pieces of the Quilt, an AIDS benefit theatre event, and *Skin* has been produced at the Weiss Forum in San Diego, SoHo Rep in New York, and Dallas Theatre Center, where it was awarded best play of the season by *The Dallas Observer*. Ms. Iizuka's plays have received readings and workshops at the Playwrights' Center's PlayLabs, New York Theatre Workshop, the Public Theater, Audrey Skirball-Kenis Theatre, Bottom's Dream, and the Actors' Gang in Los Angeles. She is the recipient of a 1995 Jerome Playwriting Fellowship, a 1996 Many Voices Multicultural Collaboration Grant and a 1996 McKnight Advancement Grant through the Playwrights' Center in Minneapolis.

HUMANA FESTIVAL PRODUCTION

Polaroid Stories was first performed at the Humana Festival of New American Plays, March, 1997. It was directed by Jon Jory with the following cast:

D (dionysus)	Scot Anthony Robinson
Philomel	Monica Bueno
Eurydice	Kim Gainer
Persephone (also semele)	Denise Casano
Orpheus	Bruce McKenzie
Narcissus	Michael Ray Escamilla
Echo	Miriam Brown
G (zeus, hades)	Nelson Vasquez
The Lydian Sailor (also theseus, pentheus)	Danny Seckel
Ariadne	Caitlin Miller

and the following production staff:

Scenic Designer	Paul Owen
Costume Designer	Marcia Dixcy Jory
Lighting Designer	Greg Sullivan
Sound Designer	Martin R. Desjardins
Properties Designer	Mark J. Bissonnette
Production Stage Manager	Debra Acquavella
Assistant Stage Manager	Cind Senensieb
Dramaturg	Michael Bigelow Dixon
Casting	Laura Richin Casting

Polaroid Stories was commissioned by En Garde Arts, Anne Hamburger, Producer.

CHARACTERS

D (dionysus)

EURYDICE

PERSEPHONE (also SEMELE)

ORPHEUS (also TEREUS)

PHILOMEL

SKINHEADgirl (a.k.a. neon girl)

NARCISSUS

ECHO

SKINHEADboy (a.k.a. oklahoma boy/speedracer)

G (a.k.a. zeus, hades)

SETTING

a pier at the edge of the city.

TIME

the late 1990s. night.

POLAROID STORIES

ACT ONE: fucked up love songs

PROLOGUE

> *in the darkness, Philomel begins to sing. a fragment of an old song, familiar and haunting. her voice is solitary, unadorned, child-like.*
>
> *the sound of the streets grow around her voice: traffic like the ocean, trains rumbling underground, a pay-phone ringing and ringing, pieces of radio, a bass line, glass shattering, a faint siren faraway. in a sea of noise, Philomel's song is gradually lost.*

THE FATE OF THE LYDIAN SAILOR—the story of oklahoma boy

> *a small light in the darkness. shadows like fish underwater. a light. D appears, a figure in the darkness.*

D: this is how it begins, this is where—
  i seen him out of nowhere, crazy amped out boy crazy oklahoma boy,
  i found him up by port authority,
  scheming and scamming, nickel diming what he can—
  i watch him a while, see him get all's he can get,
  and then he goes, he gets high on spray. oklahoma boy likes spray.
  spray's cheap, he says, and then he smiles like a psychopath.
  tell you what, he says to me, i ain't got a friend in this whole world,
  are you my friend, he says to me,
  what you got for me, friend? i got a kingdom, i says to him,
  behold my kingdom, and he thinks that's the funniest thing.

he laughs so hard he falls down.
and then we get high. we fly.

oklahoma boy likes speed,
he likes it cause it makes him go so fast
it makes him go fucking speedracer fast with them fucking speed racer
eyes.
one night, he rips me off, digs around till he finds my stash,
i hear his fingers, i hear his eyes clicking in his head, i hear him
laughing in the dark
so high he can't hardly stand, he can't hardly breathe,
and then he takes my stuff, he goes away—
pockets full of quarters, he finds some arcade, video world is all
there is all there ever was, oklahoma boy disappears for days,
all speedracer eyes, big eyes, black as night, full of laser beams and
showers of light, galaxies and planets, whole worlds exploding in
his head, and it's so bright,
what it is, right, it's so bright, for a second you think you can see
then all there is is black—

(darkness.)

A LIST OF MINOR GODS AND GODDESSES

voices in the dark call out. they call out from every direction. sometimes the voices cut each other off. sometimes they overlap. a sea of names spoken fast and loud. the names are statements, taunts, teases, fighting words.

M3: my name is bandit
F1: my name is tina
M2: my name is blondboy
M1: my name is ramon
F2: my name is mohawk girl
F3: my name is lupe
M4: my name is viper
F4: my name is lisa j
M5: my name is crazy todd
M1: my name is ninja b

F5: my name is desiree
M2: my name is david c
F1: my name is rochelle
M3: my name is tiny
M4: my name is paco
M5: my name is skater pete
F2: my name is mai thai
F3: my name is baby punk
M1: my name is tiger
M2: my name is little ray
F4: my name is candy
F5: my name is loca
F1: my name is skinheadgirl
M3: my name is baby j
M4: my name is nazi mike
M5: my name is tweeker shawn
F2: my name is nothing girl
M1: my name is oklahoma boy
F3: my name is jamie b
M2: my name is zero
M3: my name is shadow
M4: my name is scratch
M5: my name is nicky z
M1: my name is dogboy
M2: my name is skinhead steve
F4: my name is happy girl
M3: my name is marco
M4: my name is psycho john
F5: my name is melody
M5: my name is scarface
M1: my name is kaos
F1: my name is disappear

(the voices reverberate, echo. and then there is silence.)

HOW EURYDICE CROSSES THE RIVER OF FORGETFULNESS—the journey between two worlds

Eurydice is crossing the river of forgetfulness. she walks through the water. ancient trash floats across the water's surface. the water's surface gleams black as oil.

Persephone waits for her on the other side. she is the queen of the dead.

EURYDICE: my name is disappear. my name is disappear.

PERSEPHONE: hey! who do you think you're talking to, disappear?

EURYDICE: i'm talking to anybody's who's listening

PERSEPHONE: is that right?

EURYDICE: i'm talking to somebody who knows how it goes—
you know how it goes, i know you do, too— see it in your eyes. so you
tell me then, cause i want to know, tell me about the places i've never
been to, tell me about all the places i'm gonna go to

PERSEPHONE: don't you start that song with me, little girl

EURYDICE: i said to him, this town is too damn small for me
this town ain't good for nothing—
i want to get out of here
i want to see the world
i want to see some fireworks in this life, is what i said to him

PERSEPHONE: you ain't telling me nothing new, nothing i ain't heard before

EURYDICE: i want to be famous
i want to sleep in satin sheets

PERSEPHONE: girl, please

EURYDICE: i want to dance and dance all night long
i want to go someplace in this damn life, is what i said to him—

PERSEPHONE: heard that, heard that, heard that all before

EURYDICE: but see, it's like this: i got a man like a bad dream
follows me no matter where i go

PERSEPHONE: heard that, too

EURYDICE: i feel his eyes on my back
i feel his breath on my neck, no matter how far i get to
(Orpheus appears out of the shadows. he approaches.)

EURYDICE: and he's all

shut up, you ain't going nowhere, what are you thinking, girl, who are
you kidding?
and i'm looking at him
and all i can think is
who
are
you
to
me?
who were you ever to me?
like you matter to me
like anything you say is going to make a difference to me
like i want to stay in that nowhere town doin nothing all my life
like i want to be with you forever
like i want that

PERSEPHONE: little girl

EURYDICE: i ain't no little girl

PERSEPHONE: little girl is all you are—

EURYDICE: i ain't no little girl, all acting like you know me.

PERSEPHONE: i know you, little girl. i know you like i know myself.

> *(Orpheus comes so close to Eurydice. a chain link fence is all that separates them.)*

ORPHEUS: what are you thinking, little girl—
 —you ain't going nowhere—

EURYDICE: —you can't touch me—

ORPHEUS: —is that right—

EURYDICE: —where i'm going to, baby, you ain't never going to find me—

ORPHEUS: —shut up—

EURYDICE: —how do i look walking away?

ORPHEUS: —you ain't walking away—

EURYDICE: —how do i look walking away from you, baby, how do i look to
you—

> *(Orpheus tries to follow her. he climbs the fence and falls, crashing to the ground.)*

ORPHEUS: baby—

EURYDICE: i take the bus across a thousand miles

ORPHEUS: i can see you

EURYDICE: i sleep i sleep

ORPHEUS: i can see the veins under your skin, i can see your heart beating

EURYDICE: i sleep i sleep, i sleep like a dead person. it's like i disappear. and when i wake up, i'm a thousand miles away, and it's all like "where you from, you got a place to stay, how'd you like to come spend the night, how'd you like a little of this, how'd you like a taste just a taste, come on, baby, this shit is good—"

PERSEPHONE: ain't nothing new, i know how this goes:

ORPHEUS: hey, girl

PERSEPHONE: "hey, girl"

ORPHEUS: i'm talking to you

SKINHEADboy: "hey girl"

PERSEPHONE: "hey girl"

ORPHEUS: i'm talking to you

PERSEPHONE: "yeah, i'm talking to you—you got a name? where are you from? you got a place to stay? you need a place to crash a while—hey—"

ORPHEUS: hey, girl—i'm talking to you, ain't nobody else in the world but you—

PERSEPHONE: "how'd you like to spend the night, how'd you like a little of this"

ORPHEUS: i can see you, baby, i can see straight through you

PERSEPHONE: "how'd you like a taste, just a taste"

ORPHEUS: don't you walk away from me

PERSEPHONE: "come on, baby, this shit is good"

ORPHEUS: don't you walk away from me when i'm talking to you—hey—hey, i'm talking to you—bitch—

(the sound of a woman singing through a sea of static snow. Orpheus tries to climb the fence one more time. he falls, crashing to the ground. he tries to climb again and again.)

EURYDICE: you look like someone who knows how it goes, so i'm going to tell you how it goes,

i'm high, right, and this guy

he says to me, where are you from—bitch—

he wants to touch me, get inside of me, know everything about me.

he wants to know how i got all these scars on my pretty little body.

i tell him, sweet as i know how: baby, i forget.

i drink from the river of forgetfulness.

i forget the names i forget the faces i forget the stories i forget all kinds of shit.

when he's asleep, i roll him, i kick his ass, take his cash, take his fancy
watch
and i'm looking at him
and all i can think is
who are you to me,
like you know me
like you think i'm going to tell you the truth
like you think i'm going to give you that—

yeah, baby, i got scars
i got scars all over, but i don't even know their story, see.
ain't no story, cause i forget.

*(Eurydice gets to the other side of the river, and disappears with Persephone
into the darkness.*

*on the other side of the chain link fence, on the other side of the river,
Orpheus watches Eurydice disappear. he has blood on his hands from where
the chain link cut his skin.)*

THE STORY OF NARCISSUS—gazing in the mirror

*Narcissus is a skinny beautiful boy in dirtied up rave wear. Echo is a run-
away girl, plain and unwashed.*

NARCISSUS: yeah, so how it goes, right, how it goes is like: and then and then
ECHO: and then and then and then and then
NARCISSUS: it's like it's like
ECHO: it's like it's like
NARCISSUS: it's like this, check it out: i meet this guy, right, and we go to his
    place and it's phat it's plush
ECHO: it's phat it's plush
NARCISSUS: it's all glass and chrome
ECHO: glass and chrome
NARCISSUS: black leather, plush pile, big screen tv with surround sound
ECHO: surround sound
NARCISSUS: mirrors everywhere, on the walls, in the hall, on the ceiling, look-
    ing at myself

ECHO: looking at myself

NARCISSUS: and we're kicking back
    and it's cool

ECHO: it's cool

NARCISSUS: and he's like, are you hungry? and i'm like, yeah, i'm hungry, and
    so we order in, and i eat steak and eggs and fries and some pizza and all
    this ice cream and shit, and i'm eating like a pig cause i'm starvin

ECHO: i'm starvin

NARCISSUS: and we're drinking all this wine, and he's like, this is nice wine,
    and i'm like, yeah, it's ok, nothing special

ECHO: nothing special

NARCISSUS: and he busts out this big fat doobie, and i'm like, alright, and we
    get high

ECHO: we get high

NARCISSUS: and i say to him, dude, if this is the high life, dig, the high life is
    ok by me, and that makes him laugh so hard, and i see his teeth like tiny
    pearls all shiny white, and i'm like, dude, you are so ugly

ECHO: you are so ugly

NARCISSUS: and he laughs, and he's like, how about a movie, so he pops in a
    tape, and it's like scar face, and it's like my favorite movie, i love that
    movie, that movie is so excellent

ECHO: so excellent

NARCISSUS: "say hello to my little friend"

ECHO: "little friend"

NARCISSUS: and i'm like kicking back, watching the movie, and i'm so high, i
    feel like i'm coming out of my skin, and i look up at this mirror and i see
    the dude, he's on his knees, and he's like sucking me off, and i can't even
    move, and al, my man, he's like blowing all these punks away, a whole
    fucking army of em, booyah booyah, and i'm so high, this chump's giving
    me head, and i'm just like, whatever

ECHO: whatever

NARCISSUS: and then later, dude gives me some cash, and he's like, hey, this
    was fun, and i'm just like, uh huh yeah whatever

ECHO: whatever

NARCISSUS: see ya—chump

ECHO: chump

NARCISSUS: and then i'm out of there, i'm gone—

(Narcissus goes. Echo follows. darkness.)

PHILOMEL'S STORY—fucked up love song

> *Philomel is singing in the darkness. she sings an ancient song filled with nostalgia and longing. Orpheus listens. he cannot see the singer, though he hears her song.*
>
> *a siren from faraway approaches. Philomel stops. then silence. the siren passes, fades into the night.*

ARIADNE IN THE LABYRINTH

> *SKINHEADgirl moves through the darkness. an echo chamber, voices and laughter bouncing off cement, the origin impossible to gauge. stuff spills out of SKINHEADgirl's bag, a string of things.*

SKINHEADgirl: hey. hey. are you there? can you hear me?
> *(silence.)*
SKINHEADgirl: hey. hey, it's me—quit fooling, say something—
> *(a long, high whistle in the dark. the sound of beer cans clattering on cement. shower of beer.)*
SKINHEADgirl: hey—hey—
> *(silence.)*
SKINHEADgirl: man, i swear when i find you i'm going to kick your ass, for real i am
> *(laughter and voices resonate. an echo chamber.)*
SKINHEADgirl: yeah, you think this some kind of goof, you think this some kind of big fat joke, well, fuck you, cause i ain't laughing, i'm sick of your stupidass games, fuck you, man, fuck you—

> *(a storm of noise. SKINHEADgirl moves on into the darkness.)*

THE SEDUCTION OF HYACINTHUS (book X)

darkness. a match is struck. a small light in the darkness. D and SKINHEAD-*boy.* SKINHEAD*boy is whistling, making noise in the dark. his voice echoes through the space. the echoes delight him.*

D: behold my kingdom

SKINHEADboy: tss. kingdom of shit

D: behold my castle, my mansion, my taj mahal

SKINHEADboy: man, this place is a pit. it fucking stinks in here.

D: man, you stink

SKINHEADboy: hey, fuck you

D: i stink, too. yeah, i do, and that's the truth.
    but, see, i like the stink. it smells of home.

SKINHEADboy: home? man, this ain't no home.

D: this is my home.

SKINHEADboy: that is so fucked up. anybody tell you how fucked up you are?

D: i ain't fucked up, i'm a god

SKINHEADboy: tss, you're a goddamn wingnut

D: i'm a god, and that's a fact. this is my kindgom. welcome to my kingdom,
    oklahoma boy

SKINHEADboy: that ain't my name

D: skinhead boy

SKINHEADboy: dude, i ain't no skinhead

D: it don't matter to me what you are.

SKINHEADboy: i ain't no skinhead. that ain't my trip.
    see, check it out.
    *(*SKINHEAD*boy shows him crude lettering tattooed inside his arm.)*

D: "fuck na zi scum."

SKINHEADboy: see, now, that's the real deal. for real for real. this girl i know,
    she did this tat for me. i got my ass kicked in eugene, oregon on account
    of this tat. six skinhead brothers, fucking twelve steel toes. i almost kicked
    it that time, truly i did.

D: "fucking twelve steel toes." bullshit.

SKINHEADboy: hey, fuck you. you believe what you want. just don't be calling
    me no skinhead. freak.

D: little brother, i'm a god

SKINHEADboy: yeah, whatever

D: so what do you want this god to call you by, little brother

SKINHEADboy: you call me whatever you want. it don't make no difference to me. it ain't like i'm going to be around that long.

D: is that so?

SKINHEADboy: that's a fact. i'm outta here monday. i got a plan. i got it all set up. i hate this city, man, this city is bunk. till then, you know, i'm just killing time.

D: so what if i call you speedracer

SKINHEADboy: tss

D: speedracer—now that's a radass name, fucking demon on wheels

SKINHEADboy: yeah, no shit. fucking demon on wheels.

D: you like that?

SKINHEADboy: speedracer is where it's at, and you know it, too. speedracer flies, man, he goes so fast, he goes so fucking fast, zero gravity fast, feel his head explode—pow powpow pow pow

D: hey yo. speedracer

SKINHEADboy: yeah, that would be me

D: you want to get high, speedracer?

SKINHEADboy: hell yeah, i want to get high.

D: speedracer likes to fly

SKINHEADboy: damn straight

D: he likes to go real fast

SKINHEADboy: he likes to go so fast, till he's like a blur, and nobody sees him, nobody can get near him, nobody can touch him, and then he's gone

D: i hear that, i know what that is

SKINHEADboy: for real for real. so bust it on out. what you waitin for? let's have us a party. i feel like a party.

(in the darkness, D and SKINHEADboy *get high.*

in that same darkness, Philomel slips through and follows the trail of things that spilled out of SKINHEADgirl's *bag. she picks up a small transistor radio, and turns it on. the sound is scratchy and old. she switches stations. a collage of radio fragments. they grow louder. Philomel listens, captivated.)*

ORPHEUS AND EURYDICE—the wedding feast

Philomel's love song turns into music from a boombox. the sound of laughter. Eurydice and Orpheus at the foot of a chainlink fence. remains of a fast food feast.

ORPHEUS: ok, ssh, ssh. check it out, i love you.

EURYDICE: ok, ok, hold up. ok. i love you.

ORPHEUS: i love you

EURYDICE: i love you

ORPHEUS: i love you

EURYDICE: i love you

ORPHEUS: i love you

EURYDICE: goof

ORPHEUS: how much do you love me?

EURYDICE: i don't know, goof

ORPHEUS: how much?

EURYDICE: i don't know. a lot.

ORPHEUS: like about how much?

    (Eurydice spreads her arms as far as they will go.)

EURYDICE: like about—this much

ORPHEUS: yeah?

EURYDICE: times a hundred million billion

ORPHEUS: that's a lot

EURYDICE: that's a hella lot

ORPHEUS: i love you on account of your true loveliness

EURYDICE: oh yeah?

ORPHEUS: on account of your hella pure heart

EURYDICE: tss—i love you on account of your goofiness

ORPHEUS: yeah?

EURYDICE: on acount of your goofy freakiness

ORPHEUS: uh huh

EURYDICE: on account of your snooty groovy wackiness

ORPHEUS: i love you

EURYDICE: yeah, i love you, too

ORPHEUS: for real?

EURYDICE: yeah

ORPHEUS: i mean it, for real?

EURYDICE: yeah, sure

ORPHEUS: say it then

EURYDICE: for real—goof

ORPHEUS: when you sleep, i read your mind. it's like we're lying real close,
skull to skull, and our brains meld, they become all siamese twin like, and
i'm like sucking the thoughts right out of your head, swirling them
around, seeing how they taste

EURYDICE: yeah, and how do they taste?

ORPHEUS: good

EURYDICE: yeah?

ORPHEUS: juicy

EURYDICE: yeah?

ORPHEUS: juicy fruit

EURYDICE: juicy fruit

ORPHEUS: passion fruit. brain juice

EURYDICE: that is so nasty

ORPHEUS: it's the flavor, it's the key flavor

EURYDICE: oh, is it key?

ORPHEUS: it's so key

EURYDICE: tss—baby, you are too much fun

ORPHEUS: yeah? you havin fun?

EURYDICE: yeah, i'm havin fun

ORPHEUS: are you happy? do i make you happy?

EURYDICE: i don't know. i guess

ORPHEUS: i make you feel good?

EURYDICE: sure

ORPHEUS: i make you feel like nothing else?

EURYDICE: yeah sure whatever

ORPHEUS: so like what are you thinking right this second?

EURYDICE: i don't know—nothing

ORPHEUS: come on

EURYDICE: read my mind

ORPHEUS: no, i'm askin you

EURYDICE: no, i'm serious—read my mind—

ORPHEUS: —i'm askin you—

EURYDICE: —suck my thoughts right out of my head—

ORPHEUS: —i'm askin you—

EURYDICE: —come on, brain juice man—

ORPHEUS: —i'm askin you—

EURYDICE: —brain juice juicy fruit passion fruit—

ORPHEUS: —shut the fuck up—fuck

EURYDICE: ok, ok. see, what i'm thinking, what i'm thinking is: you are so like this guy i used to know back home—man, i couldn't get far enough away, i couldn't put enough miles between—this was a thousand years ago—look like him, talk like him, fucked up in the head just like him—i look at you, it's like i'm looking at him.

ORPHEUS: i love you. i love you—

EURYDICE: —yeah whatever

ORPHEUS: i love you, for real

EURYDICE: hey look, i gotta go—

ORPHEUS: —wait—

EURYDICE: —i got shit to do, baby, i got all this shit to take care of—

ORPHEUS: —hold up—

EURYDICE: —i'll see you around, ok, i'll see you real soon, i promise—
    (Eurydice goes.)

ORPHEUS: hey. hey, wait—fuck—

(Orpheus follows her. darkness.)

PROMETHEUS STEALS FIRE—a song of whispers

darkness. the sound of things crashing. the sound of breathing. light on SKIN-HEADgirl and SKINHEADboy. he's rifling through D's things, looking for D's secret stash, trashing everything. SKINHEADgirl watches.

SKINHEADgirl: —fucking big man, fucking full of plans, fucking thinks he knows everything about everything

SKINHEADboy: fuck

SKINHEADgirl: "don't worry, baby, you wait here, i'll be back, i got it covered, i'll take care of you, trust me, baby"—my ass

SKINHEADboy: shut up

SKINHEADgirl: you shut up—and that's the last time you leave me like that, get high on my time, cause i ain't goin to come lookin for you next time, and i sure as hell ain't going to wait around till you sleep it off—asshole—

SKINHEADboy: —i saw him put it right here, i saw him

SKINHEADgirl: well, it ain't there now

SKINHEADboy: fuckfuckfuck

SKINHEADgirl: give it up—it ain't there—

SKINHEADboy: —shut up—

SKINHEADgirl: —quit telling me to shut up—

SKINHEADboy: —i know it's here, i saw him stash it, i saw him—
(sounds in the labyrinth.)

SKINHEADgirl: —shit—ok, come on, let's go—let's go, what's wrong with
you—

SKINHEADboy: —shut up—

SKINHEADgirl: —we got to go, come on, i want to get out of here, i want to go,
i'm scared—

SKINHEADboy: —just shut up—

SKINHEADgirl: —fuck you, i'm scared
(SKINHEADboy retrieves a bag from the gash in the wall. it rips. colored pills
fall, scatter. they are like jewels—emeralds, rubies, sapphires, opals—pharma-
ceutical treasure. he grabs as many as he can.)

SKINHEADboy: holy shit—i told you, i fuckin told you—

SKINHEADgirl: —ok alright, let's go, please, let's get out here—come on—

(SKINHEADboy and SKINHEADgirl run. darkness.)

PHILOMEL'S STORY—transistor radio song

in the darkness, SKINHEADgirl is running for her life. the headlights of passing
cars cut through the darkness, and then disappear into night. they catch her in
the glare and then lose her again, like a strobe.

her footsteps and her breathing are gradually swallowed by the sounds of traffic, trains rumbling underground, voices, laughing, a pay phone ringing and
ringing, glass shattering—

the sound of breathing like a pulse. Orpheus emerges from the darkness. he's
looking for Eurydice, but she's nowhere to be found. he finds Philomel's radio
on the ground, picks it up, puts it to his ear. the love song from before is playing faintly. it grows louder. Orpheus listens for a moment. Philomel watches
him. Orpheus looks up, and sees her watching him.

music from a passing car, thundering bass. it drowns out all the other noises. darkness.

THE STORY OF SEMELE—a bedtime story

faint salsa music. Perephone is transforming into Semele the woman she used to be. in the darkness, Semele tells stories to her unborn child. D sees her when he dreams. he sees her now, though she never sees him. in his dreams, he can never make her see him.

SEMELE: story of a girl who turned into an echo
story of a girl who turned into a shooting star
story of a girl who crossed the river of forgetting
how she crossed the river of forgetting, and never came back
story of a girl who fell in love with a god—
(the salsa music begins to distort, becoming something foreign and strange. D approaches Semele.)
D: and how this god, how he loved her back
SEMELE: loved her so much he promised to give her anything she asked for, anything in the world
D: and she said to him, i want to see you, i want to see you for real, i want to see you as you truly are, that is my wish
SEMELE: and the god, he said, wish for something else, anything else, but she didn't want nothin else, and so he kept his promise, and when she saw him, she saw how he was pure fire, so bright, like the sun in the sky, and when she touched his face, she burned

(D is so near to Semele he can almost touch her. and then bright light like a flash. the music ends. darkness.)

THE STORY OF SEMELE—a magic trick

Semele stares into the dark. inside of her is a baby, an invisible pulse. G is watching her.

SEMELE: what? what are you looking at? don't just stand there like you made of stone, cause you ain't made of stone. damn, say something.
G: girl, you are so sweet, you are so fine—

SEMELE: —tss—

G: —"you are so fine, you blow my mind." see, girl, you are the one, you are my queen, my lady love—

SEMELE: —save all that. see, cause i know what it's worth.

G: what can i say to make my girl smile? what kind of love song can i sing to her? what kind of magic words can i say to her to make her open up for me like some kind of beautiful flower?—

SEMELE: look, i ain't gonna play this game with you. where's my stuff?

G: baby, all i got for you is love. ain't nothing deep, ain't nothing special. love is what it is. simple as a shoe.

SEMELE: baby, i don't need no goddamn shoes.

G: alright, girl, how about i give you my heart?

SEMELE: your heart? is that what you just said to me?

G: yeah, it's a big meaty heart. what more can you want from a man?

SEMELE: try, say, a big screen tv, try say a jeep cherokee and a trip to miami beach with the sunshine and the palm trees and the white sand and the ocean so blue you can see every goddamn fish there is, and no flea bag motel, i want luxury accommodations, first class all the way

G: is that all you want from me?

SEMELE: oh no, baby. that ain't it, uh huh. what i want, dig, what i want is love, love, love, tss—

G: what the fuck's the matter with you?

SEMELE: let go of me—

G: girl, how much shit do i got to swim in to get to you?

SEMELE: you're hurting me.

(G lets go.)

SEMELE: yeah, you best let go of me, fuckin kick your ass, fuckin kill you. love—fuck that. i don't want none of your love. tell you what i want. truly. enough rock to do me for eternity. i want a snow mountain, my own beautiful snow mountain, and i'm the only one knows where it is. i climb this mountain and i disappear. i get lost in more white than i can ever dream of.

(G turns to go.)

SEMELE: baby? baby, wait. baby, don't go. baby, i'm sorry, i'm sorry. i love you, right, i love you. yeah, i do. you know i do. you the one. you the only one. i love to be with you, be close to you, i love you, you know i do—

(G and Semele embrace.)

SEMELE: baby?

G: yeah?

SEMELE: baby, you love me back?

G: yeah.

SEMELE: yeah, you do?

G: yeah, i do.

SEMELE: baby, where's my stuff? i know you got it, you can tell me—

G: —later—

SEMELE: —tell me now—

G: —i'll tell you later—

SEMELE: no, you tell me now.

G: what?

SEMELE: where's my stuff? fuck. where's my fucking stuff? tell me now, you tell me now, fuckin tell me now—

(Semele goes after G with her hands. she tries to tear him apart.)

SEMELE: fuck you. you love me, huh?

G: yeah.

SEMELE: how much do you love me?

G: you know how much. why are you askin me?

SEMELE: because i want to hear you say it. say it.

G: with all my heart.

SEMELE: what would you do for me?

G: anything. you know that.

SEMELE: then you give me my stuff. if you love me, give it to me.

G: don't ask me that. ask me for anything else.

SEMELE: ain't nothing else, ain't nothing else 'cept how much you love me. how much do you love me?

(G gives Semele her rock, and she smokes it up. the smoke rises and envelops Semele. like some girl in a fucked up magic trick.)

THE BIRTH OF D—smoke

Semele is dancing in the smoke, faint and far away. in the darkness, the sound of strangers breathing, coughing. the faint sound of salsa. G is in the shadows. as he speaks, Semele continues to dance. she is turning back into Persephone. by the end of her dance, she is once again Persephone. as Persephone, she disappears into the darkness.

G: i used to love this girl. this was a thousand years ago. i seen her in the park, and she's dancing with some other guy, and he's playing some kind of salsa kind of music, and it's summer, and she's wearing some little dress with flowers, and she's dipping and turning, smiling at nothing, just smiling, the sweetest smile—i tell her, "baby, you are the one, you are my lady love, you are my queen. ask me anything, girl, i'm like a god. i have powers—anything you want in this world, i can get it for you. just ask me to, and i will." but she don't want nothing else.
(the salsa music grows louder. the music becomes distorted. D appears. he has been watching and listening.)

G: i used to love this girl, and she and me, we had a son. i seen him one time before i go away. little boy, beautiful boy, tiny fists and eyes shut tight, shakin, his whole body shakin, shakin so hard, like he's filled with all kinds of strange dreams.

(G recedes into darkness.)

BACCHIC SONG

the sound of a woman singing through a sea of static snow. AM radio in the late night hours. an ancient recording, scratched and crackling. Philomel begins to sing, a human voice alongside the radio song.

Eurydice emerges, and dances by herself. she dances as Semele danced, an echo of another woman. Orpheus appears, and approaches Eurydice. the two dance together.

D: stories she told me, whispered to me like secret things,
   before i was born, before i even remember—
   story of a girl who turned into an echo

story of a girl who fell in love with a god
and how she died and crossed the river of forgetting,
how she heard this girl on the crossing, stranger on the other side,
how this girl, how she sang this song—
sad song
love song
some kind of fucked up love song—

(Orpheus's and Eurydice's dance turns into a struggle. Eurydice breaks away, and goes.)

PHILOMEL'S STORY—wordless song

the sound of breathing underneath Philomel's singing. a pulse. the pulse grows.

Orpheus is alone. he sees Philomel. she stops singing. the sound of breathing. a pulse.

ORPHEUS: girl, what are you looking at? why are you looking at me like that? what do you see when you look at me? tell me. what did you see? what did you see in me?

(Orpheus moves towards Philomel. Philomel flees. Orpheus follows her. as he hits the chain link fence, a sudden explosion of techno music—a bass line, and a woman singing, looping back on itself like a record stuck in a groove. bursts of light like shooting stars. bodies moving in the darkness. they are like shadows underwater, caught for a second in slivers of light, body parts, then swallowed by the dark.)

techno music underneath. in the labyrinth. inside the labyrinth, a monster is breathing. voices from different corners of a dark space call out. SKINHEAD*boy and* SKINHEAD*girl are moving through the labyrinth. shadows. Echo is an echo, an aural illusion.*

SKINHEADboy: hey
ECHO: hey
SKINHEADboy: hey
ECHO: hey
SKINHEADgirl: hey
ECHO: hey
SKINHEADgirl: hey
ECHO: hey
SKINHEADboy: hey
ECHO: hey
SKINHEADgirl: hey
ECHO: hey
    *(*SKINHEAD*boy disappears in the labyrinth.)*
SKINHEADgirl: hey
ECHO: hey
SKINHEADgirl: hey
ECHO: hey
SKINHEADgirl: hey
ECHO: hey
    *(*SKINHEAD*girl disappears into the labyrinth. Echo follows her. the music changes. a pulse. Orpheus appears. he stares into the darkness. he sees shadows, figures he thinks he recognizes.)*
ORPHEUS: hey
    (an echo.)
ORPHEUS: hey.
    (an echo)
ORPHEUS: hey.
    (Orpheus disappears into the labyrinth.)

techno music underneath. the sound of breathing. an echo chamber. the sound of a boy and a girl running, shrieks and laughter echoing. silence. the sound of hard breathing. SKINHEADgirl is tripping out in the darkness.

SKINHEADgirl: hey. hey. where did you go, where the fuck did you go?
   (a sound—a whistle.)
SKINHEADgirl: i can't see.
   (a sound—a whistle.)
SKINHEADgirl: i can't see, i can't see—fuck you, i can't see
   (SKINHEADboy comes up behind SKINHEADgirl, grabs her.)
SKINHEADboy: yo, wake up, bitch
SKINHEADgirl: fuck you. i hate you.
   don't you fucking laugh at me.
   man, you are such an asshole.
SKINHEADboy: what's the matter? you scared?
SKINHEADgirl: no, i ain't scared
SKINHEADboy: bullshit
SKINHEADgirl: go to hell
SKINHEADboy: you were out-of-your-mind scared just now
SKINHEADgirl: i wasn't.
SKINHEADboy: you lie you lie.
   (SKINHEADgirl starts tripping again.)
SKINHEADboy: hey. hey. what's wrong with you?
SKINHEADgirl: nothing.
SKINHEADboy: you lie.
SKINHEADgirl: whatever—
SKINHEADboy: what?
SKINHEADgirl: i don't know. i don't feel good.
SKINHEADboy: tss. you are such a lightweight.
SKINHEADgirl: fuck you
SKINHEADboy: you're such a girl
SKINHEADgirl: man, fuck you
SKINHEADboy: nah, it's cool. it's cool cause i'm around, and i'll be there, right, i'll be there to love and comfort you—
SKINHEADgirl: shut up
SKINHEADboy: girl, for real, you are so lucky i'm around.

SKINHEADgirl: is that right?

SKINHEADboy: hell yeah. cause i'm the man of your dreams, girl. i'm the shit.

SKINHEADgirl: oh yeah, are you the shit?

SKINHEADboy: you know it. i'm the one's going to save you from the monsters.

SKINHEADgirl: tss. ain't no monsters, not for real.

SKINHEADboy: girl, you don't know what you're talking about. you're ignorant.

SKINHEADgirl: you're so fucked in the head.

SKINHEADboy: nah, shut up, cause you don't know. this is the darkness

SKINHEADgirl: hey—

SKINHEADboy: this is where the monsters live.

SKINHEADgirl: ain't no monsters. not for real.

SKINHEADboy: girl, they're real. and they're all over, too, hiding out, waiting. we can't see them, but they see us, girl, they're looking at us, laughing at us, they want to fuck with us, rip us off, but i ain't going to let that happen, see, cause i got a plan, i know how it goes, i'm watching out, i watch my back, i keep moving, ain't nothing going to catch me, i'm fast, i'm so fuckin fast—girl, i go so fast, i fly, i'm like a blur, i'm like invisible.

(SKINHEADboy's voice gets fainter and fainter as he speaks. the darkness closes in, warm and immense, and wraps SKINHEADgirl in its folds.)

SKINHEADgirl: ain't no monsters. not for real. i don't believe in fairytales. i don't believe in magic shit. i don't believe in monsters. ain't no monster, not for real. ain't no monsters 'cept the ones in your head. hey. hey. where are you? where did you go? say something.

(silence. SKINHEADgirl is alone in the darkness.)

SKINHEADgirl: man, fuck you. i'm sick of your stupidass games.

(a sound in the darkness.)

SKINHEADgirl: is that you? hey. hey, are you there? say something—

(SKINHEADgirl turns around. a sharp intake of breath like a girl about to dive underwater. darkness.)

THE STORY OF NARCISSUS—an echo

techno music underneath. Narcissus is stranded. he's drinking a forty by himself. Echo keeps him company, at a distance. he ignores her.

NARCISSUS: what? what are you looking at? cause, girl, i ain't no tv show. what? what? what are you looking at? tss.

ECHO: tss.

NARCISSUS: fuck it.

ECHO: fuck it.

NARCISSUS: forget you

ECHO: forget you

NARCISSUS: girl, don't you be fuckin with me. cause i ain't in no mood, right. what? what? fuck. ok, you want to know how it is? yeah? you want to know how it goes? ok

ECHO: ok

NARCISSUS: ok. so this is how it is, this is how it goes for real. i see this guy tonight, right, this guy i used to know, and i see him, and he's coming out of this lincoln towncar and he's this old guy, right, but he's looking good

ECHO: looking good

NARCISSUS: built, nice suit, the hair

ECHO: the hair

NARCISSUS: and i see him from across the street, right, and so i cross like four lanes of traffic and i'm running to catch up, and all these cars are all honking at me, and finally i get right up next to him

ECHO: i get right up next to him

NARCISSUS: and i'm walking next to him, and he's walking fast, and i'm like close enough i can smell his skin

ECHO: i can smell his skin

NARCISSUS: i can smell the gel

ECHO: i can smell the gel

NARCISSUS: in his hair

ECHO: in his hair

NARCISSUS: and i'm like, hey, man—

ECHO: —hey man—

NARCISSUS: —what's up—

ECHO: —what's up—

NARCISSUS: —where you been—

ECHO: —where you been—

NARCISSUS: —what's going on, what's happening—

ECHO: —what's happening

NARCISSUS: and i'm talking to him just like that, nothing deep, and everything's cool

ECHO: everything's cool

NARCISSUS: but it's like this guy, right

ECHO: this guy

NARCISSUS: he don't hear me so good, so i keep talking and talking

ECHO: and talking and talking

NARCISSUS: and i'm talking so loud, it gets so like i'm shouting, i'm practically
shouting in this guy's ear, and finally i'm just like, damn, you must be
going deaf, old man, you must need a fucking hearing aid or something,
and right as i'm saying this, right, this big fat guard, he comes out of this
building, he's all telling me, take a walk, man, do yourself a favor, get
lost, and i'm like "shut up, rent-a-cop, ain't nobody talkin to you" and
i'm lookin at this guy i used to know, right, and he's just standing there,
and he don't say a word. it's like he's looking right through me, it's like i
ain't even there, and finally i'm just like, fuck it, this ain't worth my time,
this asshole, he ain't worth my time, none of this is worth my time—tss.
who am i talkin to? i don't even know why i talk to you—girl, get out of
my face, get lost. i said, get lost, disappear—

(Narcissus tosses his empty glass. glass breaks. Echo goes. darkness.)

ORPHEUS' LOVE SONG

*techno music underneath. late night. Orpheus has been drinking for a long
time. he's looking through a chainlink fence at Eurydice. as he speaks, she
approaches.*

ORPHEUS: i love you like a hurricane
i love you like a moth loves fire
i love you like a sweet perfume
i love you like a fucked up flower
i love you like a dog loves bones
i love you like a bear loves honey

i love you like a bird loves sky
i love you like a big hot sun
i love you like a ball and chain
i love you like a dumb love song
i love you like a cold hard drink
i love you like a secret key
i love you like a super hero
i love you like a sad-faced clown—you look so pretty

EURYDICE: you're drunk

ORPHEUS: these are the ways i love you

EURYDICE: freak

ORPHEUS: i'm writing you a love song. i'm writing it in blood like an oath

EURYDICE: don't bleed for me, don't even

ORPHEUS: cross my heart. hope to die, stick a needle in my eye—
i'm going to win back your heart, swear i will

EURYDICE: baby, i'm heartless, ain't you caught on yet

ORPHEUS: i love you like a burning fever
i love you like a crown of thorns
i love you like a hungry lion—

EURYDICE: —give it up, chump

ORPHEUS: it's like i have loved you forever into eternity and back, it's like i
knew you from another life

EURYDICE: oh yeah?

ORPHEUS: it's like we were joined together in this other life, we had different
names—see, we were different people, we had completely different lives,
different destinies—you know what i'm saying—but you knew me and i
knew you, and we fell in love, and we got married and shit

EURYDICE: and then i died

ORPHEUS: no, see, you ain't dead

EURYDICE: dead to you, freak

ORPHEUS: you went away, you know, for a little while. you needed your space
and shit, but you'll come back. girl, i know you will.

EURYDICE: i died, baby. i went to hell. that's my new address—you gonna
come visit me in hell, baby?

ORPHEUS: i'm going to come bring you back.

EURYDICE: tss. i got news for you, i don't want to come back.

ORPHEUS: i know that ain't true.

EURYDICE: this is my life, right here, and you don't know what i want, you don't know me

ORPHEUS: i'm going to rescue you

EURYDICE: tss, in your dreams

ORPHEUS: i'm going to follow you to the ends of the earth, to the afterlife

EURYDICE: i really ain't got the time for this—

ORPHEUS: —hold up, hold up, wait a sec—

EURYDICE: —i gotta go, i'm outta here—

(Eurydice starts walking away. Orpheus follows her alongside the fence.)

ORPHEUS: —you're always fuckin outta here—

EURYDICE: —i ain't got time for this, i ain't got time for you—

ORPHEUS: —and what is that supposed to mean? what're you doing that so fuckin important?

EURYDICE: —man, curl up and die—

ORPHEUS: —what is that, what is that? why are you always so fuckin smart with me?

EURYDICE: —i said, drop dead—die, freak—

(Eurydice walks away.)

ORPHEUS: baby, i know you don't mean that, i know you don't. girl, can you hear me? girl, i'm talking to you. i'm going to rescue you, see, i'm going to pull your ass outta the flame, i'm going to rescue your ass—hey. hey. where are you going to, where the fuck are you going to, don't you walk away from me—bitch—

(Orpheus tries to follow her. he climbs the chainlink fence and falls, crashing to the ground. Eurydice disappears into the darkness.)

THE STORY OF SEMELE—medusa song

techno music underneath. the sound of a girl breathing.

late night. Persephone is trashing a public bathroom. outside, voices and laughter. the slam of a stall door. then silence. a mirror. Persephone speaks to a reflection, wasted.

PERSEPHONE: yeah yeah yeah, fuckin song sung blue—tss. so what do you want to know about me, cause i'll tell you everything, right, i got a thousand stories to tell, and i'll tell them for free, i'll fuckin give them away. so what it is, right, i had a baby. he ain't with me now or anything. i gave him up. i was pretty messed up at the time, but that's a whole nother story. when he was born, my baby, he had something wrong with his heart, with the way his heart was put together—fuck, i don't know. it's been so long, you know, i forget. anyway it ain't like i think about him everyday or anything—it ain't even like that. just sometimes, i think about where he is now, you know, and what he looks like, if he looks like me, if he remembers me, stupid shit like that.

(Echo comes upon Persephone, she notices Echo, looking at her in the mirror.)

PERSEPHONE: yeah, what are you looking at? i see you looking at me, like you got some kind of problem, you got a problem? what the hell are you looking at? you want to piss me off, bitch? you better get out of my face before i kick your ass, cause i ain't none of your business to be looking at—what are you looking at, huh, what the fuck are you looking at—

(Echo goes. Persephone gazes at her reflection, and slowly turns to stone.)

PHILOMEL'S STORY—blood song

techno music underneath.

Philomel emerges from an empty building onto the street. the sounds of the street: traffic, a telephone ringing, the sound of glass breaking, the sound of a siren. the sound of breathing. a pulse.

Philomel opens her mouth. no sound comes out. blood instead of sound. she touches the blood with her fingers. and then touches the chainlink fence, the cement, the walls. and everywhere her fingers touch, she stains the world red. in the darkness, the red turns into blood red flowers.

techno music grows louder.

techno music underneath. SKINHEADgirl is sleeping. she's been sleeping for a long long time. SKINHEADboy is dancing in circles to boombox music. he's wearing a wig, long platinum hair. D watches him. the music stops. and he stops dancing.

D: hell, don't stop, man. you just got into some kind of groove.

SKINHEADboy: fuck you—

D: oh man, you got the flair, you got all the moves, you got it all down

SKINHEADboy: shut up—

D: i watch you, too. i like it. i like to watch you dance.

SKINHEADboy: i said, shut up, faggot. fuck this shit anyway, stupid shit.
  (SKINHEADboy takes the wig off, and chucks it. D picks up the wig and puts it on.)

D: how do i look?

SKINHEADboy: fucked up.

D: yeah? you think so?

SKINHEADboy: yeah, i think so. tell me why are you so fucked up. how'd you get to be that way?

D: little brother, i ain't fucked up enough. i ain't even close.

SKINHEADboy: born to fry, born to die, born to lose

D: tss

SKINHEADboy: yeah, what's your problem, faggot?

D: man, you make me laugh.

SKINHEADboy: oh yeah—faggot? tell you what, some faggots i'd like to kill.

D: yeah, is that right?

SKINHEADboy: i see them sometimes on the street or something, and i see them looking at me, all checking me out, and i know what they're thinking, too, and i'm thinking to myself i'd like to kill one. fucking cut one up, come up from behind, and slice him.

D: yeahyeahyeah

SKINHEADboy: kicked the shit out of some old geezer last night.
  he shit his pants. he smelled so bad. he didn't even have a dime.
  you think that's funny. you think i'm funny.

D: yeah, i think you're funny, man.

SKINHEADboy: yeah, well, fuck you, too

D: what's the problem, funny man?

SKINHEADboy: ain't got no problems. ain't you noticed. i'm fuckin care free.

D: tss. you feel like getting high, funny man?

SKINHEADboy: yeah, whatever

D: i know you feel like gettin high.

Man, you always feel like gettin high.

SKINHEADboy: i said, whatever.

(D goes looking for his stash hidden in the walls.)

D: what's up with girlfriend?

SKINHEADboy: i don't know.

D: she sick?

she dead?

SKINHEADboy: who the fuck knows, man. i don't know what's wrong with her, like i'm supposed to know her story.

D: maybe girlfriend got a little greedy. maybe girlfriend huffed a little too much joy.

SKINHEADboy: what she is ain't none of your business, man, she ain't none of your business, so just shut the fuck up about her. *(to SKINHEADgirl:)* yo, wake up, bitch. i said, wake up. wake up wake up, fucking wake up.

D: hey hey hey—relax

SKINHEADboy: man, i am so relaxed. you don't even know. i'm so goddamn relaxed right now, i'm fuckin bored. don't nobody ever tell you how boring all this shit can be. same ole same ole. gets so i feel like taking somebody down, just to hear the way they sound, the way their body sounds, just to hear their heart beat, just to know they ain't all fuckin zombies staring right through you like you ain't even there. damn, i fuckin hate this place.

it stinks of piss.

it's cold.

it's dirty.

i'm fuckin sick of this place.

but, see, what it is, i got a plan, right

i got it all worked out

i ain't about to let shit get me down, i ain't about to let nothing get me down, cause i know what i'm doing, and i got it all figured out

D: somebody been in my stash, somebody ripped me off.

SKINHEADboy: yeah? man, that's too bad.

D: yeah—tss. yeah, it is.

SKINHEADboy: we're going, you know. like in the morning. for real, man. she's got family in pennsylvania. her mother's sisters. cousins and all her cousins' kids. it's a big fucking family. they live out in this place called rome. i never heard of it. out in the goddamn country. fields and farms and shit. she got us bus fare, me and her. and when we get out there, we're going to get us jobs, get us some money together, and then we're going to get married and like that. that's what it's going to be like for us. man, i didn't take your shit

D: be real with me now

SKINHEADboy: i didn't take nothing from you

D: because the thing being this: i see in the dark, i read your mind

SKINHEADboy: it's this fucking city, man

D: can't turn your back

SKINHEADboy: this city is bunk

D: can't trust nobody

SKINHEADboy: i fucking hate this city, man. this city is all fucked up. it's full of thieves and fuckin perverts

D: junkies and drunks. speed freaks. everybody's wet for something. sweet sweat. man, you smell like you been speeding.

SKINHEADboy: get out of my face, faggot.

D: how fucked up are you now?

SKINHEADboy: i ain't fucked up. i told you that.

D: how dumb do you think i am?

SKINHEADboy: listen, man, you're my friend. i don't steal from friends, right. that ain't my trip.

D: boy, you are so full of shit.

SKINHEADboy: yeah, and what do you know about me, talking shit about me like you know me, like you got that right

D: you don't care about nothing 'cept getting high, i know that much

SKINHEADboy: i didn't take a fucking thing from you.

D: don't lie to me. ain't nothing i hate worse than a liar.

SKINHEADboy: i ain't a liar, faggot. you watch how you talk to me. i could kick your ass.

D: what did you say to me?

SKINHEADboy: i could kill you.

D: ain't about dancing around. ain't about talking big. you got to touch me to kill me. we got to be that close.

SKINHEADboy: yeah? you feel like dying, you feel like dying tonight, faggot?
    (*darkness. and then pieces of light. D is holding* SKINHEADboy *up against the*

wall. the light cuts up his body. chest arm neck mouth. pieces of skin. D whispers to him like a lover.)

D: listen up, baby, this faggot is a god. my daddy was a god and so the fuck am i. my mamma, she wanted to see a god up close, she wanted to feel that thing. she burned, boy, so you be careful what you say to me, you show me some respect. now, did you take my shit? answer me.

SKINHEADboy: no.

D: boy, what do you take me for? who do you think i am?

SKINHEADboy: man, fuck you. you ain't nothing to me. ok so i ripped you off, and i'd rip you off again. i ain't scared of you.

D: who do you think i am, punk, stealing from me? i could kill you with my hands.

SKINHEADboy: bring it on, man, cause i don't care. fuck you. cause i ain't scared, i ain't scared.

(darkness. in the shadows, D breaks SKINHEADboy into a thousand pieces. the sound of blows. the sound of breathing. light. SKINHEADboy is alone in an ocean of darkness. the face of a boy. the sound of a breathing. a pulse.)

SKINHEADboy: i ain't scared, i ain't scared

i ain't scared, i ain't scared

i ain't scared, i ain't scared—

(the sound of a woman singing faintly. the sound of breathing.)

SKINHEADboy: i was born in grand island, nebraska, west of omaha. my mother was this beautiful queen like in some kind of fairytale. i don't know what my father was. i forget his name. he skipped town when i was like a baby, went to denver or something. when i was seven, some guy my mom was shacking up with tied a rope around my middle and put me in this well out back. he wasn't angry. he wasn't nothing. it wasn't like that. i stayed in the well for eight days. i couldn't see in the dark. i didn't never think about dying. i listened. i waited. i heard the sound the trees make, the way they—ssh. and the bugs in the ground, rubbing against the dirt, whispering. and the water, the way the walls bled water was this sound, so much sound. later, my mother was holding me. she was breathing so close to me. warm and wet, her face so close to me. she kept saying, i'm sorry, i'm sorry, i'm sorry like it was the words to some song. she held me so tight it hurt. she held me like i was coming apart.

(darkness. the bottom of a well. buried in a mother's embrace. the sound of breathing.)

outside on the street, bodies disperse, going in separate directions into the night. the smell of weed and sweat, the sound of glass breaking, the sound of voices growing fainter—

Philomel sings in the darkness. she has no tongue. she sings in a foreign language filled with nostalgia and longing.

a siren from faraway approaches. Philomel stops. then silence. the siren passes, fades into the night.

END OF ACT ONE

ACT TWO: polaroid stories

THE MYTH OF PROTEUS

light. Narcissus talks into the light. an interview with a stranger.

NARCISSUS: alright alright, here it is, alright, check it out: how i got on the streets is like this: it's like this: once upon a time, like a long time ago, i was left in this dumpster outside phoenix, i was like a little baby, nobody wanted me, and then this pack of wild dogs dug me out, fed me, took care of me, taught me how to hunt and shit, i didn't know what human was—
ok ok never mind, that's b.s.

how it is, it's like this: i fell out of the sky over salt lake city, utah—
no wait, it's like this: i washed up on the shore of the mighty mississippi—
no wait, it's like this: i was left for dead in a room in palm springs
i was left for dead in a room in las vegas
i was left for dead in a parking lot in tucson
i was left for dead on the steps of the fucking lincoln memorial—
no wait up, wait up, that ain't how it goes—

ok, check it out, it's like this: i was left for dead in this stripmall outside san ysidro, right, and this poor mexican family found me, and took me back over the border to tj, and raised me as one of their own

—nah, that ain't true neither, i'm just playin you.
what really happened, it's like this, and this is for real—

when i was like a little kid, the building where i lived at, it caught on fire, mmhm, and my mother, she held me out the window, and she was all like: "fly away fly away fly away, little bird," and then she let go—only thing was, i wasn't no little bird, and i didn't fly, i fell, and i don't know what the bitch was smokin, cause if i didn't die from the fire, i shoulda straight up died from the fall—'cept the thing being i landed on this big old mattress somebody threw out with the trash—fuckin fate, man, was on my ass—and then later this old wino found me, and took care of me

for a while till his liver gave out, and then i was on my own, i was all
alone, and that is the truth, i swear to god—

(darkness.)

G AND EURYDICE—zeus seduces a maiden

night. Eurydice makes her way through the darkness. G watches her.

G: hey, baby, hey, sugar,
    where you goin to, sweet thing, pretty thing?
    hey, baby, i'm talkin to you.
    don't you know how to talk?
    what's the matter with you, sweetheart? ain't you got no tongue?
EURYDICE: come again, old man?
G: i said: ain't you got no tongue.
EURYDICE: old man, everybody's got a tongue. some folks, they know how to
    keep it from flapping around all the time. some folks know how to give it
    a rest.
G: girl, i know what you're saying.
EURYDICE: oh yeah, you know what i'm saying? tss.
G: yeah, i do see, i knew a girl with no tongue, for real. some crazy guy she
    knew, he cut it right out of her head with a knife.
EURYDICE: —man, that's some sick shit that i don't need to be hearing—
G: —baby, this story ain't even what you think it is. this story's got one happy-
    ever-after, righteous ending. see, some god up high, he saw that girl, saw
    how her tongue, how it got cut out, and how she bled, and in his heart,
    he felt for her, and turned that girl into a bird, songbird, and she sang this
    crazy fucked up song, so strange and true, folks couldn't help but stop
    and listen.
EURYDICE: man, i don't belive any of that.
G: girl, believe it. see, i been all around, and i seen all kinds of crazy shit go
    down.
EURYDICE: tss, whatever you say, old man.
G: i ain't that old, baby, you better take another look.
    (Eurydice looks. G smiles and it's like sun through the clouds.)
G: what's your name, sweetheart?
EURYDICE: i forget.

G: come on, baby, what's your story? where you come from, where you headed, where you been?

EURYDICE: baby, i forget.

G: baby, you forget a lot.

EURYDICE: baby, i have drunk form the river of forgetfulness. i forget the
names, i forget the faces, if forget all kinds of shit—

G: girl, you forget what you want to forget.

EURYDICE: hell yeah, i do.

G: but see now, some things, they don't let you forget. they mark you, no matter how far you run, no matter how far you get.

*(G gently touches the side of Eurydice's face. his voice is a whisper, a spell that
stops her in her tracks.)*

G: it's like i look at you, and what i see, right, i see all these scars. girl, i see so
many scars, new ones over old, some ain't even mended yet, and i'm
thinking to myself, how does a girl get all them scars, how does that happen to somebody she ain't even grown yet. i want to know their story,
baby.

(Eurydice moves away.)

EURYDICE: you're out of luck, old man. ain't no story, cause i forget.

G: now i know that's a lie, i know that for a fact.

EURYDICE: old man, get away from me. i ain't playing with you no more.

G: baby, i got scars myself, more than i can even count. i can still feel each one,
i can feel the way the skin's gone all see-through, like if you looked real
hard, you could see straight inside me.

EURYDICE: you lived to tell, huh?

G: always, baby. i'm like a god, can't snuff me out.

EURYDICE: you lookin for a date or what?

G: i'm lookin for something.

EURYDICE: what you lookin for, baby? you lookin for a little love?

G: i'm lookin for something.

EURYDICE: something is a lot of things.

G: what you got to give?

EURYDICE: old man, i ain't got nothing to give, ain't nothing free in this life.

G: now that's the hard truth. i like a woman who tells the truth. you always
tell a man the truth?

EURYDICE: it ain't like i'm makin no promises.

G: no promises, no lies. ain't that how the song goes?

EURYDICE: i'll tell you what , old man, if you know all the words to that song, you ain't as dumb as you look.

G: tss. how about you take a little walk with this old man, kill a little time— come on, sweet thing, pretty thing, what you got to lose?

(Eurydice follows G into the darkness.)

INCIDENTAL TRANSFORMATIONS—songs orpheus sings to the queen of the dead and D

darkness. the sound of voices and laughter. D, Persephone, and Orpheus. the remains of fast food wrappers and beer bottles.

Orpheus is humming.

PERSEPHONE: man, shut up!

ORPHEUS: how about i tell you a little story about love—

PERSEPHONE: tss. i ain't listening to none of that. cause, see, baby, i'm done with love. love, for me, that's fuckin ancient history. for real, what's some story about love goin do for me?

ORPHEUS: make you smile

PERSEPHONE: tss

ORPHEUS: make you cry

PERSEPHONE: baby, i got plenty to cry about. i don't need no story to make me cry.

D: what up? you got a story, jack? you got somethin you dyin to say?

ORPHEUS: yeah, i got something i want to say. see, what it is, it goes like this: this guy i used to know, he loved this girl, but she didn't give him the time of day. she thought she was hot shit, she thought she was all that.

D: tss. heard that, jack. heard that all before. that story is so old.

ORPHEUS: man, i wasn't talkin to you. that story was for the lady.

PERSEPHONE: baby, that girl was a fool, and a fool stays no matter what. why should i give a damn about what happens to some fool?

ORPHEUS: baby, all of us are fools

PERSEPHONE: but that was one fucked up story though, huh?

ORPHEUS: but see, baby, that's how love goes most of the time

PERSEPHONE: tss, seriously. tell me somethin i don't already know by heart

D: ok, alright, listen up, i got one for you—girl, are you listenin?

PERSEPHONE: oh yeah uh huh, yeah i'm listenin—i'm hangin on your every word, baby, i can't wait—

D: i'm serious, don't be giving me none of that. you listen up, cause you goin like this one: story of a man who loved to love too much

D: he loved the girls so much, but he was old, dig, and the girls, they'd be all like, "old man, get away, you're too old for me—" but he didn't care, he told them: "girls, i ain't a man, i'm a god," and a god can turn into any damn thing he pleases. he can turn into the gold chain dangling around your neck, he can turn into the red cherry candy melting in your mouth, he can turn into some racy, lacy thing you wear right up close against your skin—"

PERSEPHONE: —man, shut up, cause that is so nasty—

D: —that old man had something going on, see, he was cagy and sly, ticklin and touchin, squeezin and kissin, getting all the love he could get, and that old man, he found love in some of the strangest places, sniffed it out like some old hound dog, and i swear, he lived happily ever after, the end.

PERSEPHONE: tss, sounds like the story of one dirty old man.

D: baby, you miss the point entirely. that man was sly, he had a plan—

ORPHEUS: give it up, man. that story sucked.

D: yeah, what do you know, jack?

PERSEPHONE: what i wanna know is why is it anyway the girl's always gotta be a fool?

D: tss. i don't know for sure, but baby, i can guess—

PERSEPHONE: —don't you go there, baby, cause you won't like it one bit—

D: —see, cause girls, dig, girls are fools when it comes to love—

PERSEPHONE: —you ain't no girl, baby, what's your excuse?

D: —tss—anyway—

PERSEPHONE: —fool—

D: —anyway—how about it, girl? you got a story or you just giving me sass

PERSEPHONE: yeah, i got a story. i got one better than all y'all's. story of a man who couldn't keep it in his pants, and how his woman got so sick of it, she got a little potion form this haitian girl she knew, found her old man's little missy, put that potion in the little missy's drink, turned that little missy into a pit bull bitch—beautiful little bitch, all sleek and chocolate brown, staring out at the world with these sad, dog girl eyes. everybody was all like, "where'd you get that dog, that's a nice dog," but she didn't say a word. tied her up in back with a big old chain, and that bitch, i'm telling you, she howled night and day. heard tell later, she ran away, nobody knows where she got to in the end.

D: is that a true story?

PERSEPHONE: what'd i say? hell yeah it's a true story

D: tss. i don't believe a word

PERSEPHONE: baby, you best believe what i say, cause i know it all

ORPHEUS: you know it all, huh?

PERSEPHONE: everything and then some

D: tss

PERSEPHONE: ain't nothing i ain't heard of, i've heard it all before

ORPHEUS: baby, i got a story i bet you ain't heard. true story.

D: man, ain't no such thing as a true story. and this girl, here, she lies

PERSEPHONE: —man, shut up.

ORPHEUS: this story is true, story of a man who loved this girl so much he followed her straight to hell. brought her back alive, too, tricked the devil, sang a song, made the devil cry

PERSEPHONE: tss. what kinda song would that be, that would make the devil cry?

D: must have been some kinda very special song

PERSEPHONE: uh huh

D: must have been some kinda crazyass song

PERSEPHONE: uh huh

D: must have had the devil shakin and groovin

ORPHEUS: no, man, that ain't how it was, it wasn't like that: the man, he sang this song, all about how he loved his girl, more than money, more than pride, more than his own sorryass life—one love, powerful love—and the devil, when he heard the song, he cried, from some place deep in the pit of his heart, he cried, and all the lost souls in hell, they cried, too, so that all hell echoed with their crying, saddest sound the man ever heard, cause they knew that song, they knew it in their bones, and what it was to have this pure, precious thing, to have and to hold in your hands, and then to lose it, cause you wasn't even thinking right, and you wasn't holding on, cause you're stupid and fucked up, and you could've done things different, but you blew it anyway.

D: damn. man, what are you trying to say? cause, see, no offense, but that story sucked. and if that story is true, man, tss, my name is mud—

PERSEPHONE: —well, then fuck you, your name is mud, mud.

D: my name ain't mud, bitch.

PERSEPHONE: why don't you get lost, mud—

D: —shut up, bitch—

PERSEPHONE: —and don't be callin me bitch—

D: —anyway—

PERSEPHONE: —fuck you, bitch, party's over—

D: —anyway then, i guess i'm going now—

PERSEPHONE: —yeah, you're going now, you got that right, unless you want to be gettin into it, you better get out of here—

D: tss. right. i'll see you later then. i'll see you around, jack. later for you, too—bitch

(D goes.)

ORPHEUS: fuck him

PERSEPHONE: you got that right

ORPHEUS: forget him

PERSEPHONE: forget who?

ORPHEUS: there you go. how about i tell you another little story about love

PERSEPHONE: yeah, baby, i'm listenin, tell me all about love, tell me all about that shit, i'm all ears.

HOW SKINHEADgirl TURNS INTO A STAR—the story of ariadne

in darkness. SKINHEADgirl wakes up from a deep sleep. she is alone. her bag has been rifled through. her things are spilled all over. she looks for her stuff, but it's all gone. SKINHEADboy is gone.

SKINHEADgirl: fuck—fuckfuckfuck—i can't believe this, i can't believe this shit—

(SKINHEADgirl throws her shit against the wall.)

i don't care, i ain't scared, cause i'm like this princess in this fairytale, this fuckin radass fairytale and i don't get scared ever, cause the princess always lands on her feet, she always ends up ok in the end, for real, yeah, she does—

(SKINHEADgirl is holding it together. she begins winding through the labryinth. her words are a thread to guide her through the dark.)

once upon a time, once upon a time, once upon a time, this princess, she falls in love with this guy named roger, cause roger he was like her first true love, man, roger was her knight in shining armor, he was her prince, and they woulda lived happily ever after, too, 'cept that roger, roger turned out to be this total headbanger freakazoid freak, listenin to deep purple in his mamma's basement all day long, full of bullshit about the end of the world. loved to smoke weed. roger was a pig for weed—man, she ended up hating that guy.

on the road, the princess met up with chilly, and the princess, she kinda liked chilly—she got chilly willy tattooed on her in honor of him. on her ankle. little tiny chilly willy. cost her forty bucks, too. chilly was sweet. but he had real bad teeth. his teeth, they were all blue. she said to him, chilly, man, why are your teeth blue? what kind of freak are you to be having blue teeth? later, she found out chilly was drinking bleach for the buzz—not enough to kill him, just enough to turn his teeth blue. later they all fell out, every single one. guy was nineteen and not a tooth in his head. the princess left chilly on account of the teeth thing, cause the teeth thing, that was way too deep.

after that, the princess met jesus. she met him hitching back from wisconsin. she gave him shit on account of that name. she said to him, no white guy is named jesus, not for real, but she liked him, she really did. he was tall and he had long arms he could wrap around her, and he smelled like peppermint and the princess, she thought he was like the real deal, until the night he ripped her off, and left without a word, and then she realized jesus probably wasn't even his real name, and he was just another loser like everybody else she ever knew, and she was so deep in the shit this time, there wasn't nobody going to be able to bail her out, cause she was shit out of luck, she was truly fucked—no, hold up, that ain't how it goes, that ain't it—fuck. fuck.

(SKINHEADgirl *becomes only a voice in the darkness.*)

once upon a time, speedracer, he comes along from straight out of nowhere, and he rescues her, and they live like happily ever after, and all that—fuck. never mind. that ain't it, that ain't how it goes. and after a while, the princess, she just stops, i just stop, and it's like i've been here all my life, and i begin to feel some piece of something, something big as the whole night sky, heavy and full, like how the air gets right before a storm, all electric-like, closing in on me, darkness all around me, and inside the dark, inside the inside, i see all these lights, tiny and sparkling, thousands and thousands of lights, like stars in some faroff galaxy, and i'm thinking to myself, bow beautiful they are, and i'm so close i can almost touch them, so close, i can't even tell where i stop and where they begin—

(SKINHEADgirl turns into a star, bright and glowing, a neon girl, a constellation in a sky full of stars. she lights up the dark, flickers, and then burns out. darkness.)

THESEUS IN THE LABYRINTH

darkness. the sound of water dripping. eyes watching. SKINHEADboy is moving through the darkness. he's bruised. his clothes are dirty and torn. D is watching.

SKINHEADboy: hey. hey girl, it's me. you sleepin, you still sleepin? —yo, wake up, wake up—girl, i know you're here, i know you are. come on, girl, say something. just say something, hey—

(a sound. SKINHEADboy thinks he sees something moving fast, a light, on the periphery of his vision. but when he turns, there's nothing there. he runs away. darkness.)

THE STORY OF ECHO AND NARCISSUS

Narcissus is looking in his mirror—a little girl's mirror encased in bright red plastic, salvaged from somebody's trash. he slowly puts on eye-liner, lipstick. he looks tired and drawn like he's been awake for a thousand long nights. Echo watches Narcissus.

NARCISSUS: yeah? what? what are you looking at?
ECHO: nothing
NARCISSUS: what? what are you looking at, what?
ECHO: nothing
NARCISSUS: "nothing"—i'm going to start calling you nothing girl. nothing girl with nothing to say, nowhere to be, nothing worth nothing to nobody. you got a smoke for me, nothing girl—i know you do—give it up, give it here—
(Echo gives him a cigarette. Narcissus lights up, sucks in smoke.)
NARCISSUS: tss, menthol. menthol sucks. i knew this guy back in l.a., smoked

egyptian cigarettes. that guy was so fucking loaded. girl, he had so much blow. dude had this red ducati, beautiful machine. we rode down to baja. we'd go so fast. i felt like my head was about to come off. the wind'd make me cry, and he'd look at me and laugh, he'd say—are you sad, little man—but i wasn't sad for real, it was just the wind. what? say it.

ECHO: nothing

NARCISSUS: i got a sugardaddy
    i got plans
    i got the keys to a room uptown
    i got a thousand dollars in my pocket right now
    (you don't believe me, fuck you)
    and i can sing, i got a beautiful fucking voice—
    i'm going to have a party in my new place real soon, and i'm going to get high high high, me and all my girl friends—what?

ECHO: nothing

NARCISSUS: don't be looking at me like that. always checking me out—

ECHO: i ain't doing that—

NARCISSUS: —you think i'm hot—girl, you want me, i know you do—

ECHO: —you don't know what i want—

NARCISSUS: —who are you kidding, girl? please. following me around, staring at me all the time—you want to jump my bones, but that ain't going to happen not in this lifetime, that's for sure—

ECHO: i don't want nothing you got.

NARCISSUS: oh yeah is that right, is that a fact—

ECHO: —that's a fact. all skinny and bony and shit—

NARCISSUS: —fuck you—ain't like you're anything anybody's gonna want to be looking at anyway, so just don't even—

ECHO: —shut up—

NARCISSUS: —and, girl, get away from me because you smell—

ECHO: —shut up—

NARCISSUS: —i can smell you way over here—

ECHO: —shut up—

NARCISSUS: —it's like this, dig, you got an ok face, you got an ok body—
    you ain't beautiful, but it ain't like you're ugly.
    i'm saying you ain't butt ugly
    i'm saying you ain't an all-out hound
    i'm saying you ain't a total skank
    i'm saying you ain't half bad—what? what?

ECHO: nothing.

NARCISSUS: oh fuck. relax. it's a joke is all, what's your problem? what?

ECHO: nothing.

NARCISSUS: girl, you got a thin skin. that ain't no way to be. that ain't the right attitude. look at me. think positive. belive in your own self, believe you are all that, like they say—be all that you can be. how do i look? what? what? fucking say it.

ECHO: you look nice.

NARCISSUS: fuck you. i look more than nice. i look beautiful. i look at myself, and i think, girlfriend, i am looking at the man of my dreams.

i got a sugardaddy

i got plans

i got the keys to a room uptown

i am so beautiful and i got a body that will not stop

and i can sing, i got a beautiful voice—

ECHO: yeah, you do. you got a beautiful voice

NARCISSUS: yeah, i do. i know i do.

ECHO: you could be like a star. i know you could.

NARCISSUS: girl, i'm on my way—star search, dig? i'm all over that shit—man, ed mcmahon, he ain't even heard nothing like me before. i sing like a fuckin angel. what?

ECHO: nothing.

NARCISSUS: girl, you say that to me one more time, i swear i'm gonna scream. and why are you always lookin at me like that?

ECHO: like what?

NARCISSUS: like what, like what—like that. sad. you got sad eyes.

ECHO: what do i have to be sad about?

NARCISSUS: oh, girlfriend, don't even get me started. all kinds of shit.

ECHO: but see i ain't like you.

NARCISSUS: yeah? and what is that supposed to mean?

ECHO: i don't know.

NARCISSUS: "i don't know."

ECHO: i don't.

NARCISSUS: "i don't."

ECHO: fuck you.

NARCISSUS: ok, fuck me, fine, fuck me, whatever. only don't be all like "nothing. i don't know." i swear to god, one day all that's gonna be left of you is just this little voice saying "nothing. i don't know."

ECHO: shut up—

NARCISSUS: —whatever—

ECHO: it's like, it's like, it's like you see all these things, it's like you look out into the world, and you see all this shit, and you're like: i want that and that and that, it's like it ain't never enough for you. as long as you got eyes in your head, it's like you're always wantin shit.

NARCISSUS: girl, i deserve the moon, i deserve the stars, i deserve all of it.

ECHO: yeah, well, i ain't like you.

NARCISSUS: what's wrong with wantin shit? no, i'm serious. what's so wrong with wantin shit? tss. forget this. forget you.

ECHO: it's cause there ain't no point.

NARCISSUS: what? there ain't no point in what? say it, just fuckin say it.

ECHO: there ain't no point in wantin shit you ain't never gonna get.

NARCISSUS: come again.

what am i never gonna get?

you think i'm just some kind of fuckin blowhard? is that what you think? is that what you think when you look at me?

girl, you must think i'm some kind of sorryass loser—

ECHO: —that ain't what i mean, i didn't say it right—

NARCISSUS: —no, you said it right, and i heard it right, too—

ECHO: i don't know what i'm trying to say.

NARCISSUS: —just shut up, alright?

ECHO: cause you do have a beautiful voice, i've heard you, and i know you could be a star, you could totally be a star, and i'd be so happy for you, too. i'd be like somebody who knew you when, i'd be like somebody you used to know. and when you came on the tv, i'd be all like, i know him—

NARCISSUS: —look, whatever, alright?

ECHO: no, i mean it, for real—

NARCISSUS: —just don't, don't even—cause, girl, what it is, see: you're right. you ain't like me. all you want, when it comes down to it, you just want to get along, you just want to hang back, take it as it comes, don't be wantin shit, don't be askin for shit, don't be gettin up in nobody's face, don't be makin any noise, don't be makin nobody uncomfortable, don't be sayin what it is you got to say—just hang back, fade away, be real quiet, and get by, pray you get by, like that's all you get in this life, like that's all you deserve—well, fuck that, fuck that.

(Narcissus' reflection explodes as through a rock had been thrown into a pool, distorts, breaks up. Echo flees. darkness.)

THE STORIES OF NARCISSUS—interviews with strangers

> *in the darkness. Narcissus' reflection is shattering, refracting, prices of himself breaking up in a dark pool. voices in the darkness overheard like the rushing of some underground stream, fragments of interviews—overlapping, incomplete.*

M1: fuck that
F2: fuck that
M2: fuck that shit
F2: how it is—tss, fuck it
M5: how it is, right
F3: you want to know how it is
M2: fuck that shit
F4: you want to know how it is
F3: psycho bunched me for everything i own
M1: psycho took all my shit
F2: psycho ripped me off
M2: psycho fucked with my head
F2: psycho called me liar
F3: slut
F4: loser
F2: thief
M5: psycho kicked my ass
F3: psycho sold me bad shit
M2: psycho sold me out
F4: psycho made me sick
M1: psycho took all my shit
F2: psycho laughed in my face
M2: psycho kicked me out
M5: psycho beat me up, broke my jaw
F2: psycho ripped me off
M5: psycho turned me loose
F3: psycho bunched me for everything i own
M2: psycho waited till i was asleep

F4: psycho took all my stuff, everything i own
M5: psycho wasn't even angry, it wasn't even about that
F3: psycho left me in the middle of nowhere
M5: psycho kicked my ass
F2: psycho took all my stuff, everything i own
M2: psycho looked right through me
F5: psycho beat me up, left me for dead in the middle of nowhere, psycho forgot all about me, but i didn't die, right. i didn't die.

(the sound of dead air on tape. the sound of breathing. Narcissus is a reflection growing fainter and fainter.)

AND OTHER INCIDENTAL TRANSFORMATIONS

late night. Orpheus, Persephone, Echo and SKINHEAD*boy are on the periphery of a circle, listening to music on the boombox. they are each in their own worlds.*

ORPHEUS: i used to know this guy, he got cut up, he bled all over everything, and the next day, you could see where his blood stained the ground, all these flowers sprung up out of nowhere, bright red flowers, right up through the cracks in the cement, flowers like nobody's ever seen before, beautiful flowers, nobody knew their name.
PERSEPHONE: i used to know this girl, she cried so hard, she turned into a river. that's what they said. cried and cried till all that was left was water.
ECHO: i used to know these girls downtown, somebody put a hex on them, turned them into bats. they fly around, you can see them sometimes down in the tunnels, little black bats with sad girl faces.
SKINHEADboy: i used to know this girl, she disappeared. i don't even know where to. i figure maybe she went home or something. and then one night, i see her, out of nowhere, and she's up in the sky, and it's like she ain't even human anymore. it's like she's turned into this star, all bright and sparklin, filled with all this fire and light, and she's so faraway, it's like she's a thousand galaxies away, and i don't even know, where she is, if she can hear me.
(Persephone, Orpheus and Echo fade away. SKINHEAD*boy is alone in the darkness.)*

THE STORY OF SKINHEADboy—the transformation of iolaus

last song on the tape. SKINHEADboy talks into the light. an interview with a stranger. D is watching him.

SKINHEADboy: yeah, i don't know where girlfriend went to for real. i used to see her around sometimes, but i don't no more. we had this big blow up. i told her, "fuck you, i like dope a hella better than i like you, so deal with it or get lost," and that used to be the truth, too, but it ain't the truth no more. i'm gonna be all clean-living from now on, straight-edge and right-eous to the bone—you don't believe me? yeah, well, whatever.

this lady the other day, she comes up to me, she says, "i want to help you, young man" and i'm like, "that's great, lady, i need all the help i can get," and then she's all like, "do you believe in god?" and i'm like, "hell no." and that was the end of that, jack. she didn't want to help me no more after that—whatever. cause, see, i don't even believe in god anyway. i don't believe in nothing. i mean, what i believe is you can't believe in nothing, and if you do, you're gonna lose for sure, cause shit happens. ain't no big answer to why shit happens, it just does, and you gotta deal with it, or maybe you say, i'm checking out, ain't nothing to it really—that's how it is sometimes, and that's the straight up truth.
(light fades. the after-light of a flash. the last song ends. sound at the end of a tape. SKINHEADboy walks away.)
D: hey. hey. hold up. hey. where you goin? hey—

(SKINHEADboy disappears. darkness.)

G and EURYDICE—eating the fruit of the underworld

the sound of breathing, a heartbeat. G is sleeping. Eurydice is going through his pockets carefully. she finds matches, paper, an orange—nothing of value to her. she searches for a watch. no watch. she sees a charm around his neck, starts to pull. G grabs her hand. Eurydice breathes in—the sound of a girl taking a breath before diving underwater.

G: girl, what the fuck are you doin?
(Eurydice extricates herself.)

EURYDICE: i wasn't doin nothin.

G: you think you gonna steal from me?

EURYDICE: baby, don't flatter yourself. you ain't got nothin to steal.

G: steal my soul.

EURYDICE: i don't want to steal your soul, old man.

G: steal my heart.

EURYDICE: i don't think so.

G: steal my little good luck charm. yeah? you like that, huh? fourteen karat gold.

EURYDICE: it's pretty. it's like something a girl wears.

G: baby, i ain't no girl.

EURYDICE: i know that. see, that's what i'm saying. i'm a girl. you could give it to me, and then, i don't know, i'd be like your girl or something.

G: you want to be my girl, huh? what if i don't want you to be my girl?

EURYDICE: hey, man, fuck you.

G: now, why you got to talk like that: "fuck you, fuck you"?

EURYDICE: i talk like i want. and i don't even want to be your girl anyway.

G: well, make up your mind, little girl.

EURYDICE: i don't want to be your girl, old man.

G: tss. you takin it the wrong way.

EURYDICE: i don't even know what you're trying to say.

G: i'm tryin to say, maybe things ain't always what they seem. i'm sayin maybe you got to look a little harder.

EURYDICE: i'm lookin real hard at you right now.

G: oh yeah? and what do you see?

EURYDICE: you old—

G: —uh huh—

EURYDICE: —but you ain't that old.

G: i ain't that old, i ain't that young. baby, i'm like a god

(G picks up the orange, and begins to peel it.)

EURYDICE: tss. man, i don't believe you're a god. you're too dirty and snaggle-toothed to be a god.

G: uh huh, well, maybe this god ain't that pretty. you think a god's got to be pretty all the time? you think he's got to smell sweet and shit gold? is that what you think?

EURYDICE: i don't know. i don't think about stuff like that.

G: yeah, i know that. that's cause you're young and dumb.

EURYDICE: man, fuck you.

G: "fuck you fuck you"

EURYDICE: man, what do you want from me?

G: for real? girl, i want a good night's sleep.

EURYDICE: that's it?

G: that's it.

EURYDICE: that ain't nothing.

G: now, that says to me, you ain't never had a good night's sleep—

EURYDICE: —tss—

G: a good night's sleep, that's a treasure. rest your weary bones, free yourself from all earthly cares. but, now, i ask you, how can a man get a good night's sleep when his woman's got one eye open, waiting to rip him off, slit his throat. that ain't no way for a man to live. if a man can't trust, it'll drive him crazy, it'll piss him off, make him meaner than hell. here, you want some orange?

EURYDICE: no.

G: it's good.

EURYDICE: i don't want no fuckin orange.

G: it's good. florida orange, girl, fresh off the tree. here.

EURYDICE: man, you are so weird. i can't figure you out. i can't follow how you think. i can't get inside your head.

G: i like to be able to sleep easy.

EURYDICE: so sleep easy, baby. i ain't gonna stop you.

G: can't sleep easy unless you got some trust. i like to be able to give a person trust.

EURYDICE: tss. can't trust nobody

G: now that ain't true. anybody says that, they don't know. i feel sorry for them. if they can't trust, it's like they ain't even truly lived.

EURYDICE: man, that's bullshit. you got to watch your back all the time. everybody's runnin some scam, for real. everybody wants something. and some folks, it's like they think they can get it for free. they're all like, i love you, shit like that.

G: girl, why you got to talk like that?

EURYDICE: man, shut up

G: cause, see, love ain't shit. it's somethin real and pure and true.

EURYDICE: yeah, that's what they all say. but that ain't even it, see. it's like they want to tell you how it is, tell you how it's gonna be, and they ain't even lookin at you. it's like they're lookin right through you like you was a ghost or something.

G: maybe they see somethin inside you, you don't even know is there yet.

EURYDICE: man, they see what they want to see. it's their own fucked up trip. ain't got nothing to do with me.

G: girl, you're talkin about love, right, and love is mental. even in the good times, it's gonna make you crazy. and in the bad times, i swear, it's gonna make you wish you could put a bullet through your brain, put yourself out of your own damn misery. and then when it's all gone, you gonna wish you could do it all over again.

EURYDICE: man, for a god, you don't know shit.

G: yeah, yeah, yeah. i'm a fuckin fool for real.

EURYDICE: i'll tell you what i know, for real: don't let nobody get too close, cause i don't care how nice somebody is, fuck nice, you let them get close enough, they'll take everythin you own, your own self even. ain't nobody who won't.

G: some will, some won't.

EURYDICE: tss. ok, you believe what you want, buddha man.

G: i believe that.

EURYDICE: yeah, you believe in love and all that shit.

G: yeah, i do.

EURYDICE: why? you got somebody you love, old man? you got some girl you love?

G: i used to.

EURYDICE: yeah, and what? she broke your heart? she take off, she leave you high and dry?

G: yeah, she broke my heart, but that was a long time ago. she was my lady love, she was my queen, and i loved her with all my heart. so yeah, i believe in love and all that shit.

(Eurydice tries to pick up the stuff she took from G and return it to him.)

EURYDICE: here, that's yours. i messed up all your stuff, i'm sorry.

(time slows down. G gives Eurydice a piece of orange, and she eats. he gives her another, and she eats. and as she eats, she transforms into something softer, something of who she used to be.)

EURYDICE: it's good. where i come from, there's these orange groves, all along the freeway, and the orange trees, they have these little, white flowers, all tiny and lacy like. man, i ain't even thought about this in so long. i used to go out there all the time, with this guy i used to know, this goofy guy i used to know, and sometimes we'd be out there, and there'd be this wind, and all the flowers, they'd start falling. we'd close our eyes, and laugh so hard. for a little while, nothin else mattered, and everythin was perfect, cause when the wind got up and the flowers started falling, it was like it was snowing, and the air smelled all of orange, and we thought it was so cool, we thought it was the coolest thing in the whole world.

(G caresses Eurydice like a god caresses a maiden. Orpheus slowly appears like a shadow of the past. Eurydice sees him. and the peace and tranquility is broken. the pulse begins.)

EURYDICE: look, i got to go, i got to get going.

(Eurydice resumes picking up G's stuff, and gives it back to him.)

G: you always going, huh? that must be a hard thing to always be going.

EURYDICE: sometimes, it's like if i can just keep moving, nothing bad'll happen, sometimes, it's like if i stop, i'll die.

(Eurydice goes.)

G: —hey, hold up. what're you afraid of?

EURYDICE: i ain't afraid.

G: what're you so afraid of?

EURYDICE: i ain't afraid of nothing.

G: that ain't true. i know it ain't. cause it ain't about love. it ain't even about that. you hear what i'm saying? ain't about nothin 'cept getting out alive.

(G takes out a knife.)

G: here.

EURYDICE: i don't want that. i don't want that.

G: girl, ain't nowhere left to run, ain't nowhere left to go. here, take it, go on—take it.

(Eurydice takes the knife from G. darkness.)

ORPHEUS IN THE UNDERWORLD—last song for the queen of the dead

Orpheus and Persephone are alone. Orpheus is in the middle of a story he tells over and over again. boombox music, low and melancholy.

ORPHEUS: i used to love this girl. she was crazy insane.
  i used to love this girl. she was a liar and a thief.
  i used to love this girl. she was a wicked little speedfreak.
  i used to love this girl. she ripped me off, told me all kinds of lies.
  i used to love this girl. we used to fight. i tried to kill her one night.
  i used to love this girl, i got her face tattooed on my arm when i was fif-

teen years old, looked just like her, like a fucking photograph—burned it off myself when i was twenty-one. now i just got a scar, looks like i walked through a raging fire.

PERSEPHONE: —tss. man, you are so drunk.

ORPHEUS: girl, don't say that. it breaks my heart to hear you say shit like that to me

PERSEPHONE: tss

ORPHEUS: girl, why are you always breaking my heart?

PERSEPHONE: man, just shut up. what you're saying, you ain't even makin sense no more.

ORPHEUS: i'm telling you what's in my heart.

PERSEPHONE: baby, if you could hear yourself—you're so fucked up right now, it's almost funny.

ORPHEUS: fuck you.

PERSEPHONE: man, what, what is it? you want me to feel sorry for you? you want me to cry for you?

ORPHEUS: i was going to tell you all about love, remember? i was going to tell you a story about love.

PERSEPHONE: yeah, well, fuck that—i'm sick of your stories, i ain't interested in no more stories about love.

ORPHEUS: oh yeah, you're so hard. you're so tough.

PERSEPHONE: fuck you.

ORPHEUS: girl, why do you talk to me like that?

PERSEPHONE: man, just back off.

ORPHEUS: who do you think you are, who do you think you are talkin to me like that?

PERSEPHONE: o man, fuck this shit.

(Persephone starts to go.)

ORPHEUS: girl, where are you going, where the fuck do you think you're going? *(Orpheus follows her.)*

PERSEPHONE: man, just back off or i swear i'll cut you up. i'll cut you to pieces.

ORPHEUS: damn. damn, that is so cold.

PERSEPHONE: then call me cold, motherfucker, just don't be getting in my face.

ORPHEUS: girl, o girl, what am i doing? what are you doing to me, i can't believe what you're doing to me. you look so pretty. it breaks my heart. you got such pretty eyes.

PERSEPHONE: tss.

(as Orpheus speaks, he draws closer and closer to Persephone. a whisper. Persephone listens as though in a spell. music begins.)

ORPHEUS: i could stare into those eyes for the rest of all eternity, i could get lost in those eyes and never come back again—girl, you got eyes that have seen all kinds of shit, all kinds of hurt, you know all about hurt, all about what it is to have that thing, some pure and precious thing, what that is, to hold it close and lose it anyway, cause it could've been something else, it could've been different, everything could've been different. i know you know what i'm talking about, cause i know you. girl, i know you like i know myself—

(the music grows louder, becomes distorted. Persephone strikes at Orpheus with the broken bottle. Orpheus stops the arc of the blow. Orpheus an Persephone struggle. Orpheus cuts her, and she bleeds, she falls away like a shadow.)

ORPHEUS IN THE UNDERWORLD—the shotgun blast of memory

the music continues as a pulse underneath. Orpheus is walking towards daylight, blood on his hands. as he speaks, Eurydice appears out of the darkness. she walks behind him like an inverse shadow.

ORPHEUS: i used to love this girl. i loved her more than money, more than pride, more than my own sorryass life—
i used to love this girl. and then she ran away. i followed her to hell and back, and everywhere i was, i saw a thousand girls she could've been. i held them close, and looked into their eyes. i said, are you the girl i'm looking for, are you the one, is she hiding in your skin? baby, i know that's you.

EURYDICE: don't you turn around.

ORPHEUS: i know the feel of your breath on the back of my neck. i know the feel of your eyes, i know you, i know everything about you.

EURYDICE: you used to know me. you don't know me no more.

ORPHEUS: girl, i have missed you so bad
i have loved you with all my heart
i have never stopped loving you, not for one second
i want to look at you.

EURYDICE: don't you turn around.

ORPHEUS: or what? what are you going to do to me?

EURYDICE: i will turn your heart to stone, i swear i will.

ORPHEUS: i want to see your face.

EURYDICE: man, you wouldn't know me to look at me.

ORPHEUS: don't say that. girl, listen to me. you can come back with me. come back to me and we'll start all over, we'll make it be alright—

EURYDICE: i ain't coming back with you.

ORPHEUS: girl, what are you saying?

EURYDICE: i ain't going nowhere with you.

ORPHEUS: what are you saying to me?

EURYDICE: i forgot you a lifetime ago, you're a bad dream i'm still trying to wake up from, is what i'm saying

ORPHEUS: you're breaking my heart.

i have loved you, i have never stopped loving you—

EURYDICE: —don't you turn around—

ORPHEUS: —or what? what are you going to do to me?

EURYDICE: —don't you turn around—

ORPHEUS: —or what, bitch? what are you going to do to me that you ain't already done?

EURYDICE: i will tear you apart.

ORPHEUS: oh yeah?

EURYDICE: i will blow your soul to pieces.

ORPHEUS: yeah, is that right, is that how it's going to be? girl, you won't ever get away from me.

EURYDICE: you think i won't, you turn around and see.

(Orpheus turns around and sees Eurydice. the music shifts to an ancient song filled with nostalgia and longing. they dance for a short time. something of who they used to be, a flickering happiness from a long time ago. and then Orpheus looks into Eurydice's eyes, and she sees who he is and who he has become. the present comes back in a flash. she stabs him with G's knife. blinding white light. the shotgun blast of memory. Orpheus is illuminated, shot through with light. music ends. sound at the end of a tape. darkness.)

THE STORY OF PYGMALION AND GALATEA

a flash. a moving picture projected into the void, scratched and ancient. no sound except the buzz of a projector. a home movie of a young girl who could have been Eurydice once, a long time ago. the girl is a small figure, squinting into the sunlight. she waves, smiles out into the future. the camera moves away from her, held by loving and unsteady hands.

G: story of a girl i used to know
　　story of a girl who turned into an echo
　　story of a girl who turned into a shooting star
　　story of a girl who crossed the river of forgetting
　　story of a girl i used to know
　　story of a girl who almost died
　　story of a girl who came out on the other side
　　story of a girl i used to know
　　story of a girl who walked away
　　story of a girl who got out
　　story of a girl who walked away, and never looked back
　　and how she changed into something else
　　and how the old scars, how they grew new, smooth skin—

(Eurydice is walking away. G watches her go. darkness.)

THE TRANSFORMATION OF THE LYDIAN SAILOR

a flash. another moving picture snaps into focus. no sound except the buzz of a projector. a home movie of SKINHEADboy playing dead—arms splayed, sunlight streaming across the lids of his closed eyes. and then his eyes open, and he smiles. SKINHEADgirl enters the frame, shoves him and they wrestle on the grass, all hands and arms and faces, laughing eyes. soundless laughter.

D is alone in the darkness.

D: i used to know this boy. this was a thousand years ago. he jumped off a bridge on the other side of town. he flew so fast. nobody saw him, nobody heard him. he flew so fast, he died before he hit the water. i dream about him every night, and in my dream, he's coming apart, he's breaking into a thousand pieces, and i go and i catch the pieces with my hands, and hold them to the light and in my hands, the pieces turn into something else:

each one tiny and shimmering—

each one a perfect, living thing—

and then they slip through my fingers, and swim away. i watch until they disappear and all is green black water.

(the moving picture ends. scratched whiteness at the end of the film. then darkness.)

METAMORPHOSES—an epilogue

voices in the dark call out from all different directions. sometimes the voices cut each other off. sometimes they overlap. the dark goes back farther than anyone can see. light on a wall of polaroid pictures like an anonymous shrine somebody left behind. as the voices call out, the polaroids gradually come clear. from out of the black green surface emerge the faces of thousands of kids. they stare you down.

M3: my name is bandit

F1: my name is tina

M2: my name is blondboy

M1: my name is ramon

F2: my name is mohawk girl

F3: my name is lupe

M4: my name is viper

F4: my name is lisa j

M5: my name is crazy todd

M1: my name is ninja b

F5: my name is desiree

M2: my name is david c

F1: my name is rochelle

M3: my name is tiny

M4: my name is paco

M5: my name is skater pete

F2: my name is mai thai

F3: my name is baby punk

M1: my name is tiger
M2: my name is little ray
F4: my name is candy
F5: my name is loca
F1: my name is skinheadgirl
M3: my name is baby j
M4: my name is nazi mike
M5: my name is tweeker shawn
F2: my name is nothing girl
M1: my name is oklahoma boy
F3: my name is jamie b
M2: my name is zero
M3: my name is shadow
M4: my name is scratch
M5: my name is nicky z
M1: my name is dogboy
M2: my name is skinhead steve
F4: my name is happy girl
M3: my name is marco
M4: my name is psycho john
F5: my name is melody
M5: my name is scarface
M1: my name is kaos
F1: my name is disappear
M3: peace
F5: peace
M1: peace
F4: peace
M3: peace

(silence. a wall of polaroids in brilliant color. darkness.)

END OF PLAY

Waterbabies
by Adam LeFevre

BIOGRAPHY

Adam LeFevre is a writer and an actor. His full-length plays include: *Yucca Flats*, produced at Manhattan Theatre Club; *The Crashing of Moses Flying-By*, produced at Theatre Three in Dallas; *Grant at Windsor*, most recently given at the University of North Carolina at Chapel Hill; and *Ethiopian Tooth*. His shorter plays include: *Window Washers*, produced at Manhattan Punchline Theatre; *Americansaint*, produced at Actors Theatre of Louisville; *Seneca Hollow Rescue*, *Mona Lisa* and *The Defenestration of Citizen Candidate X*. *Waterbabies* was co-winner of the 1995 Heideman Award. *Everything All at Once*, a book of his poetry, was published by Wesleyan University Press. As an actor he has appeared in many plays off-Broadway, at regional theatres (1987 Humana Festival) and on Broadway in *Our Country's Good* and in revivals of *The Devil's Disciple* and *Summer and Smoke*. He lives in New Paltz, New York with his wife Cora, and children, Tate and Isaac.

HUMANA FESTIVAL PRODUCTION

Waterbabies received its professional premiere in the Humana Festival of New American Plays, April 1997. It was directed by Simon Ha with the following cast:

Emma . . . . Kate Goehring
Liz . . . . Jennifer Hubbard

and the following production staff:

Scenic Designer . . . . Paul Owen
Costume Designer . . . . Kevin McLeod
Lighting Designer . . . . Ed McCarthy
Sound Designer . . . . Martin R. Desjardins
Properties Designer . . . . Ron Riall
Stage Manager . . . . Juliet Horn
Assistant Stage Manager . . . . Andrew Scheer
Dramaturg . . . . Michael Bigelow Dixon

FIRST PRODUCTION

Waterbabies premiered at Actors Theatre of Louisville in the Apprentice/Intern Showcase in December, 1995. It was directed by Simon Ha and featured the following cast:

Emma . . . . Jennifer Bohler
Liz . . . . Elizabeth Dwyer

CHARACTERS

EMMA
LIZ

WATERBABIES

Lights up. A small office in the newly constructed wing of a YMCA complex in a medium-sized American city. An institutional metal desk with chair, a small couch, a bookcase with a few books for and about children. On the wall, a big daisy made out of construction paper, each petal a different color, each bearing the name of a child—Becky, Andrew, Travis, etc.—and a painting, a seascape, perhaps a print of a Winslow Homer. Emma sits quietly on the couch. In her lap, a swaddled little body. Enter Liz, as if turning from one corridor to another. She holds a scrap of paper in her hand, referring to it as she talks to herself.

LIZ: Right, down the third green hallway. That was the third green hallway. First blue door on the left. Whose left? God, I don't have a clue where I am. Blue door. *(She turns and sees Emma.)* Oh! Hi. Water Babies? Am I here?

EMMA: He's almost down.

LIZ: Uh oh. Nap time? Am I late?

EMMA: His eyes are open. I don't know.

LIZ: There was traffic everywhere. Central Avenue closed entirely. The arterial backed up to Henshaw. Flashing arrows funneling traffic into one lane. Normally nice people, they get behind a wheel in a situation like that, presto!, swine. Total maniac piglets. And forgive me, this new wing, it's gorgeous, but it's not the Y I remember. These color-coded corridors, I cannot fathom.

EMMA: *(Speaking to her bundle.)* No, no. Shhh.

LIZ: Ooops.

EMMA: Don't do this to me. It's my life now.

LIZ: I'll whisper.

EMMA: Don't worry. Once he's down, he sleeps like a...like a...lo...like a law... Damn! Like a lull...

LIZ: Is this a bad...

EMMA: Lobster! A lobster. He sleeps like a lobster. There. Bingo.

LIZ: Cause if this is a bad time...

EMMA: It's not good or bad, long as it floats.

LIZ: ...I could come back. No problem. I've got errands to do, and Jim, my husband Jim's got the baby at home. He takes Wednesday afternoons off now, which is such a blessing. A legitimate breather for me, and he gets his one-on-one Daddy time with Duncan. Am I talking too loud? How old's your little guy?

EMMA: He's...He's about...Oh God, I don't know. You know those days when everything...

LIZ: Boy, do I. I mean, having a kid...

EMMA: Everything is just so...

LIZ: Changes everything, doesn't it?

EMMA: Boneless. Unbraided. Blended in? Something with a *B* in it. *(To bundle.)* Lullabye-bye, Snookums. Sneepytime.

LIZ: What's his name?

EMMA: Oh God. Okay. It's...it's...lo...law...lolaw...

LIZ: It's not important

EMMA: It's his *name*, for Christsake! I'll get it.

LIZ: Why don't I come back?

EMMA: Blob! No! Bob! Bob. This is my boy, Bob. *(She gently tucks him under the chin.)* Bobby, blobby. Li'l puddin' face. Wow, he's really under now. I'm losing my ambivalence about the immediate future. What is it you want?

LIZ: I called you, remember? I have some questions about Water Babies.

EMMA: Oh, yes. Water Babies.

LIZ: Just some quick ones, you know, about the philosophy of the time-frame, you know. What's developmentally appropriate specifically *vis a vis* Duncan, who's pretty advanced, according to our doctor, physically. It's amazing, really. He'll be eleven months next week, and he's *this* far from walking. Because I've read if you wait too long, with some kids—and unfortunately, we only just heard about your program from my friend, Diane, who, by the way, said you just had a *knack* with the little ones. *Enchantress*, in fact, was the word she used. Anyway, I read if you start too late it can be traumatic and actually instill a fear, you know, of the water and create an obstacle the child then later on down the road has to overcome. If you wait, that is. If you wait too long. Before you start. So, I was just concerned that at eleven months we may have missed the boat, so to speak, with Dunkie. But I don't know, of course. Because this is not...my area. So. *(Pause.)* I guess your Bobby's a water baby.

EMMA: It's in the blood.

LIZ: So, how old was he when he started?

EMMA: Oh God, here we go again. Okay, wait. I'll get it. Bob was...When we met he was already nearly this size, so that would make him...It's conceivable he was younger, by a breath or two. Maybe. But you know he's not really mine so none of this is written in stone.

LIZ: Oh. He's adopted.

EMMA: Listen. You hear that?

LIZ: No.

EMMA: He doesn't get that from me. Does your son speak?

LIZ: Oh, yes. Lots of words. Doggie. Horsey. Moomoo.

EMMA: Horsey and Moomoo. Wow. Think I should worry about Bob?

LIZ: No. I mean, well...how old is he? No. I mean, no. Each one is just different. Each has his or her own way. Like my sister-in-law's little boy, Wade. He didn't say a word till he was nearly three and a half years old. Then, all of a sudden, one morning, this torrent of language just poured forth from this child's mouth—all these words they had no idea where he'd even heard them, as if they'd been dammed up inside his little brain and finally on this particular day, the dam just burst.

EMMA: This morning I thought I heard him say *waffle*. But he was just choking.

LIZ: Dunkie says *waffo*. And *maypo suppo*.

EMMA: I had to give him a real smack on the back.

LIZ: He calls it *maypo suppo*.

EMMA: Calls what *maypo suppo*?

LIZ: Syrup. Maple syrup.

EMMA: Don't worry. He'll get it.

LIZ: I'm not worried.

EMMA: Bob doesn't talk. He kind of transmits. You gotta stay on your toes.

LIZ: Have you been doing this a long time?

EMMA: What?

LIZ: Teaching infants to swim.

EMMA: Oh. I've been involved in aquatic education all my life. When I was a kid, I tried to teach myself to breathe through my eyes. I just thought I could do it.

LIZ: Aw. That's cute.

EMMA: No, I was absolutely serious about it. I sensed inside me this skill, this ancient, lost skill which I was sure I could salvage from the deep of my memory. I practiced in the bathtub. Kept my mouth and nose just below the surface of the water, and concentrated on bringing air in through my tear ducts, and around my eyes...I never got it. Swallowed a lot of water too. But I learned...that the breath...cannot be contained. It must circulate, always and forever. And that I could not disappear...into what contained *me*...and remain...myself.

LIZ: Wow, so you've really developed a philosophy, haven't you. It's not just the doggypaddle and back-float anymore.

EMMA: The brain is 80% water. Does that answer your question? That wasn't your question, was it. Damn. I'm sorry. What is it you want to know?

LIZ: Is Duncan too advanced for Water Babies? Jim is very gung-ho. I'm just ...I may be a little over-protective, I guess. I just don't want anything bad to happen.

EMMA: Well, I don't know then. You see, it's like a dream. In a liquid environment, there are no guarantees.

LIZ: I mean, he's just a baby. I don't want him traumatized. I don't want him set back in any way. As a mother you know what I mean.

EMMA: No. No I don't. You think this is the Marines?

LIZ: No, of course not...

EMMA: Just what do you think I intend to do to little Dunkie?

LIZ: You misunderstand me...

EMMA: Roast him and eat him like a Peking duck.

LIZ: No, please, I just...

EMMA: Lookit! Ol' Dunkie and me will get along just fine so long as he leaves the *moomoo doggie* out of it. We're swimmers here, not talkers.

LIZ: I'm not worried about you. I'm worried about the water.

EMMA: Oh, well. That's different. It is always wise to cast a cold and narrowed eye upon the water. Water can take you places from which, unless you're very careful, there is no return. Places so deep, so quiet, so beautiful, it's more than the human heart can bear. It's always good to pause at water's edge. Hesitation, as they say, is Wisdom's crippled child. For Duncan's sake, let's be perfectly quiet for a moment. No words in the world for awhile but water's words.

LIZ: I...

EMMA: Shh! *(There's a considerable pause. Emma cocks her ear towards Bob.)* You hear that? Didn't that sound like *waffle?*

LIZ: I have to talk to Jim.

EMMA: How would he know?

LIZ: About Water Babies for Duncan. We just have to discuss it a little more before we can make an informed decision.

EMMA: That's a mistake. Men don't trust water. They can't fix it. It eludes them. Not their fault. Just the way it is. Jim'll steer you wrong on this, believe me. The hell with Jim is my advice. Though I'm sure he's an excellent man.

LIZ: We're a team. That's the way we do things. Sorry, I'll just have to get back to you when we decide what to do. Is it the same phone number?

EMMA: I should have told you. There's no space left in this session anyway. All filled up. Just before you arrived a baby crawled in here and formed a complete sentence. Crawled right up into my lap and said, you believe this, without a trace of a lisp or coo, said, "I shall test the deep." I mean, talk about *advanced*. I was just bowled over by the presence and self-possession of this little fry who couldn't have been more than a handful of moons old. So I said, "Bless your soul, child, you're in! You're my last water baby." So, you see, there's just no room. Unless someone drops out. Or drowns.

LIZ: I'm sorry.

EMMA: Maybe next session.

LIZ: Maybe.

EMMA: Or not. Your choice. I'm pro-choice. *(To Bob.)* Don't. Don't. Lullabye-bye. Lullabye-bye.

LIZ: He's waking up?

EMMA: Dreaming. I think he's dreaming. His eyes are open, but he looks very far away.

LIZ: Can I take a peek? I just adore babies.

EMMA: No. No!

LIZ: Okay. Is everything all right? Is your baby all right?

EMMA: Sometimes you have to listen with your feet to hear the S.O.S. from your heart. You don't understand, do you?

LIZ: I'm a mother. Like you. I just want my child to be healthy and happy and safe. That's why I came. That's why I wanted to talk to you. Because I thought you would be able to advise me.

EMMA: I did my best, my level best.

LIZ: Thanks for your time.

EMMA: It was nothing.

LIZ: I hope I can find my way out of here.

EMMA: Just keep turning as the colors change—blue to green, green to yellow,

yellow to red, red to white. At the end of the white there's a big glass door. That's it. That's out.

LIZ: Thanks. Blue to green, et cetera. Thanks. Diane, my friend Diane, she says you're an extraordinary teacher. She recommended you. I thought you might like to know.

EMMA: Diane? I don't remember. So many babies, so many mothers. It's hard. I've already started to forget you. It just goes on and on.

LIZ: Goodbye. Good luck with all your water babies. *(Exit Liz.)*

EMMA: *(She looks down at the swaddled Bob.)* Luck. Luckabyebob. I remember it. Like an arrow. The first time I saw you. Flash of silver as you arced into the sunlight. The thrash sending white spray high over the gunnels into my bloodied sheets. Like being struck by an arrow. God. My heart stopped. Then it started beating backwards. I should've thrown you back. I should've thrown you back right then. Now it's too late. I've been struck by your silence. I need to know your secrets. Talk to me. Stop dreaming. Bob? Bob? Say *waffle. Waffle.* Say it. Say *waffle.*

END OF PLAY

Stars
by Romulus Linney

BIOGRAPHY

Romulus Linney is the author of three novels and many plays produced throughout the United States and abroad. They include *The Sorrows of Frederick, Three Poets, Sand Mountain,* and *Heathen Valley.* Plays at Actors Theatre of Louisville are *Shotgun, 2, Holy Ghosts, The Love Suicide at Schofield Barracks, The Death of King Philip* and *Childe Byron.* His many awards include two Obies, the Award in Literature from the American Academy, Guggenheim and Rockefeller Fellowships and two NEA Awards. He teaches in the Actors Studio MFA program at the New School in New York.

HUMANA FESTIVAL PRODUCTION

Stars was first performed at the Humana Festival of New American Plays, April 1997. It was directed by Frazier W. Marsh with the following cast:

He .... William McNulty
She .... Karen Grassle

with the following production staff:

Scenic Designer .... Paul Owen
Costume Designer .... Kevin McLeod
Lighting Designer............................ Ed McCarthy
Sound Designer........................ Martin R. Desjardins
Properties Designer.............................. Ron Riall
Stage Manager .... Chris Lomaka
Asst. Stage Mananger .... Andrew Scheer
Dramaturg .... Liz Engelman

CHARACTERS
HE
SHE

PLACE:
Manhattan

TIME:
The present

STARS

A penthouse terrace. A summer night. Stars. He and She, drinking wine.

SHE: Stars.

HE: Great penthouse.

SHE: Like the party?

HE: Very much.

SHE: Like me?

HE: Very much.

(Pause.)

SHE: When people. *(Pause.)* What I mean is. *(Pause.)* Do you think suicide is more anger or sorrow?

HE: I have heard both.

SHE: I met a man named Norwood in Southampton at a club called The Dunes. It went out of business but that was the afternoon it opened, and my husband and I came from a rental on Shelter Island to a party in the bar and he left me there.

HE: What for?

SHE: My husband is very effective.

HE: I know that. You know I know that.

SHE: Drink, kiss. "Enjoy yourself." Off talking to a client.

HE: He's very effective.

SHE: So there I was. Five o'clock Saturday afternoon, Hamptons, smiling and bored. Norwood Struther wore a blue linen blazer, a red and yellow tie, silly and snappy. He didn't say a word. Men liked him, slapped him on the back, called him Squeaky, kidded him about being a bachelor, fondly, but with some kind of something else about it, I couldn't tell what. Well, I was so sick and frustrated with my husband, mad at the world and my utterly asinine position that summer in the Hamptons, hello, there, Norwood, you squeaky bachelor, how are you, say something, and he did. He did have this stutter and high weird voice. I was desperate. I said, "Norwood, take me home?" He said, "Yes." "Bartender, tell my husband I've gone to the movies." I was in Squeaky's bedroom in half an hour. He lived right on the beach, million dollar real estate Bridgehampton. Bedroom whole side wall open to the sea. God. God, you could hear the surf roaring and pounding. Wonderful. Kissing, hugging. He undressed me. Grand. But it took him a while to undress himself. It took me a while to notice it, then to see that he was choking, face red as a lobster, mortified, in that ravishing home, in his beautiful bed by the sounding sea. He had a very small sexual organ. *Very small.*

HE: Oh.

SHE: He tried to apologize. I kissed him and said stop, it doesn't matter.

HE: Did it?

SHE: Of course. He wouldn't talk to me afterwards. Mumbled something about reality I couldn't understand, stuck his head under a pillow, like a little boy. I had betrayed my husband—again—this time with a poor wretch lying ungenerously bestowed next to me in abject misery. Outside on the beach, we could hear the surf pounding. The sea, powerful and potent, alive with cruelty and beauty. All that creation, and us. There was even moonlight, gorgeous, ravishing, with me and Norwood in his bed. And my husband, who hoped I liked the movie.

HE: What does this have to do with suicide?

(Long pause.)

SHE: Look at the moon.

HE: All right.

(Pause.)

I'm in a bar on Columbus Avenue. I meet a woman who says she's a schoolteacher. We have fun, a really good time. She takes me home. It's good. I leave about eleven, she's looking at me like I'm an angel from heaven. Four o'clock in the morning, my telephone rings. It's her, sounding terrible. Help! Right now! So I go back to her apartment and she is looking at me like I'm a demon from hell. "What's the matter?" "Did you call me on the phone?" "When?" "Right after you went home." "No." "You swear?" "I swear." "Oh, my God, my God!" "What happened?" I said. "What a *fool* I am! What a fool I am!" she said. "*What happened?*" "Well," she said, "about eleven thirty a man whose voice sounded I thought just like yours called me. You, I thought it was you, said you had a way of making us both some money right now but you needed two hundred dollars first, and didn't have any cash, did I? Yes. Would I lend it to you. Oh, I had such a good time with you, I liked you so much, so I said yes, I have that, come get it. You, I thought it was you, said, no, you wanted me to meet a man and give it to him, with whatever else he asked for. "What?" I said. You told me to go to a children's playground off Central Park West at midnight, and just sit in a swing and wait. You hoped I would do this for you. I was speechless, and God help me, I was excited. I got the money and went. There were shadows of people at the playground, coming and going in darkness, there for sex. I was frightened and disgusted with myself and terribly, terribly alive. He was wearing a cowboy hat. When he came up to me and when I saw it wasn't you, I was horrified and thrilled. I gave him two hundred dollars and he pulled on his belt and I knelt down and gave him sex. He thanked me and was gone, leaving me there on my knees. I felt—well—debased but delivered. Then I thought, was that really like you? What if it wasn't you who called me? Was it? Oh, tell me the truth! We did meet in a bar but you were decent, weren't you? You wouldn't do that to me, would you? But who else could have? Nobody knew about us. It has to be you! "No it doesn't," I said. "It could be somebody in the bar." "Oh," she said. "But I don't go there often. I don't!" "Sometimes?" "Well, yes." She thought a minute. That man, with the cowboy hat, he could have heard us, heard I was taking you home." "Right." "But that means it was somebody who knows me, my phone number, and everything." "That's the only other possibility." "Oh, God," she said. "I don't know what to believe. Was it some man who's been watching me in that bar? Or was it you? Who did that to me?"

SHE: Do you expect me to believe this?

HE: It's true.

SHE: *Was* it you? You sent some man to do that to her for two hundred dollars? Which he kicked back to you?

HE: No.

SHE: Then who was it?

HE: I never knew. If she does, I never did.

SHE: It was you.

HE: Probably. But it wasn't.

SHE: I believe it was.

> (Pause.)

HE: Did you keep up with Norwood?

SHE: I read about him, in a Long Island newspaper, two years later. In that beach house, with majestic surf and the ravishing moonlight, with two

big pistols, one at each side of his head, both at once. Paper said there was
nothing left of his head but the top of his neck.

HE: We have reached the point of this conversation?

SHE: Yes.

HE: Not yet. Two years later?

SHE: About.

HE: It was the day after.

SHE: A week.

HE: A day.

SHE: A day.

HE: I stole her money? You laughed at him?

SHE: Neither? Both? Did she die?

HE: Oh, no.

SHE: You saw her again?

HE: We married.

SHE: What?

HE: Yep.

SHE: You told me that awful story about your wife?

HE: She's in there now.

SHE: You're not going home with me?

HE: Not tonight.

SHE: Do you like your wife?

HE: Very much.

SHE: Then why are you here?

HE: Why are you?

SHE: I wish I knew.

HE: The moon.

SHE: Those stars. I'm shaking.

HE: I don't feel very good either.

SHE: I'm really upset.

HE: So am I.

(Pause.)

SHE: 858-5492.

HE: 858-5492.

SHE: Mornings.

HE: OK.

SHE: OK.

HE: Stars.

SHE: Bright.
HE: Hard.
SHE: Cold.
HE: Still.
SHE: They never change.
HE: They never will.

(He holds out his hand to her. She takes it, presses it, gets up and leaves. He looks at the stars and shivers.)

END OF PLAY

In Her Sight
by Carol K. Mack

BIOGRAPHY

Carol K. Mack is a New York playwright whose work includes: *The Accident, Territorial Rites, Postcards, Borders, A Safe Place,* and *Esther,* which premiered respectively at the American Repertory Theatre, American Place Theatre, Ensemble Studio Theatre, Prima Facie at Denver Center Theatre, The Berkshire Theatre Festival in association with the Kennedy Center, and Lucille Lortel's White Barn Theatre Foundation. Ms. Mack's awards include a Stanley Award, Beverly Hills Theatre Guild/Julie Harris Award, Playwright's Forum Award. Her work was selected for *The Best Short Plays-1985,* Chilton; *The Best American Short Plays, 1990* and *1993-94,* Applause; *Postcards & Other Short Plays,* Samuel French. Ms. Mack received a Master of Arts degree in Religious Studies, 1992, at New York University where she teaches fiction writing. She is a member of The Dramatists Guild, Inc. and P.E.N..

Ms. Mack gives special thanks to the Rockefeller Foundation for her residency at the Bellagio Center to work on *In Her Sight,* and to Michael Dixon, Bob Scanlan, and James Carse for their invaluable contributions.

HUMANA FESTIVAL PRODUCTION

In Her Sight was first performed at the 1997 Humana Festival of New American Plays, March, 1997. It was directed by Robert Scanlan with the following cast:

Marie Theresa Paradies . . . . Angela Reed
Franz Anton Mesmer . . . . Jonathan Epstein
Karl . . . . Tommy Schrider
Ben Franklin/Baron Anton von Storck . . . . Fred Major
Dr. Jan Ingenhousze/Josef Paradies . . . . Allen Fitzpatrick
Frau Mesmer/Ensemble . . . . Toni Gorman
Stroller/Ensemble . . . . Dianne Archer
Street Entertainers . . . . Brian Carter, Christine Carroll

and the following production staff:

Scenic Designer . . . . Paul Owen
Costume Designer . . . . Marcia Dixcy Jory
Lighting Designer . . . . Greg Sullivan
Sound Designer . . . . Robert Murphy
Properties Designer . . . . Ron Riall
Stage Manager . . . . Carey W. Upton
Assistant Stage Manager . . . . Megan Wanlass

Dramaturg . . . . Michael Bigelow Dixon
Casting . . . . Laura Richin Casting

CHARACTERS

MARIA THERESA PARADIES: 18-26. Intense, riveting, almost eerie attentiveness. She is without agenda, guile, transparent, rather than "innocent." A blind musician-artist.

FRANZ ANTON MESMER: 42-48. Charismatic presence, his centered stillness is powerful. He is utterly confident, passionate, and obsessed. A maverick-scientist.

KARL: 15-23. Observant, vulnerable, and lame, adolescent. He is the apprentice of Mesmer and also his valet. He becomes THE BEAR who is also MOZART.

ENSEMBLE: 2 MEN & 2 WOMEN:
One man portrays JOSEF PARADIES, Maria Theresa's father (42), a weak, cunning bully. This actor also plays DR. JAN INGENHOUSZE (40s), a cold, academic (visiting physician) from Holland. The actor playing BEN FRANKLIN (70s) also is BARON ANTON VON STOERCK (50s)–worldly physician, mentor to Mesmer. Both become CONCERTGOERS and STROLLERS in Paris and Vienna. TWO WOMEN play: Mesmer's wife, MARIA ANNA VON POSCH (50's), wealthy, handsome, proprietary; various relatives of Maria Theresa; and CONCERTGOERS and STROLLERS in Vienna and in Paris.

BEAR is played by an actor in bear costume. In Scene 22, when the bear speaks and turns out to be MOZART, and in final scene of play, the bear is played by the actor who plays KARL.

SET

The action of this play begins and ends at a concert in the Jardin des Tuileries, Paris, April, 1784. It revisits a concert hall in Vienna, December 1776. All other scenes take place in Vienna during four months (January, February, March, and April) 1777, in Franz Mesmer's home in the Landstrasse; in its clinic, drawing room, and on its Belvedere overlooking Schonbrunn Park.

The scenery is minimal, as this is a memory play, impressionistic locations created fluidly by the move of a candelabra or light shift. Chairs and other props are carried on and off by actors; a cyclorama can be used for projections (such as stars); a small five octave piano (circa 1776) remains in place throughout. At the top, a period billboard advertises in French: "Concert of The Blind Pianist." The billboard on the other side is the same in German.

The ensemble is always an integral part of the action, and never leave stage. In their various aspects, they form the web of society, the historical worldview, in which Maria, Mesmer, and Karl are caught. As this is a psychological memory piece, costume should be minimal and impressionistic as set.

There is music and/or sound throughout the play—especially, the haunting sound of the Glass Armonica, a wood-framed instrument holding water-filled glass tumblers that are turned by foot pedal and are played with moistened fingers (in the way that one "plays" rims of crystal glasses).

There is no intermission.

Note: This is a true story. All events in this play are part of a famous case that was documented in great detail by historical figures who are in play, but all the why's are fictional.

IN HER SIGHT

PRECURTAIN

Downstage, a billboard advertises the "Concert of the Blind Pianist" in French. On piano, a vase of roses. The piano, U.S., is circa 1784. She is to play (on billboard) Premiere of Mozart's Piano Concerto # 18 (K456): "The Paradies Concerto." It is April of 1784 in the Tuileries, Paris. This audience becomes that audience as it assembles, Onstage and in the house. To sounds of an orchestra tuning up, a bear descends onto the stage in a basket held by ropes (attached to unseen hovering hot air balloon). Bear climbs out of basket, ties ropes to stage, stands, and with opera glasses, observes all. Ben Franklin enters, wearing small spectacles, signature marten cap, a Parisian woman on his arm, and a cane. Bear sits, invisible to players.

Maria Theresa Paradies, 26, blind, enters. She wears a powdered wig, formal gown, small, dark glasses, poised, U.S. Maria stands a beat, dependent on piano edge, then, confident, but obviously blind, walks Downstage to applause, then curtsies formally. Franklin's hands mid-clap, freeze:

There is a sudden silence and into the vacuum comes a whispered sound: "Maria Theresa" ..louder. Alert, she backs up a step, starts to turn to the piano as,

A man enters slowly from the house. He observes Maria intensely as she begins her turn, and he walks slowly toward her. He, Mesmer, is a powerful pres-ence, a man who both creates and commands a space between himself and others. Mesmer is utterly still, gazes at Maria, who seems to sense him. The whisper arises all around the stage. "Maria Theresa!"

Lights up to full.

SCENE 1: SIGHT UNSEEN

MESMER: Maria Theresa!

(Maria, riveted, breathes, as ensemble moves in the moment. Play begins.)

FRANKLIN: *(To the audience which is his audience.)* There is a wonderful lot of credulity in the world. That's why crackpots thrive. Magnetism. Mesmerism. *(Pointing cane at Maria.)* Look at the outcome of it. She's living proof.

MESMER: *(Turns at bait.)* Mr. Franklin!

FRANKLIN: Dr. Mesmer! The Royal Commission tested your "discovery" and you know what we found? Nothing. Not even enough nothing to raise the hackles on a hound dog.

MESMER: Sir. I must be present at any test of my discovery.

FRANKLIN: We find the influence of Animal Magnetism entirely due to the Imagination.

MESMER: My cures speak for themselves.

FRANKLIN: And "The Blind Pianist," is she one of your famous "cures"?!

MESMER: *(With utter conviction.)* Yes.

(At this, Maria turns to face Downstage, riveted.)

FRANKLIN: Are you calling her a fraud, sir?

MESMER: No...

FRANKLIN: Is she or isn't she blind?

MESMER: I cured her. Then...

FRANKLIN: Yes or no, sir. Day or night. Hard science! Can she see? *(With great authority.)* We'll have no more magnetic fluid, or phlogiston, or pixie dust! The Royal Commission's all here. *(Looking out at house.)* Lavoisier, Dr. Guillotin...it seems everybody's here today. *(He checks pocketwatch.)* Since Mozart will arrive soon for the premiere, and I expect the Queen is with him, we'll put the matter to rest now. *(Gently but firmly engaging Maria.)* Fraulein Paradies, this concerto Mozart's written for you, will you be playing it from memory, dear? *(At Maria's slow, affirmative nod.)* And you must have a prodigious memory, child. I understand you can play sixty concertos by heart.

MARIA: *(Stands, flatly without affect.)* It was February 9, 1777, the day I began seeing. I saw the doctor first and then...

FRANKLIN: Yes, yes, so we've read, but prior to that alleged event, had you not been treated for your condition by other physicians in Vienna?

MARIA: *(Less certainly, clenching her fists.)* I, don't remember, I think...They used the leeches. Valerian root, and...then your cure.

FRANKLIN: My cure?

MARIA: *(Quietly)* No...please...

MESMER: *(With intense distaste.)* Electrotherapy. Your friend, Jan Ingenhousze, brought it to Vienna.

MARIA: NO!

(Maria's anguished cry causes a blackout. A clap of thunder is heard, and the cyclorama flashes with lightning as her entire memory returns and the stage goes to black, a beat, then:)

SCENE 2: CREATURES

Lightning. Ben Franklin and his kite are in pinlight Downstage. Franklin is preoccupied with a model apparatus in hand. He is fascinated with his kite.

FRANKLIN: *(Dispassionate humor, "curious" anecdote, playfully.)* Ingenhousze, my dear friend. Here I am in America again and have had a most ridiculous accident with a turkey! I tried to kill it by the shock from two Leyden jars containing as much electrical fire as forty common phials. But I forgot once again to let go of the chain and nearly did myself in! They say there was a great flash and a crack loud as a pistol! I remember nothing. I think I had again become a lightning rod! The turkey got away.

(Franklin exits. Lights full. Seated on chair, on bare stage, is Maria, without wig or formal attire. She wears a simple shift, and her face is lit by the flashes of light. She appears very frightened. Doctor turns her to face Upstage and then Doctor moves away He sets up a Leyden jar near her and connects her head with metal plates (one on forehead, one at lower back of head) to wires to jar. Entire stage is "hospital". Mesmer enters "hospital" and sees the patient being treated during below by Ingenhousze.)

INGENHOUSZE: *(With academic interest to what has now become "Academy Amphitheatre" audience.)* The patient has been for many years under the care of Dr. von Stoerck and Dr. Barth of the esteemed faculty...they find the optic nerve intact, healthy, yet the state of blindness persists, chronic spasms of the eyes and occasional bouts of delirium have not responded to the usual purgative measures. We will use the equivalent of seventy-five common phials. *(He administers shock. Lights flicker, Maria, seated in upstage chair, shudders.)* She reports light flashes. She says she sees crowds of we don't know quite what, but the fact is that she sees something is evidence the treatment may prove efficacious. We'll try this round a charge equivalent to one hundred phials. *(Lights flicker, Maria shudders.)* Nothing. Nothing now. We may have to stop. Disturbance overly excites the humours. Convulsions set in. We will bleed her. No operation of surgery is so frequently necessary as bloodletting. We use it at the start of all fevers, and always in the apoplexy. With this patient we have a classic case of too rigid fibres. As we know from the great Dr. Boerhaave himself, my own teacher, the nerve fibres are tubular and carry in their hollows, subtle fluidim which the cerebral cortex separates from the blood. In the case of too rigid or too lax a fibrous system, pathological states often result. Bloodletting eliminates the rigidity, drains off the dense portion of blood which congests and engorges the bodily mechanism, slowing the solid components...Dr. von Stoerck.

VON STOERCK: *(Enters, nods, to medical audience house.)* That should alleviate the convulsions. And after, of the antispasmodics: powder of earthworms when necessary, chamomile infusion, cream of tartar, the usual chalybeate waters for strengthening. Powders of arum root, crabs-eyes, amber, cinnebar, etc., etc.

INGENHOUSZE: To which I might add the bark of China root, salt of wormwood, and cumin for their mild balsamic qualities.

VON STOERCK: *(Soothingly.)* Yes, and after, a change of air perhaps. Gentle exercise. Avoiding the North wind and the Southerly east of course. Moderation.

INGENHOUSZE: The key is moderation. And diet. For ten days, pullet broths at supper cooked with oats, violets and wandering poppy...Electrotherapy, our most modern treatment is of no use in this case. *(Exit.)*

VON STOERCK: *(Shakes head.)* Unfortunately she's of the sanguine choleric temperament. Richness in blood, thinness of vessels. We can account for the tremors and the spastico-convulsive nature of the sickness. But as for her blindness, the Academy regrets, the patient will remain blind.

(Van Stoerck exits resignedly. In pinlight Maria turns, pale and shaken, hair all matted, sticking out. She's like a very bewildered creature. Mesmer stands, silent, witness to the entire proceedings. He is left alone onstage with her. They both stand a beat, as a dancing bear is led across the empty stage by actor in a clown costume and

Lights shift as

Pine boughs are hung festively across the stage, now a concert hall in Vienna. Concertgoers stroll by as the blind, fragile-looking Maria, wearing veil now, is led Onstage by Josef. A dress she is helped into covers her shift. She is without will. A billboard is turned around. It now reads in German: Blind Pianist, etc. She begins to play.

Dancing bear is led across the concert hall again to delight of the gathered crowd. Maria plays, unaware of its presence.

Concertgoers laugh, throw coins, applaud. Maria sees nothing. She plays throughout above, utterly lost in her music until Josef Paradies follows Baron von Stoerck as he crosses downstage calling: "Doctor!" Josef takes Maria by the hand, pulls her up from the piano bench and tows her behind as he goes.)

SCENE 3: PERFORMING BEARS

JOSEF: Doctor, pardon, but my wife asked if...

VON STOERCK: *(Curtly.)* Herr Paradies, leave the girl be, as I've advised your wife at least a dozen...

JOSEF: But we only wanted our daughter to, to have a normal life!

VON STOERCK: *(A blink of impatience, coldly.)* Come now! She's a prodigy. The Queen-Empress awards her a large pension. Salieri calls her his prize student. And now young Mozart plans to dedicate a concerto to her! What's "normal" about that?!

JOSEF: *(Sotto voce.)* But Doctor, look at her!

VON STOERCK: Balance her one impairment against her great good fortune. *(Pointedly.)* Not to mention your own!

JOSEF: *(Pursues him.)* That's what we're sayin', y'see. *(Slyly.)* Now the spasms stop only when she plays! Since your treatments, Doctor, she's worse 'n ever!

VON STOERCK: *(Interrupts, fatigued authority.)* Electrotherapy may have influenced those very subtle tremors. But I assure you they'll pass. Patience is the best prescription. Failing that, sir, use the water D'Arquebufode applied with silk compress.

(Stoerck dismissingly exits when Josef spots Mesmer just crossing stage with

Frau Mesmer. When Josef sees Mesmer stop, riveted by Maria, he approaches cagily.)

JOSEF: Doctor? *(Bowing.)* Josef Paradies, father of the girl there...*(As Mesmer looks at him and beyond, at Maria.)* My wife and me, we heard all about your remarkable cures...

MESMER: It's your daughter who's remarkable, sir. A marvel.

JOSEF: *(Insinuating himself immediately for sympathy.)* But after those three thousand shocks entered the poor girl's eyes...*(Grabbing Mesmer's arm firmly.)* she's having fits she's so nervous. Those spasms stop only when she plays...Please, Doctor, they do nothing! And now look at her! *(Confidentially, much too close.)* These spasms are distracting. For the audience. Y'know, a celebrity like her's always in the public eye. I mean we've all got to worry about appearance, but them more than anybody!

MESMER: *(Repulsed, looking past him at Maria.)* She plays like an angel.

JOSEF: Not everybody's discerning as you, Doctor...it's the nervousness, y' see. Makes her disagreeable lookin'. Could ruin her appeal and then what!? She's got a Paris concert comin' up! Huge tour! Way beyond Vienna, sir! It's the world!

MESMER: *(Resisting, turns away from Josef.)* I can't involve myself in her case, sir. I'm sorry.

JOSEF: *(To Mesmer's back, loudly, attracting Frau Mesmer's attention, and she turns, not happy at encounter.)* We don't expect much only maybe you could stop the shaking, y'know...that's all we asked them just ta make her look normal and now will ya look what they've gone and done?! Nobody's going to blame you if it don't work out! Everybody knows she's absolutely incurable!

(Mesmer tenses, gazes a beat at the sightless but riveted Maria, as Frau Mesmer turns sharply to look, he decides as light shifts to clinic.)

SCENE 4: SURPRISE

Mesmer turns as Karl helps a fragile-looking Maria. She seems very reluctant to enter clinic. She walks in tentatively, tenses as Mesmer takes a step toward her. Noting that, then:

MESMER: I won't hurt you, Fraulein Paradies. I am Dr. Mesmer. *(Observes as Maria turns her head away, scared.)* Think of me as one of your great admirers. *(She is overwhelmed with compliment. He watches response intently, then:)* I give my word I'll never hurt you. *(As Maria again flinches when he approaches, realizing:)* Shall I always tell you first what I intend to do? *(At her nearly imperceptible nod.)* Good. Then, now I will...why don't I play something for you.

(He begins to play the Armonica, glancing at Maria for response. As odd sound begins, her body becomes riveted. Expression fills with delight and wonder.)

MESMER: It's my Glass Armonica *(Watches her intently as he plays.)* It was invented by Benjamin Franklin. A true genius. *(Remembering.)* When I played it for him I said, Music of the Spheres, that's what it's like. And you know what he replied? "It keeps a tune. That's all. You don't ever have to tune it." He said, "Time is money." *(Watching her.)* I'd like to show you how to play it because you would do it justice...you play incomparably, Fraulein. *(Plays, always watching her reaction.)* Gluck bids me improvise. He says, "Never use artificial compositions when you touch the glasses."

MARIA: *(Her face lights up suddenly with comprehension.)*...surprise!

MESMER: *(Very surprised at her first spoken word, slowly:)* Yes. Precisely what he said: Be always surprised.

MARIA: Yes...!

(She rises to approach sound and crashes into Mesmer and instrument.)

MESMER: Fraulein! Wait... *(Maria, oblivious, feels Armonica eagerly.)* First, I'll dip your fingers in water. *(Held by her actions, takes her hands, helps her to wet her fingers in water and touch glasses.)* So. Yes...there. You run your fingertips lightly, yes...round the glasses. As they turn...softly. Good. Round and round, till...

MARIA: *(At sound of glass, joy lights her face.)* Oh!

MESMER: *(Playing a chord with her, close now.)* If you'll allow me, I'll barely touch your eyelids with my fingertips. Perhaps I could relax your eyelids this way...like so. *(As Maria surrenders to his touch.)* Good. *(Touching her eyelids, running his fingers over them, then, soothingly:)* Good. Fraulein, how long has this condition...*(Rephrasing as he seats her.)* How long...have you been, unable to see? *(No response.)* Your parents report that you could see normally till the age of five and then one morning you awoke without sight... *(She nods slightly. Continuing to examine her.)*

MARIA: *(Flatly, affectless.)* They say it was winter, December ninth.

MESMER: And before...when you could see? What do you remember? *(He continues to examine her eyes during below.)*

MARIA: *(Responding to newness of question, tentatively.)*...Colors.

MESMER: *(Gazing at her intently.)*...Colors?

MARIA: Music colors. I see them when I play.

MESMER: *(Powerfully touched, stops.)* Can you describe these music colors?

MARIA: Sometimes they're, very warm and...but at times like cold rain rush...or...OH! Oh...oh what is that...? *(Her head jerks back violently.)*...something's pulling! Tugging at...my head!
(Below speeches overlapping.)

MESMER: It will be all right.

MARIA: Make it stop! / I can't...

MESMER: It's all right /...all right.

MARIA: ...oh.

MESMER: ...now I'll bring it into equilibrium. Good. I will place my hand on your left temple. I'll put my fingers near your eyes. Now I'll run my fingers around and round like the music glasses. There. Yes? Isn't that better now?

MARIA: *(Calming down.)* Yes /... yes.

MESMER: Good /... Now what else do you remember? *(Preparing to take notes.)* People...Your parents? *(During below he is surprised into abandoning notes entirely and listens intently.)*

MARIA: *(Tentative, then gaining odd, intense energy.)* I imagine, people when I, hear their clothing—rustle—silk sweeps velvet, soft. Like cats. And at tea, voices. Voices. Like, like doves the ones outside Salieri's room, when I have a lesson, he, plays for me and then I play what he plays and then in between is when I hear the doves...Low, hum deep deep inside them, friendly-sounding, small changes from bird to bird, person to person. Humming, and then I play, and the music has a, has a greater sound that...that swallows them all! And it rises up so bright I hear nothing else. And the music fills my entire BEING until...*(She stops dead, very embarrassed.)*

MESMER: *(Fascinated.)* Until... ?

MARIA: *(Quietly, discovering state herself.)* I'm...inside. Until, I'm not here anymore. *(She senses him freeze. Tensely reaches out to touch him.)*...What?

MESMER: *(Thoughtfully.)* Yes.

MARIA: What?!

MESMER: Yes, I know. I know that sensation well, Fraulein. *(Backing off slightly.)* I'm quite familiar with that...effect of music.
MARIA: *(Ingenuous.)*...so peaceful here, Dr. Mesmer. I so, like, this, room.
MESMER: *(Keeping her in his gaze throughout, slightly puzzled by her and her effect on him.)* Good.
MARIA: You know, I...I think I love this room!
(Light shift. As she stands in place, waits, sightless, Mesmer in note-taking, observation tone, gives testimony in his light, Maria stands in pinlight.)
MESMER: *(As Testimony.)* It was a complete amaurosis attended by spasms in the eyes. That is what we call the condition, "amaurosis" or gutta serena, when the eye, with no manifest fault, can discern nothing at all. It's often brought on by illness...The parents claimed she was never ill. *(Pausing, thoughtfully over mystery.)* In fact, the day before onset, she was so well, they took her out in the carriage through Schonbrunn Park and visited the new zoo...Then, perhaps something frightened her, the night before onset. Again they say nothing unusual occurred. Very odd, such an extended amaurosis with no originating malady or severe fright. *(Seeing Karl, idea, into moment, light shift.)* Karl, bring a long mirror to surgery, will you? And we will try an experiment.

(Light shift.)

SCENE 5: REFLECTIONS IN THE MIRROR

Maria turns to listen to Doctor Mesmer.

MESMER: With conventional treatment all I could do at best would be to alleviate the spasms...*(To Maria, as he seats her.)* and that's all they expect...
KARL: *(Bringing mirror in.)* Doctor?
(Karl sets mirror in the space. It sends out glints of light.)
MESMER: Fraulein? *(To her, always watching her closely.)* There is a long mirror near you...it has a lovely golden frame carved all around with cherubim...
MARIA: Cherubim?
MESMER: You feel them...? *(He moves her hand over the carving, watches her face.)*...then in the center, is a mirror.
MARIA: Cold. Yes, I know, "Glass."
MESMER: A looking glass. In which you can see your own face. Now. *(He holds thin rod like a wand, hands it to her.)* I have in my hand a wand. Here.

With it I'll touch you very lightly. *(Touching her shoulders, head and arms. She trembles in response.)* There. There. Now concentrate very hard on the wand as it travels. I am moving the wand now and I am pointing the wand. I'm going to move it again. Now I want you to follow it. Follow it. Follow. Where am I pointing the wand now?

MARIA: *(Without will, quietly, following wand.)* At my face. You are pointing it at my face in the glass.

KARL: *(Whisper in surprise.)* Doctor?

MESMER: *(Nods at Karl to observe, then:)* Now, follow it, again. Slowly... there... and *(Maria moves her head in the direction of the wand, and back again.)* There. Excellent. That's enough now. Rest now...*(He nods to Karl to roll the mirror offstage.)* I think, Fraulein, I can do something more for you. Would you like that, Fraulein, do you want to see?

MARIA: More than anthing...I want to see just as you do. I want to see this room...to see you!

MESMER: *(Deciding.)* We will arrange to have your piano brought here. You will be staying with us until you're cured.

(A joyous expression lights her face. Lights shift immediately as Karl moves with the candelabra to illuminate drawing room area. Mesmer's mentor, Dr. von Stoerck, enters, cool. Mesmer turns to him. A tension exists between them.)

SCENE 6: SEEING IT OUR WAY

VON STOERCK: *(Understated, testing for truth of story.)* So, the mother's spread rumors all over town. Claims she's moved the girl here at your request.

MESMER: Yes.

VON STOERCK: Of course you know the mother's a slander-spewing shrew. Disgusting temper, fickle, untrustworthy...or perhaps you missed all that when you were out of town?

MESMER: *(Challengingly.)* When I travel other academies are intrigued by my cures.

VON STOERCK: *(A burst of anger.)* Who really cares what Bavarians think about anything. This is Vienna! If you wish to continue here you will use what you can see, measure, and prescribe. Those were the conditions set!

MESMER: Anton, listen...

VON STOERCK: You really try my patience, Franz! You have an enviable practice. Then you set out on this capricious tour, get yourself followed about by peasants like some faith healer! A great embarrassment to the Academy. This time I singlehandedly convinced them not to dismiss you. Barth and Ingenhousze are dead set against you. So's De Haen.

MESMER: *(Intense.)* But I'm on the verge of something here! I need the use of the Spanish hospital. I need your observations, all of you, especially you, my friend. Something happens.

VON STOERCK: Oh dear God.

MESMER: Between me and the patient. Some, transfer of force!

VON STOERCK: This occult streak of yours must be curbed. Patients report you have a basin of magnetized water in the garden...They think you're a wizard.

MESMER: I claim no special powers, Anton.

VON STOERCK: You point, we're told, and "magic" happens.

MESMER: You can also do this...

VON STOERCK: Thank you very much, but I'd rather not. Nor do I wish to be involved! The magnets were at least something tangible—a bit whimsical but harmless. Then you take these mineral magnets away and leave us with what?! Some ephemeral thing your hands do? Worse, you claim it's not your hands, no! The air itself is full of "invisible influences" floating about like chimney soot!

MESMER: What about the dozens of so-called incurables I've cured then? Facts! One acknowledges facts even if their cause is not yet understood! They liked me well enough until I took their patients. Now they won't even look at my notes.

VON STOERCK: Clinical notes signify nothing unless anchored to a proven system.

MESMER: What about my cure of Frau Oesterline here in Vienna. Did that prove nothing?

VON STOERCK: We're not empirics anymore.

MESMER: *(Intensely.)* Listen, Anton, we know from experience with art, with music, that what stirs us profoundly is invisible and can't be weighed or measured. *(At von Stoerck's look.)* Yes, I know that won't do. I must find a proper scientific explanation for the phenomenon. But of this I am sure: anyone can utilize this agent that I've named Animal Magnetism to produce beneficial crises and recovery from nervous disorders. It is as powerful a force as Franklin's Electrical Fire!.

VON STOERCK: Notoriety's far more powerful. And dangerous.

MESMER: *(Beat, then:)* What if I could cure her?

VON STOERCK: But she does well because she's blind. It's her specialty. Take away her blindness, what do you have? Just one more virtuoso.

MESMER: She plays like an angel.

VON STOERCK: In Vienna angels are usually meringue. *(Putting drink down.)* We love novelties, music boxes filled with bonbons, Mozart! But when he grows up...he's finished! Believe me, Franz, if you were to cure her, you'd end both her career and your own. *(Rises to go.)* So! You will repair her tremors with conventional methods, and quickly. She'll be off on her tour soon as Mozart's new concerto is ready. I shall tell them you see it our way...yes.

KARL: *(Entering, with Maria, not seeing von Stoerck at first.)* Doctor...? She's having pains again, near her eyes...*(Mesmer holds his hand up to stop Karl.)*

VON STOERCK: *(With final warning.)* I shall tell them you've given your word.

(Von Stoerck exits and scene continues in drawing room. Mirror is upstage as part of its decor. When lit it can either be transparent or be reflective.)

SCENE 7: EMERGING INTO LIGHT

KARL: Doctor?

MESMER: *(In answer to Karl chooses to go ahead.)* Her eyes begin to discern light, even if for now they're tender against it. We will move her very gradually from the darkness, by degrees...*(To Maria, who stands with bandages over her eyes.)* Fraulein, only when you can endure it, will we introduce full daylight. You will let me know how much light you can bear...For now we will keep your eyes bandaged to stop the light, so you can play the piano.

MARIA: Was that Dr. von Stoerck?

MESMER: Yes.

MARIA: Did you tell him you will cure me?

MESMER: No, I, think that must be our secret. *(Very gently.)* Go on then, Fraulein...*(She sits at piano. He crosses as she begins to play beautifully. This is the only time we hear her play without interruption. He listens, delighting in the music, he notetakes. He speaks in light as Testimony.)* After one week of treatments the spasms finally were eradicated and the convulsions and vomiting of the crises ended. But the pain persisted behind her eyes, from the occiput to the temples, and worsened...yet when she played.

(Listening, back in the moment.) The effect is immediate and continuous. No matter how severe the pain, it vanishes in the presence of music.

KARL: *(Blurting out passionately.)* Maybe now you should end the experiment! Set her free!

MESMER: Karl?

KARL: I have a terrible feeling.

MESMER: Go on then, what is it?

KARL: It's nothing I can explain, only...

MESMER: What? *(Music stops abruptly, beat.)* Fraulein Paradies?

MARIA: *(Stands.)* I am ready. *(She progresses by holding the chair tops, then sits, bandage over eyes.)*

MESMER: *(He unwinds bandage.)* Good. *(Interested.)* Does the light begin to bother you now?

MARIA: A little.

MESMER: Karl, one candle... *(He waits, bandage in hand. As Karl snuffs all but one candle, lights dim.)* Now, how is it?

MARIA: Better.

MESMER: Keep your eyes closed until I tell you to open them. *(He takes off the last bandage. He sits opposite Maria.)* Very slowly then, very slowly begin to open your eyes. *(Maria does. Amazement begins almost imperceptibly.)* *(In front of her.)* Now , follow my hand please.

MARIA: What.

MESMER: *(Realizing, touches her hand.)* Your hand, Fraulein. Your hand... *(Taking her hand in his.)* My hand.

MARIA: *(Very still, astonishment, realizing what she sees.)* This..."hand"... Ah!

MESMER: Yes. My hand.

MARIA: *(Getting it, with utter astonishment.)* Hand. Yes! Hand. And OH!

MESMER: Tell me! What is it? What do you see?

MARIA: LIGHT...all...fields of light! Brightness...and, there...There. Bright, blurs all moving round! Wild confusion. Moving, all around. Dancing!? *(Surprise as she focuses intently.)* Oh...?

MESMER: Do you see me?

MARIA: *(Leaning very close to him, puzzled.)* I...I'm not...

MESMER: What is it?

MARIA: *(With huge concentration.)*...I know it's your face because your, voice is...is coming from the bright patch, and so, the dark, must be your... *(Touching her own lips.)* "mouth." Yes! It's your mouth! Your lips... *(She moves her hand up to her nose, discovering.)* So! Then! That's your nose...And your eyes? Ah... *(Touching her own eyes like a mirror image of his.)*

MESMER: Yes...my eyes.

MARIA: *(Intensely.)* You are the first person I wanted to see!

MESMER: *(Beat.)* Yes?...but would you like to see yourself, Fraulein?

MARIA: *(Puzzled.)* Myself.

MESMER: *(Turning her to face mirror.)* Yes...Look. Over there. Turn this way...

MARIA: *(Stunned, whisper, moving.)*...there?! I'm, there...?...is it following me?

KARL: *(Blurting out.)* It's a reflection, Fraulein. Only a shadow!

MARIA: *(Understanding shape in mirror is Karl.)* Ah...it's you, then you are Karl! And you are there as well? *(Confused.)* But it's *(Touches it.)*..."Glass"!

MESMER: It's a mirror, glass coated with silver...

MARIA: Does it see me?

MESMER: No, the mirror reflects. *(Leads her away, gently.)* To "see", to see one needs first our sensorium, which transmits impressions. Then our perception of properties, our recognition. *(Aware of her innocence.)* All that comes into play. *(Then, as he realizes piano is close by her.)* But do you see that? You see what that is...?

MARIA: *(Immediately stumbles.)* Things are not where I see them! Oh, and now it's...getting very bright. Doctor, it hurts, my eyes hurt above...just here! *(She thuds into the keyboard. Discordant sound.)* Oh... ! *(She feels the keyboard slowly with eyes closed. She opens her eyes, examines it closely, with wonder, feels it, whispers reverently.)*..."piano."

MESMER: *(Gently.)* Yes, so...It's your piano.

MARIA: *(With astonishment.)*...this! Piano!

MESMER: *(With concern.)* If your head hurts, the bandages should go back on now.

MARIA: No, please, wait! I...I want to play.

MESMER: Of course. Yes, it will soothe you.

MARIA: *(Studies keyboard, readies herself to begin, hands up, sees them, and then, freezes, stunned, whispers.)* I can't... *(Turns.)* I can't. *(Light shift. As her testimony, controlled, flat.)* It was February ninth, 1777, the day I began "seeing." I saw Dr. Mesmer first and then Karl in the mirror, and then Frau Mesmer's dog and the mirror, the mirror with the cherubim on the frame, then my eyes began to hurt from the brightness. I knew every object by touch of course but not by, "seeing", and so I felt quite overwhelmed in this new sphere and being part of the doctor's secret experiment. Until this day, whenever I felt overwhelmed, I would go inside the music... *(Memory turns into immediate pain.)* But now I can see there are keys, there are keys, and I see my "fingers", and now somehow the music is...all is utterly different now, and...And I, seem to be... *(Agony of complete realization.)* Locked out!

(Light shift on discordant sound.)

SCENE 8: RECOGNITION

MESMER: *(Defensively, pained, to Karl.)* It is only that everything is new to her. It's to be expected at first. The sooner she learns to be comfortable here, the sooner she feels at home, the sooner she will recover her skill. *(Pain just under.)*...you needn't look at me like that. I am a musician myself. I had no intention of damaging her.

KARL: ...But how do we fix it then? What do we do?

MESMER: We begin by retraining her. That will be our daily task. We teach her to recognize objects and gradually she will regain her peace of mind, be less occupied with novel impressions. And as our world becomes routine...*(Thinking.)* she'll find it all a matter of habit, be less startled by it all, then her attention will turn to music.

KARL: *(With misgiving.)*...Yessir.

(Light shifts as Karl crosses and Mesmer looks after him. Drawing room where Maria is practicing by finding objects, concentrating, naming.)

MARIA: Blue...Yellow...Blue...red... *(Touching, discovery.)* Book!

KARL: *(Takes it from her gently.)* Book. But, Fraulein, try without touching it. *(Holding up book.)*

MARIA: ...Book.

KARL: Good.

MARIA: *(Looking around, fastening gaze uncertainly.)* "Chair"? *(Feeling and confirming by touch.)* yes...Armonica? *(She touches object and it is not Armonica but is sofa, corrects.)* Sofa...Table...Book...

KARL: You touch them first every time and that's cheating.

MARIA: All right. All right. You do it then.

KARL: *(Pointing.)* Cushion...Carpet.

MARIA: Faster. Faster.

KARL: Mirror. Sofa. Candles. Table...candelabra, bowl of fruit...apples.

MARIA: *(As nonsense, naming first as real then not as seen objects, but only names.)*

Chair, sofa, red...blue. Apples, cushion, candle, spoon...dizzy...I'm getting very...dogshawltablestoolcandle...

KARL: Go easy, easy now.

MARIA: *(Falling into him.)* Mirror. Maria. Mirror, book, table carpet, ANGELS dogflower sunshine and RAIN! Rain. Rain. Rain.

KARL: *(Laughing with her in game.)* Wait. Stop it! Wait, y'know it's not raining in here!

MARIA: *(Breathlessly, spinning.)* It's not? It's what? It's what? It's snowing, yes?! SNOW! Rain!

KARL: Hey, no snow! No angels, come on...only real things! *(Observing her as she slows, tense.)*...what is it? What's the matter?

MARIA: *(Tensely, different tone.)*...tigers.

KARL: *(Worried.)* Fraulein? Please be...serious, what...? What is it? *(As she becomes rigid.)* Doctor! *(Karl exits.)*

MESMER: What's wrong?

MARIA: *(Frozen with fear, quietly.)* Get them out. *(She is rigid with fear.)*

MESMER: *(Kneeling by her.)* Fraulein Paradies?

MARIA: *(Slowly, seems to awaken.)*...Oh... *(Peering, softly.)* It's you.

MESMER: *(Still kneeling by her.)* .. If you'd, go a bit more slowly...

MARIA: So much to know, Doctor, too much.

MESMER: Patience.

MARIA: *(Enraged, just under, frustrated.)* I don't know anything! And now I can't seem to play and I feel lost...so entirely lost! *(Stops, as tears are close.)*

MESMER: *(Taking over calmly as Karl backs off.)* Yes, I know, I know, only have a little more patience and soon you'll play...Karl tells me you're, very good at naming colors, is that so?

MARIA: No more today.

MESMER: *(Beat.)* Shall I leave you then and let you rest?
(Maria shakes her head "no" and grips his hand.)

MESMER: *(After a beat, takes a flower from nearby vase.)* Well then, what's this...? I found a red object. *(He kneels by her and holds up flower, pulling it away as she tries to touch it.)*

MARIA: *(Concentrating hard.)* That? is...Red. Well, it's...a... *(Sniffs, recognizes, at last slowly with delight.)* a flower...Flower.

(Lights shift.)

SCENE 9: PERCEPTION

Maria practices piano in drawing room. Practice heard under below.

MESMER: *(Crosses downstage. Testimony.)* With her eyes closed she would touch a book and know it, yet when she looked at it from a distance she could never connect the object with its name. Somehow, although she could see, she did not know what she saw. I would show her a periwig or glove and she would stare as if at some exotica and repeat the object's name with such wonder it seemed new to me as well! Ordinary things were so new to her vision that the effort to distinguish one from another seemed to exhaust her...*(Into the moment as her piano practice continues.)* This fatigue must contribute to her difficulty at the piano...

KARL: *(Intensely.)* What will become of her? She's only like a visitor here! *(The practice continues with clumsiness.)*

MESMER: *(Pulled from thought by tone.)* What do you mean?

KARL: I mean playing the piano is why she is! It's home to her.

MESMER: But I've told you her skills will return when she is more settled. *(At Karl's silence.)*...Surely you don't doubt me.

KARL: I never have, sir. I know you mean to help her...

MESMER: Karl?

KARL: *(Tortured.)* She don't doubt you! She pitched herself full into this for you! *(Hearing Maria practice, walks away disgruntled, to himself.)* She keeps that rose you gave her like some kind of holy relic!

(Light shift. Maria is at piano ending practice. None of the above practice has been successful. She stops. She looks at book on piano. Rose is in it. She turns to examine objects in mirror.)

MARIA: *(As she studies herself in the mirror, book in hand.)* I'm captured there, yet here I stand. Two of me. One I see. One I am...It confounds the mind. And this, is held in the glass and in my hand. Another marvel! Like the Armonica. *(She hears Karl, as practice when he enters.)* Karl!?...Don't tell me, don't tell me. My hair is yellow! Is that right? Is it "yellow"?

KARL: *(So she doesn't hear, solemnly, infatuated.)* It's gold, Maria. Like an angel.

MARIA: What?...Karl? *(No response. Peering closely in mirror.)* The human face leaves so much to be desired. Not like the dog. How beautiful is a dog! The way it's put together. Its ears are atop the head exactly where ears should be, and its face comes first into view so you can greet it. The confusion starts only with the tail motion it seems, then the whole dog vanishes!? Does that startle you?

KARL: *(Apologetically.)* Well, I'm quite used to dogs, y'know.

MARIA: And horses! I'd love to see a horse!...I fed one once from my hand. I can still feel it breathing hot in my palm.

KARL: Soon you'll go out and see 'em near the promenade!

MARIA: You know what else I want to see? A peacock! I heard they have eyes on their tails. Is this true?

KARL: Sure. We'll take you to the zoo in Schonbrunn Park. They've collected all the beasts of the jungle from all over the world!

MARIA: ...no.

KARL: *(Puzzled.)* But you said you'd...

MARIA: *(Flatly.)* Cages.

KARL: *(Surprised.)* You've seen them?!...Fraulein?

MARIA: *(Dazed.)*...what?

KARL: *(Concerned, humoring her fondly.)* Never mind. Never mind, I'll bring you a baby bear, how'dya like that?

MARIA: *(Peering, puzzled, noticing for first time.)* Karl?...are your *(Touching her own legs for confirmation of word.)* "legs" very different or do I see them wrong?

KARL: *(Tightly, self-conscious.)* No, you're...They're, quite different. No comparison. Apples and oranges they are.

MARIA: What makes the difference?

KARL: *(Realizing it means nothing to her, beat.)*...Y'mean why...when I was about twelve, I took sick. My little brother too. He died of it, and after, I, got lame...my mother, she took me to Dr. Mesmer for the cure but he couldn't do nothing for it. And then my mother...she didn't want me back.

MARIA: Oh...

KARL: *(Defensively, brightly.)* But the doctor said I could stay on here and work for him.

MARIA: It must be wonderful working for him.

KARL: *(Resenting her enthusiasm.)* Sometimes...

MARIA: Not always?

KARL: *(Displacing his resentment, covering.)* Well, it's not easy...I mean Frau Mesmer, for one, y'notice she never comes by? It's her way of letting him know she hates it when he takes incurables. Like me. She thinks he's wasting his time.

MARIA: *(Curiously.)* What's she like, Frau Mesmer?

KARL: Horrible jealous. Of everything that takes his time...like she owns that too. Like her mansion.

MARIA: But you truly appreciate him. You must be as important to him as you are to me.

KARL: *(Overwhelmed.)* I am?

MARIA: *(Increasingly nervous.)* Of course, with the training, and when you help me through the bad time, when it all blurs and when I'm...

KARL: Now, none of that now. It's only a matter of time. You're coming along excellent...

MARIA: No, there's always something new, something odd...

KARL: Don't start up again.

MARIA: But look! *(She pulls him back from mirror.)* Look at this. There. We change size. But how can it be...

KARL: It makes no difference.

MARIA: You just told me that your legs being different changed your life, why no difference when everything changes... *(Swinging book.)* Now big now small, it makes you faint. If that glass reflects but can't see, how can its book be different from the one in my hand, and then which is the true book, and how do I know you see the book I see when you say "book" to me, or...

KARL: Fraulein, this sort of question can make a person sick!

MARIA: *(Continues demonstrating her problem, intensely.)* But when I walk around the chair and the mirror they keep changing as I go. In fact what I see depends entirely on where I am, so! I stand here...but then I move and the room is different!

KARL: *(During above.)* Fraulein, Fraulein, listen, I'm begging you not to...just please sit down.

MARIA: *(Much too intensely.)* How can I get used to it! Nothing stops!

KARL: You'll get the vertigo again...

MARIA: But Karl, it all keeps, becoming and becoming. I'm dizzy from it.

KARL: *(Holding her shoulders, face to face.)* No, it's all this thinking gets you perplexed when you're supposed to concentrate on seeing!

MARIA: But how can you see without thinking?! *(Confronting him closely, solemnly face to face.)* It's not only the names! Your whole visible world is really really peculiar! You've lived in it so long you probably don't notice anymore.

KARL: And soon you won't either, Fraulein. Just learn your up and down, yellow and blue, apples and spoons. Hear me? This is the sort of thing that gets you ahead in the world, believe me. Thinking gives you vapours.

(Light shift. Piano scales begin offstage. Josef Paradies enters, stops, takes out card. He starts to put it on tray when he hears clumsy chords. He stops, and winces at the bad notes. Karl enters, sees him, and tries to withdraw immediately.)

SCENE 10: BEAR AT FIRST SIGHT

JOSEF: *(Catching sight of Karl.)* What's that? That's not my daughter playing...?

KARL: 'Course not! Fraulein, she's doin' very nicely, sir. You'll be delighted when you see her...

JOSEF: *(Annoyed.)* I'll see her now!

KARL: Doctor's forbidden me/I can't let anyone in the clinic...she's resting.
(Overlapping phrases shown by / lines.)

JOSEF: The doctor be hanged! / Out of my way /...Where's Frau Mesmer?

KARL: *(Blurting out, trying to stop him.)* Out...They're out, Herr Paradies, wait! Please! Listen to me, I'm not, I'm not to say anything but, sir...don't go in there!

JOSEF: Why?

KARL: *(Desperately, to stop him.)* Because...because, your daughter can see, sir.

JOSEF: *(Incredulous, quietly.)* What do you mean she can see...?

KARL: She can, it's true, but please. Please, sir, listen to me, it's a secret. No, wait! Don't, don't go in, I can prove it to you.

JOSEF: Prove it...Why would this be kept secret?

KARL: It's, the doctor, he doesn't want any interference just yet...from outsiders. *(At Josef's look.)* He wants her to stay quietlike. Look, what if I prove it to you? Would you give me your word you won't say nothing to anyone or interfere with the treatment...?

JOSEF: *(Grudgingly suspicious.)* If my daughter can really see, I'll do whatever the doctor asks.

KARL: Good. Good, then only wait till dark. Her eyes, they're still not up to daylight, sensitive y'see. But after sunset she's all right to go out, and I'll make sure she comes out on the belvedere...over there. *(Pointing.)* Wait over there. Until dark.

(As Karl points to area offstage, as lights shift to twilight Promenade. Maria stands with Karl on belvedere. She pulls her cloak close. Stops. Then she

notices strollers. They laugh and point. She turns to gaze as a bear crosses stage on leash with clown. Josef ducks into shadows.)

KARL: *(Tense, aware of Josef in offstage shadows.)* There, Fraulein, y'see? Just like I promised you...a bear. But don't worry, it's tame and very gentle. They've got 'em all over Vienna.

MARIA: *(Holding his arm, open-mouthed, pointing.)* Oh!...That! is...a bear! *(Noticing, curious, distracted from sight.)* Why are all those people laughing?

KARL: 'Cause of the bear? *(No response.)*...It's dancing, see. It's like a waltz it does.

MARIA: *(Doesn't get it.)* They're laughing at the bear?

KARL: Yes! No, more at the idea of a, of a bear dancing! Like the waltz, it got so popular even the bears are out nights doin' it!?

MARIA: *(Caught up in sight of bear.)* It's magnificent! Like a thunderstorm! How does it know to dance?

KARL: Well, that fellow with it? He's the trainer, see. He put a ring in its nose, attached a rope and he yanks it, and right off the pain makes it rise up on its hind legs! Then after it's trained, all he needs to do is reach for the rope and... *(She begins backing away during above, appalled. Karl follows, not comprehending.)*

MARIA: No! *(Exiting hastily.)* I don't want to see this!

KARL: *(Following her.)* But Fraulein... *(Stopped by Josef Paradies.)*

JOSEF: *(Stepping forward, quietly.)* I didn't believe you. *(Handing him gold.)* Here.

KARL: No, Herr Paradies.

JOSEF: *(Handing him another coin.)* Keep it. *(Josef Paradies exits.)*

KARL: No, wait...Fraulein!...Herr Paradies... *(Turns.)* Fraulein, wait!... No, wait... *(Walks toward him calling but he's gone.)* Herr Paradies... !

(Watching after Josef Paradies and then toward Maria, he stops, feels purse with remorse, looks at it alone, cyclorama darkens, and fills with stars. Karl stands in darkness. Karl is bereft, then he exits. Maria Theresa in a cloak walks out with Franz Mesmer in his cape, stand silent. Maria raises her arms and stands still among the stars in awe.)

SCENE 11: THE MOST MAGNIFICENT SIGHT

MARIA: Nothing in nature can be more magnificent than this! They touch me...starlight falls into my eyes...my mouth...so close I can drink it...so close I can hold them.

MESMER: The ancients thought they were on a ring called the Star Bearer but then came the Great Newton to show us all how the universe works.

MARIA: *(Seeing a completely different version of the universe, sheer awe.)* The Universe!

MESMER: *(Opening his arms wide.)* Vast machinery, all in places like an eternal clockwork. And we are wonderful machines that think!

MARIA: *(Taken aback.)*...are we?

MESMER: Yes. We surely are!

MARIA: Oh.

MESMER: *(Takes her hand and arm, points up with them.)* And we make a map of all these stars! We draw an invisible line between them like so, there to there, there's his belt, and there's the sword and that shape we call Orion! The hunter.

MARIA: *(Trying to discover it visually.)* The constellation Orion...I know the story of it, yes.

MESMER: *(Holding her hand in his pointing.)* Above us, now imagine a long long line, like so...Like a dipper, yes? It's called Ursa Major.

MARIA: *(Thinking through story as she tells it.)* Ursa Major! A bear with a long tail! Yes. It was once a beautiful woman named Callisto. Zeus falls in love with her. But when Hera finds out, she's so jealous she turns Callisto into a bear who has to roam the forest alone until one day a hunter, raises his bow and arrow to kill her. And at that very instant she's rescued, and sent up to the sky forever!

MESMER: *(Captivated.)* I think I'd, forgotten all those stories, a long time ago. *(Notices her expression.)*...What is it?

MARIA: *(Wiping away tears.)*...It's only. Now, it's all so beautiful. Thank you for bringing me out here tonight...(*Pinlight to Testimony.*) It was then, we stood immersed in brilliant streams, were *of* it all, within its glory, so like music, this universe, my head and soul were full of stars and no way of saying...it was then I knew that he and I saw different skies, that we were each alone. *(Tears, sorry to have ruined moment.)* I'm sorry, I...

MESMER: *(Walking away from her, very attracted to her.)* No, no don't be sorry,

Maria...I am happy we're out hre together...you're a, marvelous story teller.

MARIA: *(Looking at his back, crossing down to him.)* Someday, when they see me cured and acknowledge your discovery, we'll be linked together forever, just like a constellation.

MESMER: *(Realization of import.)* We are, linked together.

MARIA: *(Intensely.)* I want to live out here forever.

MESMER: *(Gently, touching her eyes.)* Ah, but the stars disappear by dawn, you know, and the daylight is still too harsh for your eyes...

MARIA: *(Not letting go of his hands.)*...Then, every night may we meet here?

MESMER: Maria. You'll soon be completely well...

MARIA: *(Interrupting him.)* No, don't say what you are about to say. *(Moving closer.)* Please...just hold me.

(They freeze as Ingenhousze crosses stage and lights shift as von Stoerck shouts at Ingenhousze.)

VON STOERCK: Conjecture!

SCENE 12: SIGHT OF DOCTORS

Ingenhousze crosses stage slowly with paper in hand, icy. Von Stoerck follows, looking grim, downstage of Maria and Mesmer, lights shift.

VONSTOERCK: *(During light shift, in freeze.)* It is all conjecture!

INGENHOUSZE: *(Icily.)* No! Not anymore. On February eighteenth, Herr Paradies claims his daughter saw! Dr. Mesmer, the girl tells him, *(Flatly mocking.)* "I saw the starry heavens!" *(Mesmer turns to look at them as they enter drawing room. Maria exits in light shift. Frau Mesmer enters, listens, takes paper from von Stoerck and reads with great interest, while Karl, watches nervously. Referring to paper, drily, flatly.)* Herr Paradies reports that you, quote, produced an effect that greatly surprised when my daughter followed a stick with her gaze.

MESMER: *(Calm, soberly, explains.)* Herr Paradies somehow got wind of her recovery...so I was obliged to allow him a visit. But he gave me his word he'd...*(During above Karl looks so uncomfortable that von Stoerck notices his discomfort.)*

INGENHOUSZE: *(Drily, interrupts)* Not every man's word has equal weight.

MESMER: *(With barely concealed contempt.)* Our first oath is to heal. What's the difference now... ?

INGENHOUSZE: *(Impatiently.)* Now? Now the father's testimony's on its way to the court! And Mr. Franklin writes that the news has already travelled abroad.

MESMER: *(Challengingly.)* Good! What the father writes is the Truth! She can see!

(Pause.)

VON STOERCK: *(Surprised but taking control, smoothly.)* Ah. But why have you kept this from us? This is joyous news.

INGENHOUSZE: If you can alter her vision, touch me. Touch the whole Academy.

MESMER: It happens only when two people are in rapport, which we are not!

INGENHOUSZE: Chimerical nonsense. Medieval quackery!

(Mesmer turns away, silent.)

VON STOERCK: Dr. Ingenhousze, do not be so quick to judge. *(Patting Frau Mesmer's arm, thinking fast.)* Perhaps...perhaps we've all been hasty... *(Squelching Ingenhousze's protest with a glance.)* I myself, regret having waited so long to investigate this discovery...Of course I've read the notes you sent, Franz...Oh, and about the Spanish Hospital, we may be able to arrange the enterprise if we're satisfied...

MESMER: No. You can't disturb her now.

INGENHOUSZE: Now is when the truth must be ascertained.

MESMER: She suffers from a type of nervous fatigue. Anton, she's...remember your own diagnosis of choleric temperament, she's not stable enough...

VON STOERCK: *(Lightly, reassuringly.)* Nothing exhaustive, Franz. *(Including Ingenhousze.)* A preliminary glimpse is all we need.

MESMER: *(Starting out.)* Then first I'll go have a word with her.

INGENHOUSZE: Dr. Mesmer, you must have no contact with the patient. We'll not have any tricks...

VON STOERCK: *(With an annoyed glance at Ingenhousze.)* Prejudicing the subject would disturb the science of it. How could the faculty with any integrity, vouch for the results?

MESMER: *(Appealing to von Stoerck.)* I don't want a relapse.

VON STOERCK: Nor do we, Franz. After all, we're all members of the Academy. Was it not you who repeatedly requested our observations. Here we are. Let us have a few moments alone with her.

(Mesmer, stymied, gestures them past. Light shifts to other area where Maria waits, tense.)

VON STOERCK: My dear Fraulein, you remember me, Doctor von Stoerck, and may I present...

MARIA: *(Turns, flatly.)* Speak.

INGENHOUSZE: Good afternoon, Fraulein.

MARIA: *(Looking him over coldly, expressionless.)* You are Dr. Ingenhousze, the innoculator from Holland.

VON STOERCK: So, your hearing is sharp as ever, and we're told your sight is coming along, is it?

MARIA: *(Regarding von Stoerck.)* You are "taller" than I imagined, Baron. I must look sharply up to see your face.

INGENHOUSZE: Let's begin with a few simple objects...

MARIA: Doctor Ingenhousze, why don't you take your head off. I, I mean your hat?

INGENHOUSZE: *(Startled, removes hat.)* Oh, yes...*(Picks up book.)* Now, what have I in my right hand?

MARIA: *(Touching book.)* A book, sir.

INGENHOUSZE: She touched it. Note that. Here, again. *(Holding up spoon.)* What's this?

MARIA: *(As he pulls spoon out of reach just as she tries to touch it, uncertainly.)* A...a...to eat! A fork!

INGENHOUSZE: A fork is it?!

MARIA: *(Getting slightly rattled.)* No, no, a...shiny, not a fork, a dipper...no, dipper is wrong! Sky is...not a fork, a...I can't yet always name the thing. *(As he hands it to her, watching, she feels it to confirm recognition.)* Spoon. A spoon, isn't it?!

INGENHOUSZE: You see how she does it.

MARIA: I, I saw the stars! And Ursa Major! Many wonders. And marvels. A sunset! Where is Doctor Mesmer?

VON STOERCK: He can't come in just yet until we've asked a few more questions.

MARIA: And why is that?

INGENHOUSZE: No, Fraulein, we ask the questions.

VON STOERCK: We need to ascertain the truth of certain claims.

MARIA: What claims?

INGENHOUSZE: Let us do the asking, please, Fraulein. Just tell us simply if this is a spoon, a cup, or a fork?

MARIA: *(Losing control.)* I can't always name the thing, but that doesn't mean that...

KARL: She always gets confused when she's nervous or tired, y'see...

VON STOERCK: *(Angrily.)* What are you doing here?

INGENHOUSZE: Out. *(Waits a beat as Karl exits.)* Now, let's begin again, Fraulein, what's in my hand?

MARIA: I can see. I see you, clear, standing right in front of the table...and in the mirror too.

(Ingenhousze is momentarily taken aback.)

VON STOERCK: *(Aware she sees, neutrally while deciding what to do.)* Fraulein Paradies, please tell Dr. Ingenhousze what's in his hand.

INGENHOUSZE: *(To von Stoerck, concluding with theory.)* Pure memorization is exactly what's going on...

(Despite above, there is a growing awareness she can see on part of von Stoerck, Frau Mesmer and Ingenhousze.)

MARIA: It's, it's red... *(Beat of silent discomfort which is relieved by next part and causes a laugh of relief on "apple".)* so it's, most probably an apple.

INGENHOUSZE: An apple is it? If so, how many? If not, tell us the number and forget the name. / Come come, how many now?

(Overlapping.)

MARIA: What? I...Five fingers. / I have five fingers. I'm sitting on one sofa, sir. The the ceiling is above and the book is on my my "table." An apple is, red as a rose / The egg is white. You are not, you are night! Night!

MESMER: *(Entering at hearing her raised voice.)* What are you doing?

VON STOERCK: *(Backing away.)* We've kept you too long / too long. Overstayed our welcome. *(Exits.)*

MESMER: *(Angrily after him.)* Anton!

MARIA: *(Bewildered and furious.)* Wait!...Doctor von Stoerck, take off your head and come back here! Don't you know I see you! Don't you see me?! Can't you see? Crows!

(Mesmer goes to her side, and after doctors and Frau Mesmer exit, his anger is powerful. Maria is panting with fury, only slowly recovers.)

MESMER: *(Holding onto her tightly.)* Maria / forgive me / I should have known. Maria forgive me.

(Overlapping.)

MARIA: *(Bewildered.)*...They were laughing at me / the way people laugh at the bear!

MESMER: No. No, / Not at you. Not at you.

MARIA: I know that sound. Like dogsnarls only worse, for they bare their teeth and pretend. It gives me chills.

MESMER: I'm sorry. I'm so sorry. They are fools, the lot of them!

MARIA: *(Quietly.)* Just like the bear. That's how they see me.

MESMER: *(His love showing through.)* You are so very lovely.

MARIA: *(Stops all motion.)* Am I...? *(With full attention.)* You care for me, you truly care, don't you, Franz...?

MESMER: Yes, of course I do!

MARIA: Yes, yes...of course you do, oh Franz, you're not like them! Your True Nature is that of an artist. That's how you play the glasses...yes! And how you understand music. I know you. I think I know you better than you know yourself.

MESMER: *(Almost sadly.)* Do you?

MARIA: Yes! I do. Why try to prove anything to them? They're not worth...Not worth one finger of your hand.

MESMER: *(Touched.)* But they are the Academy, without their acceptance my discovery will never be known. *(Torn, conflicted; profoundly felt.)* There is no way out.

MARIA: *(Recognizing.)* They know full well I saw them. They only play a game.

MESMER: But they'll do anything to win it, even destroy you if...oh I am sorry I involved you in this now. I thought you'd be completely well before they...what have I done?!

MARIA: *(Wondering, quietly.)* Is there no way around them?

MESMER: If we could only somehow circumvent them. We could...open the house. Invite *(Discovering idea aloud.)* the public to visit. Let them see for themselves...

MARIA: *(Finishing his sentence.)* Yes! Let them see what a great healer you are!

(Lights shift.)

SCENE 13: DAMAGES (FIRST MOVE)

VON STOERCK: *(Finished reading report, downstage.)* This report won't do.

INGENHOUSZE: *(Coldly.)* And why's that, Baron? I thought it quite clear.

VON STOERCK: *(Folds report, logic.)* If she's blind, he hasn't harmed her, as she's always been blind. If the girl can see, again, no damage...In Vienna, Dr. Ingenhousze, to have her forcibly removed from his clinic, we must prove damage... *(Fishing for alternative.)* Are you certain she didn't see something?

INGENHOUSZE: Something...perhaps, but what little vision she may have could be the late result of our electrotherapy treatments.

VON STOERCK: Can of worms. Tricky business, sight. The father's claim against ours, and the girl, who knows, the public loves her...They look to magic like savages! That's all they are, savages in modern dress. True, your vaccine was accepted, Ingenhousze, but had a plague broken out just then, you'd have been shipped to Holland in a box.

INGENHOUSZE: It's you who insisted we keep him after the last fiasco.

VON STOERCK: The Mesmer effect is not True Science, but it seemed harmless enough. I thought the Academy might utilize...

INGENHOUSZE: You thought. If his crackpot idea took hold it would destroy modern medicine. He should have been ousted! Now if my report won't do, what exactly do you propose?

VON STOERCK: Start with the report. But we must also prove damage. *(Thinks, stops, realizing plan.)*...there are, of course, other things to damage. She's young and she's, become rather attractive, hasn't she? I wonder. Why don't we have a word with Frau Mesmer?

(He turns to Ingenhousze with idea as lights shift.)

SCENE 14: SIGHT OF VISITORS

Karl steps into scene to help Maria, who is very nervous, recovering from visitors at the mirror and preparing to meet yet another round. She is playful at first with Karl and entertains him with her imitations as he laughs.

MARIA: So many visitors today. So many! Who'd have thought...It is a lovely...*"gown", they all say, it's lovely, but the... (Feels the "panniers" with eyes closed, then checks.)* "Panniers" make one look like a sofa! Oh my! And I will never never wear the mouche! I thought it was a bug on Auntie's cheek, but when I tried to get it off her, she said leave it be! Ohohoh don't touch me "Beauty Spots"! She has three of them. She says each mean to say something. The spot near her eye means "Passion!" The one on her lip means "kiss!" They're "beeyouteefool," she says and Maman says that "Rouge Parisian" is the very latest! Red circles upon the, the cheeks! *(Imitating.)* "She don't know the beauty spots nor even how to stuff the hair with wool! She don't know how to get a big head, look, her head's the smallest in town, I swear!" "She'll know it soon enough, she'll know the robe anglaise, the polonaise!" And then Uncle says: Now you'll marry and he makes that awful... *(Imitates wink for Karl.)*

KARL: "Wink," Fraulein. It's only a wink.

(Suddenly through mirror comes a flash of grotesque visitors posed behind it.)

MARIA: *(Getting more disturbed.)* It's horrid. A dog would never do it. The mouth hooks up to his eye and then he makes a hawing sound and his teeth!? Black. Oh! *(Reacting to a flash of sight of visitors in mirror.)* The smells and the air's like mist...my eyes! Oh! Now all color patches gowns blur blur. *(To ensemble who appear again grotesquely in mirror.)* So dizzy all the things! Go home. Names of all the Things and...please go away...go away...

(During the above, Karl is increasingly disturbed by Maria's behavior and exits, runs off for Mesmer. Ensemble: Aunt, Uncle, Gossips, as they move into space. They preen. They look slightly grotesque as they gawk, sit, titter, and nod in her direction. Maria walks among them, curtsies, stiff and polite. They comment on her as if she is invisible: "Looks rather like the Mother," "I think she favors the Father," "Around the Mouth," "Around the eyes." "But her eyes are .. " "Do you think she can see us?" "Have her play something." "Ask her." "She doesn't talk much." "Go ahead, dear!" "Will she play?" Maria curtsies and is breaking down as they wheel back behind mirror and the mirror images vanish as mirror becomes opaque again and Mesmer enters forcefully.)

MESMER: No more visitors. We will have no more visitors! *(To Maria, who is in state of hysteria.)* I know...I know how difficult it is for you...we'll have no more visitors...we're alone now...You're with me now. *(Trying to calm her.)* Be calm. They've gone. Be tranquil...you're better, you know. *(As she calms.)* There. There. You're so much better...be calm...there. *(She is calm.)* There...

MARIA: *(In trance state.)*...We're home.

MESMER: *(Wondering at flat odd tone of voice.)* Maria?

MARIA: Home...from the zoo...

MESMER: What are you saying? *(He moves to chair to observe, sits.)*

MARIA: ...smells of animals in my nose...Maman's angry. She throws me...ahhh...hits me...I am bleeding. The blood. Blood...Papa he attacks Maman and...they're...fighting, on the floor now. Locked together. Growls. They are animals?! Blood. Blood is falling in my eyes...smells like animals. I am afraid. I am afraid.

MESMER: Maria... ?

MARIA: Light! Hurts...Oh God, oh God, they left me here, in the cage with the tigers. The tigers will eat her. Unless she...Unless she's invisible. Invisible. *(Beat of astonishment.)* It's black now. Night. It is night. Don't move. She's got to stay here or...

MESMER: No...

MARIA: She's got to stay...

MESMER: *(Responding to content of her words.)* No, Maria. Listen. Listen to me now. Don't be afraid. You're here. You're at home with me...you're at home with me now. Open your eyes, Maria, and you'll see, you're in my house and it is a beautiful morning.

MARIA: *(As if awakening.)*...it is so, beautiful.

MESMER: Maria?

MARIA: *(Looks at him.)* There you are. *(Discovering quietly.)* The brightness doesn't hurt...so strange...you spoke to me and then I felt as if I were, the way it used to be when I played. When I wasn't here anymore.

MESMER: You spoke to me just before about tigers and...

MARIA: Tigers?

MESMER: Yes. You seemed afraid. Said you were bleeding, you don't remember?

MARIA: Bleeding...? Was it a dream?

MESMER: Or memory perhaps, of an injury. You seemed...It was not a waking state, nor a sleep, but some state of a different nature...But now, you see quite clearly?

MARIA: *(Examining her hands.)* Yes...I feel fully here now, in this sunlight, in your house.

MESMER: You seem quite transformed. *(Quietly concluding for clinical notes.)* So the magnetism facilitated a beneficial crisis without the usual accompanying tremors or convulsion...

MARIA: The tiger! How can this tiger be hidden from me, yet revealed to you?

MESMER: You must stay quite calm now and not disturb the new equilibrium.

MARIA: If it is a memory, is it both then and now? And if it is my memory, why do I not remember it?

MESMER: You are a machine that thinks much too much...

MARIA: *(Discovering.)* But that is it. The thinking part but a hidden part, yes! Somewhere in me there must be a place that I do not know and you have found...like a spring that only a diviner could unearth!

MESMER: *(Gently, crossing to her.)* Maria, wait. Remember this is a physical phenomenon caused by an agent I have already identified as "animal magnetism" which acts upon us as an elemental force. This is not magic.

MARIA: *(Uncertainly.)* Of course...*(Grateful.)* But only a magician like you could have turned a tiger into sunlight and helped me to see.

MESMER: *(Tormented.)* Would that it were magic and I could simply perform it like a trick. Control it, fool everyone, then reveal the string I cunningly pulled to effect the illusion. But this phenomenon is genuine and so powerful I can only guess at its mechanism. I may be wrong about my own discovery.

MARIA: Ah.

MESMER: And about your music. What if I'm wrong?!

MARIA: That cannot be. You said you would never hurt me and I know that is the truth...that is the truth, is it not Franz?

(Lights shift.)

SCENE 15: DAMAGES (SECOND MOVE)

VON STOERCK: *(Crossing stage, sees Karl, stops.)* Karl...I was looking for you.

KARL: *(Small bow.)* Baron...?

VON STOERCK: Perhaps you can help me. I've placed a small wager on the blind prodigy. I'm half convinced she can see...

KARL: She sees fine, sir, not ordinary seeing like you or me but...

VON STOERCK: How then?

KARL: From a different angle, from inside out. *(Pointedly.)* She sees through things, sir, clear through everything!

VON STOERCK: *(Amused.)* But not walls. Not a witch?

KARL: *(Naive.)* No!

VON STOERCK: *(Amused, sly.)* But Karl, if she can see, why is she still at the clinic?

KARL: *(Lying badly.)* I don't know, sir.

VON STOERCK: No? Perhaps she's bewitched you, hmmm? And the doctor? Has she enchanted him as well?

KARL: I really wouldn't know anything like that, sir, really. *(Tries to exit, with bow.)*

VON STOERCK: Karl, if your doctor is disgraced and you stand by him, you'll find that despite your qualifications and rare tact, nobody in Vienna will hire you. Consider your future.

KARL: *(Angrily.)* I'm a good lad, sir.

VON STOERCK: Oh, don't let that become a handicap! *(Turns at exit.)* By the way, does the doctor know yet it was you who let the cat out of the bag?

(Lights shift to drawing room.)

SCENE 16: SIGHT OF THE EMPRESS

Maria is practicing piano during shift.

MESMER: *(Angrily, throws cape on chair, paper in hand.)* I've been deserted. They've dismissed your cure as fiction and issued a report that you can't see because you misnamed some objects presented to you!

MARIA: *(Stays at piano, thoughtfully.)* But all the visitors, surely...

MESMER: They contradict each other's testimony.

MARIA: So in the end, it all comes down to table settings.

MESMER: Fools.

(Pause.)

MARIA: You don't need them. Leave them to their remedies. Don't cut your discovery to their pattern or their size.

MESMER: *(Sits.)* Ah Maria...

MARIA: *(Crossing to him.)* Or Franklin's either. You hook yourself to Franklin's kite when you could soar beyond him...

MESMER: *(Distractedly, angry.)* How could I let them take me in? My mentor, von Stoerck...

MARIA: *(Kneels by him as he sits.)* Tell them you have found a great mystery and that you will spend your life investigating it! You'll return to the lake where you lived as a child with your true believer at your side!

MESMER: *(Gently.)* Such things are not possible. What a curious creature you are...

MARIA: Of course you must stay here in your home, your Vienna, your reputation, your important work...

MESMER: Vienna is your home as well...or is Karl right. Are you only visiting us?

MARIA: Did Karl say that?

MESMER: Yes. He said you come from another realm. From the stars. From Terra Incognita.

MARIA: To save you!

MESMER: How?

MARIA: We will go directly to Her Majesty the Queen Empress and I will present you to her as my healer. She is, after all, my patroness. And what she claims true is truth itself.

MESMER: ...And how will we prove to the Empress you can see?

MARIA: But I can see. I will walk into court and I will curtsey to Her Majesty and then raise my eyes to gaze at her directly. I am certain she is beautiful as she is kind...I will tell her so!

MESMER: ...But what if she asks you to play?

MARIA: We have time still. I will practice until I forget the keys. I can do this for you. I will try again with my eyes closed and practice and practice until my fingers remember.

(She sits, determined, at the piano and begins to practice as lights shift. Practice continues as Karl enters, crossing stage with mirror. Maria hears his steps, opens eyes, pulled out of her focus.)

KARL: *(Pushing mirror across, stops apologetically.)* Frau Mesmer wants it back in her rooms. *(Stops.)* Sorry, Fraulein, she wants me to move you to another room for now. Just temporary. Don't mind it.

MARIA: *(Distractedly.)* I don't mind it, Karl. *(She attempts to return to practice but after he exits she again hears footsteps, turns.)*...Franz? *(Startled, she regards mirror and sees Frau Mesmer looking at her through the frame as visitors had in prior scene.)*

FRAU MESMER: *(On tape, augmented voice.)* You must leave my house.

MARIA: *(Whisper.)* But where could I go?

FRAU MESMER: *(On tape.)* Roam the world for all I care. But leave. This is my family home. That is my mirror. Here is my garden, my clock... *(As ticking sound starts.)* My clock. You have one week. No more.

(Mirror becomes opaque as light shifts.)

SCENE 18: SIGHT OF BELVEDERE BY DAY

MARIA: *(Tense, overwrought, pale.)* Are you angry with me? What have I done?

MESMER: *(Overlaps, torn.)* No, no...it is only that we are being watched. We must be circumspect.

MARIA: *(Irony.)* Circumspect.

MESMER: We'll have only moments alone now...

MARIA: *(Tense, looking straight ahead.)* The red spot on the green is a "robin." I knew it from its song. Now the red spot has an eye, and it looks at me, then a sudden motion and it's vanished. The robin is a moment!

MESMER: Maria.

MARIA: I prefer the belvedere at night. When dusk falls. When we can see equally well...now all's just clutter. The trees are a tangle. And the trunks walk past me. And things come at me when I approach them. I grow faint from the landscape. From the thought of leaving.

MESMER: I am sorry. I don't think you can imagine how sorry, but...

MARIA: But? I do hate that word.

MESMER: (Uncomfortably, understatedly.) Frau Mesmer insists I tend to the other patients, and that I...I'm in an awkward position, you understand? Things have been said...

MARIA: (Interrupts, angry.) There appears to be a cloud on that tree, what is it?!

MESMER: (Looking, sadly.) "Blossoms" they're called.

MARIA: (Agitated.) Blossoms. Yes. I know, blossoms...I know leaves. Buds. Those yellow patches, "daffodils," under the tree of that cloud...blossoms. Yes, but there the blossoms beneath that tree are called "petals" but were they yellow they'd be daffodils again.

MESMER: Maria, stop!

MARIA: That ribbon there, all white and shining?

MESMER: The River Danube.

MARIA: And that shining?!

MESMER: (Looking in the direction of her gaze.) Holly. A kind of tree.

MARIA: The whole thing's like the stars! Isn't it? All laid out with invisible lines and then you all agree on what to name them, and you play this stupid game! When there are important things...it's falling apart again...and I feel faint.

MESMER: (Concerned about her mental state and her physical proximity.) Let's go back inside now please.
(Pause.)

MARIA: (Pulling away.) After the presentation...will I ever see you again?

MESMER: Of course.

MARIA: Of course?

MESMER: I'll visit you. In Paris. When you begin to tour again. I'll, arrange it somehow... (At her expression.) What's the matter?

MARIA: ...What if nothing is what it seems?

(Light shifts to individual lights on Mesmer and Maria.)

SCENE 19: SIGHT OF HIDDEN NOTES

MESMER: *(As testimony.)* Gradually she had learned to recognize common objects. At times she would gaze at a tree...suddenly it loomed huge and seemed to fill the landscape or a leaf would seem ablaze in the sunlight.

MARIA: *(As testimony.)* There were many times when I was preparing for the presentation when everything would suddenly fall away...everything. I would have to touch my own face to know that even I was still here, and then touch each thing until it became real again.

MESMER: *(Continues testimony.)* Sometimes she'd see as we might in a fast coach—with all hurtling by her, transforming and she'd say it was all dancing, and who was to say her vision was less true than our own.

MARIA: *(Continues testimony.)* And all the while there was no respite. The keys and fingers are in my head now, and there is no music anymore.

MESMER: *(Hearing Karl, moves into the moment in clinic seeing Karl at his desk.)* Karl! What are you doing?

KARL: She's not herself. Her spirit's gone *(Bitterly.)* and it's all for your sake she lost it!

MESMER: What more can I do?! You see how busy I am preparing for the presentation. What?

KARL: *(With Mesmer's notes in his hand, furious.)*...You wrote here, you set out to prove your system by this case.

MESMER: Karl.

KARL: *(Snatching paper, reading furiously.)* "This 'celebrated' sightless prodigy provides me with a striking undeniable cure with which to convince the entire world!"

MESMER: *(Arrested by words, a beat.)* Those are early notes...*(Furious at himself, takes it out on Karl.)* But I didn't know I housed a little thief.

KARL: You mean to prove this at any cost? Even if she never plays again.

MESMER: *(Justifying, but anguish under.)* If that were the cost of saving thousands from suffering...

KARL: But *she's* suffering. And all for you!

MESMER: *(Angry.)* I gave her *sight*. And I gave you a home.

KARL: You lied to her. You said you'd never hurt her!

MESMER: *(Anguished.)* You could never understand. Just get out. Get out!.

(He exits. Karl stands alone. Lights shift to downstage.)

SCENE 20: DAMAGES. LAST MOVE

VON STOERCK: *(Enters, hears Karl.)* It's the messenger, is it?

KARL: *(Crossing into scene.)*...I've considered well what to do.

VON STOERCK: And you have something to tell me, don't you? *(Noting Karl's hesitancy, takes out purse.)*...How valuable is the information?

KARL: I don't want nothing from you! Nothing!

VON STOERCK: *(Putting purse away.)*...What is it then, Karl?

KARL: He's not worthy of her. I was deceived by him and so is she...

VON STOERCK: Ah?...Surely that's not all?

KARL: They plan to go tomorrow to convince the Queen that Fraulein can see.

VON STOERCK: Thank you, Karl. As Her Majesty's personal physician I'll have them stopped.

KARL: *(Blurting it out.)*...She can see, sir. She can. But she can't play, and, I don't believe he can ever fix her right again.

VON STOERCK: *(Very surprised, dead halt.)* She can't play?

KARL: He wants her to be "whole" again before the experiment ends. He thought he could heal her, but he can't! The man's not God even though he thinks he is! He's not.

VON STOERCK: How interesting...I think somehow your doctor also forgot how to play.

KARL: What do you mean, sir?

VON STOERCK: Once in a very great while, when rumor turns out to be fact, there's a certain, frisson delicieux one feels, you know?

KARL: *(Disgusted.)* I wouldn't know anything about that, sir.

VON STOERCK: Oh, but you will.

(Von Stoerck exits in light shift. Lights shift to drawing room.)

SCENE 21: THE LAST SIGHT

Karl stands stunned, morose, angry, sees Maria. She enters wearing the formal dress she wears at top of play. She is regal in her walk and able to see, but she is quite tense. Karl falls to his knees distraught and weeps.

MARIA: Karl? What's the matter?
(Karl, overwhelmed by remorse, love and anguish, throws himself at her feet, crying and miserable. Maria is shocked and bewildered, bends over him.)

KARL: I'm sorry...I'm so sorry...

MARIA: (*Stands in pinlight, as Testimony.*) It was then he told me what he'd done. And why. The concealed things about Dr. von Stoerck, the scandal, the battle Dr. Mesmer waged and how I was being used. I did not believe him...(*Lights expand into moment.*) Why did you do it?!

KARL: To save you...To save you from becoming one of them. (*Rises.*) You'll become one of them, you will! (*He runs off and nearly crashes into Mesmer, who enters with a small packet in hand.*)

MARIA: (*Calling after him, alarmed.*) Karl!

MESMER: (*Angry at Karl and suspicious.*) What did he say to you? Why are you looking at me like that?

MARIA: (*Bewildered and alarmed.*) I don't understand...

MESMER: What lies did he tell you?

MARIA: I'm not sure.

MESMER: Nevermind. (*Taking her in.*) Look at you. You are exquisite. It will be a success! I can feel it!

MARIA: Yes.

MESMER: After the audience with the Empress, when you...have no more dis-tractions, you'll be able to devote yourself utterly to music again...

MARIA: Then?

MESMER: You'll be ready for your gift.

MARIA: What is it?

MESMER: It is for the future.

MARIA: But let me see it... (*Despite Mesmer, she opens it.*) What is it?

MESMER: The new concerto. That Mozart promised for your Paris concert.

MARIA: (*Studying it as something entirely new.*) But...What are...what are all these, these black marks?

MESMER: (*Surprised.*) Maria? Notes. They're, notes...That's, the way music is written... (*He picks up her book, holds as example and keeps this book in hand until end of play.*) It's written like words in a book...But no matter, you will take the concerto to Salieri and he will play it for you and it will be as it was...(you'll)

(*She holds in her hand the concerto, astonished during the above but there is loud knocking, She turns, startled, as Josef Paradies enters noisily, in a violent temper. He is followed by a worried but controlled Frau Mesmer.*)

JOSEF: (*Sees Maria, grabs her and drags her to piano.*) Play! (*Sheets of music fall, and Maria is horrified.*) Play! Go ahead, what're you waiting for?!

(Terrified, she sits, her hands frozen. Then, contained, final, to Frau Mesmer.) Have her things packed, she's coming home at once.

MARIA: *(Anguished from piano bench.)* No, Papa, please first (let me)...

JOSEF: *(Flat, incredulous.)* What?

MARIA: I...I can't leave, Papa...not yet. Not today!

JOSEF: *(Grabbing Maria viciously.)* How dare...How dare you speak back to me.

MESMER: Herr Paradies!

MARIA: Please, Papa!

JOSEF: *(Completely losing control, throws her across floor.)* You're in collusion with this charlatan. *(He strikes Maria very hard. Mesmer crosses to her, and she holds onto him fiercely as he raises her up. Then, only very slightly abashed.)* She's going home, I say! And now! Let her go.

MARIA: This is my home!

MESMER: *(Looking at Josef, furious.)* Can't you see she's hurt?!

JOSEF: And who hurt her, you, move off! *(Mesmer is shocked, doesn't move.)* She's worthless. And why? Because of your experiments! She can't play a note! She's useless. You've ruined her.

MESMER: Herr Paradies! I'm a physician, sir.

JOSEF: Are you? Her reputation's gone thanks to you.

MESMER: *(Reacting to implication.)* They're liars and scandalmongers. You know she sees and I am trying to heal her despite all of you!

JOSEF: Will you let her go!

MESMER: You won't let me heal her!

JOSEF: You've clearly seduced her!

MESMER: *(Hopeless predicament, beat, chooses.)*...She's, only an ailment I've treated and tried to restore to health. No more. I can do no more.

(At the above, Maria becomes rigid and gestures with her arms to erase them all. She waves away all sights. Blackout. The stage becomes night. Then dreamlight night, stars. Dream Belvedere. Music. Bear enters via the mirror. Maria, in her dream, sees bear emerge from mirror.)

SCENE 22: IN BEARSIGHT

MARIA: Ah. *(Dancing bear crosses slowly and nears Maria.)* Here you are. You're as lovely as the stars!

BEAR: Now I shall play something for you!

(Bear sits on piano bench. He begins piano part of Concerto 18 #456, brilliantly. Maria listens, rapt. He stops with a flourish.)

MARIA: What a beautiful concerto!

BEAR: It's yours!

MARIA: But I can't play it.

BEAR: Come, give me a kiss. *(Maria kisses the bear. Bear takes off his head. He is Mozart.)* There! Fooled you! Trompe l'oeil! *(Laughs.)*

MARIA: *(Total astonishment.)* And you've taken off your head!

BEAR/MOZART: *(As Mozart, reaches up to his head as if to take it off.)* Wanta see me take off this one, sweetie?

MARIA: No!

BEAR/MOZART: Know what's inside?...Nothing! Nothing! *(Mozart laughs.)*

MARIA: *(Wonderment and recognition.)* You're Mozart!

BEAR/MOZART: I'm nothing! That's how the music comes through! *(Laughs uproariously.)* A joke, a joke! It's all a joke! You know what I say? I say good riddance to the lot of 'em, that's what! All of them, Fraulein, but you. *(Kneels.)* To you I bring music. I dedicate my concerto to you! Play it for me. Think of me when you play it, think of what I tell you now: pay no attention to any of them. *(He kisses her hand.)* Always remember the three important truths!

MARIA: What are the three important truths?

BEAR/MOZART: Nothing is as it seems! Only music can be trusted! All freaks are beautiful! And Everything Important is Invisible!

MARIA: That's four!

BEAR/MOZART: I was joking! A joke. A joke. *(Crackling laughter.)* Now you must pay. Must pay. So play!

MARIA: But I...I can't just now...you see.

BEAR/MOZART: And why's that?

MARIA: There are things in my head.

BEAR/MOZART: Get rid of 'em! Take off your head, sweetie! *(He laughs, kisses her, puts on his bear head again.)*

MARIA: *(Astonished, holds music sheets in hand, joy.)* Thank you! Thank you for the concerto...

(Bear helps her to piano as light shifts to the Tuileries concert, 1784. Play begins again where it left off in scene one.)

SCENE 23: SIGHT UNSEEN

The stage is exactly as it was at the top of the play. Maria is at piano. Franklin stands where he stood.

MARIA: *(Evenly.)* It was February 9, 1777 the day I began seeing. I saw the doctor first, then the visitors, the bear, my father...and I was always, surprised.

FRANKLIN: *(Almost gently at piano.)* Did you truly see, child?

MARIA: Yes, I saw it all...for the first time. I saw how I was seen. How many views could be held of a single being. How little vision...finally I saw it all.

FRANKLIN: *(Gently.)*...I'm sure you were convinced you did. And now?

MARIA: I am cured of seeing.

FRANKLIN: You have managed not only to delude her, sir. But to confuse her. *(Crosses away. Stirrings, sounds.)*

MESMER: *(Steps near piano.)* You must have known you were no ailment to me. You must have known I didn't mean it.

MARIA: *(To him.)* I knew you better than you knew yourself.

MESMER: I never meant to hurt you.

MARIA: You meant to set me free.

(Stirrings, sounds, music.)

FRANKLIN: The Queen arrives and is taking her seat. *(Crossing downstage.)* My dear, you didn't play for the Empress but now you will play for her daughter. *(He taps his cane twice. Crosses downstage.)*

MESMER: Maria, listen...

MARIA: Farewell. *(She turns to Bear who stands near her, waiting.)*

MESMER: But she's seen everything. You heard her say so! She's living proof!

FRANKLIN: Proof indeed!

(The concerto begins with opening instrumental notes. Bear bows to Maria. She dances with Bear, played by Karl, to music as Franklin crosses all the way downstage.)

FRANKLIN: *(With coolness.)* Our recommendation: ban him. Condemn anybody practicing "mesmerisme." And let us all pray that no more ideas from Vienna pollute our True Science with odd speculation! *(To audience now and then.)* People come to me all the time with useful inventions! The water closet made more efficient. The fountain pen. Great idea! And these new velocipedes all over Paris now hold promise—need bells so they won't knock folks down—but otherwise excellent for small deliveries. Saves the horses. America will lead the way in practical improvements...We're at the threshold of a new age. *(The cyclorama darkens. He continues. Then during Franklin's next speech, the sky darkens a bit more as instrumental music of opening continues behind him. The bear hands him binoculars, returns Maria to piano bench, returns to basket and lifts off.)* Even now, at this moment, the newest marvel is about to soar! And all of Paris is out to see it, here in the Tuileries and on the streets and bridges! Never before was a scientific experiment so magnificently attended. The Montgolfier balloon ascends! Who knows to what great use these flying machines will be put when the world takes to aerial voyage!...The machine rises majestically from among the trees and all eyes are gratified with seeing it fly high above the buildings...a beautiful and promising spectacle. *(Wonderingly.)* I followed it until I lost sight of it...When I last saw the balloon it appeared no bigger than a walnut. What became of this experiment is not yet known here...

(Mesmer sadly looks at the book still held in hand, and he opens it to find the rose. He places it on piano. Sadly, turns away as the piano portion of the concerto starts.

Mesmer is very alone withdraws and the lights close in on Maria, rapt, playing. Then he turns and looks up sadly to the vast sky. Stars have appeared as the cyclorama goes to black, and as the sky blackens to night, a new constellation floats near the Polar Star. Piano section of Mozart's Paradies concerto grows louder and louder in black and finally the concerto envelops all.)

END OF PLAY

Icarus
by Edwin Sanchez

BIOGRAPHY

Edwin Sanchez's produced plays include *Unmerciful Good Fortune* (AT&T On Stage New Play Award and Princess Grace Playwriting Award) co-produced by Northlight Theatre and Victory Gardens in Chicago and Frontera at Hyde Park Theatre in Austin; *Clean* (Kennedy Center Fund for New American Plays winner and American Theatre Critics Association Best New Play nomination) produced at Hartford Stage in Connecticut; *Trafficking In Broken Hearts* at the Atlantic Theatre Company in New York and *Floorshow: Dona Sol and Her Trained Dog* at Latino Chicago. His plays have been workshopped at the Mark Taper Forum, Seattle Repertory, and South Coast Repertory for which he is currently commissioned to write a new play. He is the recipient of numerous awards and participated in the 1995 Sundance Screenwriting Lab. A 1994 graduate of the Yale School of Drama, he is a member of the Dramatists Guild and New Dramatists. He is also an artist in residence at the Public Theater in New York where *Icarus* was originally commissioned.

HUMANA FESTIVAL PRODUCTION

Icarus was first performed at the Humana Festival of New American Plays, March, 1997. It was directed by Melia Bensussen with the following cast:

Altagracia	Denise Casano
Primitivo	Nelson Vasquez
the Gloria	Julie Halston
Mr. Ellis	Ray Fry
Beau	Ross Gibby

and the following production staff:

Scenic Designer	Paul Owen
Costume Designer	Marcia Dixcy Jory
Lighting Designer	Greg Sullivan
Sound Designer	Robert Murphy
Properties Designer	Mark J. Bissonnette
Special Make-Up Design	Frank Wagner
Production Stage Manager	Debra Acquavella
Assistant Stage Manager	Cind Senensieb
Dramaturg	Liz Engelman
Casting	Laura Richin Casting

Icarus was commissioned and developed by the Josph Papp Public Theater/ New York Shakespeare Festival.

CHARACTERS

ALTAGRACIA

PRIMITIVO

the GLORIA

MR. ELLIS

BEAU

ICARUS

The roar of the ocean. The sound lessens as lights begin to rise on a beach. There are some dunes in the background. To one side of the beach is a wooden staircase that leads to a beach house and its porch. Glass doors lead from the porch to the rest of the house. Underneath, the porch is shrouded in darkness. Opposite this house we see the bedroom window of another house. On the porch of the other house is a chaise lounge, a vanity and chair and a sun lamp. Alatagracia enters, her face is very noticeably deformed. She is half wheeling half dragging a wheelchair on the beach in which Primitivo sits. She stops.

ALTAGRACIA: Now this looks like a nice spot, doesn't it? Doesn't it? *(Primitivo points, with a shaking hand, to a spot, dead center. Altagracia gives him a dirty look and pulls her fist back, as if to punch him. She drags the chair to the spot Primitivo pointed to. Sarcastically.)* Oh, yeah I can see where this is so much better. Okay, on your feet. *(She tries to pull Primitivo up, but can't. He is dead weight. There is a stand-off between them. He lowers his head and begins to cry softly.)* Sssh. Don't do that. It's okay. Okay? Okay? *(She makes cooing sounds and wipes his tears away. She gently lifts his head up.)*

PRIMITIVO: I'm tired.

ALTAGRACIA: It's okay, we're here. This is, this is the very house I was looking for. How about that?

PRIMITIVO: What if this one has people in it, too?

ALTAGRACIA: It doesn't. *(To herself.)* I hope.

PRIMITIVO: They'll make us go back.

ALTAGRACIA: No, they won't.

PRIMITIVO: How do you know?

ALTAGRACIA: What did I promise you?

PRIMITIVO: That everyone would know just how special I was.

ALTAGRACIA: *(She stands by the chair.)* Ladies and gentlemen, it is my great honor and privilege to introduce one of the most, what's this "one of the most?" the most, the most beloved and famous swimmer *(Primitivo hits her.)* person, most beloved and famous person in the world. Yes, we all love him, *(Primitivo tries to stand.)* here he is, the one, the only *(He tries again and awkwardly stands.)* Primitivo! *(Primitivo stretches his right arm to the sun, his fingers splayed out wide. He takes a very tentative step and suddenly collapses in the chair. She slowly begins to undress him, starting with the shoes.)* Let's get you into the water.

PRIMITIVO: It's too cold.

ALTAGRACIA: Uh uh, let Altagracia tell you how hot it feels. Why, it's the hottest day of the year. Why it's a heat wave right in the middle of March! *(As she removes his clothing, he begins to tremble from the cold.)* Feel the sun, the heat. It feels so good. *(He slowly stops trembling.)*

ALTAGRACIA: The sun is absolutely merciless. You could just about melt. Man, you are going to get such a tan. *(Primitivo throws his head back and sighs in contentment. Altagracia rubs her hands together for warmth, then goes back to undressing him.)* And all the people here love you. Every single one of them. They came out on the hottest day of the year to cheer you on! To pay their respects to the best. You, Primitivo, are the best. Shift. *(He shifts to the side. She pulls down his trousers. He is left in only his swimsuit. He trembles from the cold.)* Boy, is it hot out here or what? *(He stands and with one hand, reaches for the sun.)* Go get it, Primi. *(With great difficulty he runs, disappearing into the water. When the water hits him, he screams. She calls out to him.)* Oh, and the water, the water is so warm. It's almost soup. *(She takes a blanket from the backpack on the back of the wheelchair. She shakes it out and begins to hum and dance by herself. Mr. Ellis enters, he is a man in his fifties wearing a hospital maintenance worker's uniform. In one hand he carries a suitcase and in the other he carries Betty, an old stuffed cat.)*

MR. ELLIS: Where is he? *(Altagracia points to the water.)* How did you get him to get into the water on a day like today?

ALTAGRACIA: I have my ways. Have you got his fan letter?

MR. ELLIS: Yeah. You know, there are just so many ways you can say, "I'm your biggest fan". *(To Betty.)* Right, Betty?

ALTAGRACIA: So what do you think of the house? It's ours until somebody kicks us out. I figure we got a couple of months before the season starts and the owners show up.

MR. ELLIS: What then?

ALTAGRACIA: I'll think of something.

MR. ELLIS: You always have.

(Primitivo comes running, stumbling from the surf. He is soaking wet and shivering. He tries a little bow to the audience before collapsing on to the outstretched blanket Altagracia is holding. He knocks her down with him. She is laughing, while drying him with the blanket. He is shivering.)

PRIMITIVO: I came the closest I've ever come to it today. Closer than yesterday

PRIMITIVO & ALTAGRACIA: but not as close as tomorrow.

MR. ELLIS: Primitivo, you crazy man, why you wanna go in that icy water for?

PRIMITIVO: *(Referring to Mr. Ellis.)* Ah, get him away from here.

ALTAGRACIA: Honey—

PRIMITIVO: Who invited him anyway?

ALTAGRACIA: Primi, we need him. Stars have entourages.

PRIMITIVO: You said we were gonna get rid of him! You said we didn't have to bring him along with us! You said it was gonna be one night and then we would lose him! You said (last time was it.)

ALTAGRACIA: *(Cutting him off.)* Well, okay! I don't care what the hell I said. He is staying.

PRIMITIVO: Then, I'm going.

ALTAGRACIA: Go ahead. *(Primitivo tries to drag himself along. He reaches for his wheelchair and Altagracia moves it out of his reach. Again he almost touches it and again she moves it out of his reach. There is a stand-off. Altagracia crouches by Primitivo.)* I need him to...do things, you know? Like carry your...throne, here. And look at those stairs. I can't drag you up there by myself.

PRIMITIVO: He's not gonna touch me!

ALTAGRACIA: Okay, okay.

PRIMITIVO: I mean it. I'll get up there by myself.

ALTAGRACIA: Fine. Get dressed.

PRIMITIVO: And he's not allowed upstairs.

ALTAGRACIA: What?

PRIMITIVO: You can have one us of upstairs, but not both of us.

ALTAGRACIA: Primi, what has he ever done (to you?)

PRIMITIVO: *(Cutting her off.)* Non negotiable.

ALTAGRACIA: Fine. *(She goes to Mr. Ellis.)* Good news, Mr. E, Primi insisted you stay.

MR. ELLIS: So I heard. We could stay under the porch.

ALTAGRACIA: No, that's (ridiculous.)

PRIMITIVO: Works for me.

MR. ELLIS: We don't mind.

ALTAGRACIA: Let me set his highness up and I'll bring you something to drink, okay? (*She turns to Primitivo.*) Come on. (*She takes Primitivo's hands, holds them in front of her and carries him on her back, slowly up the stairs. She turns to address Mr. Ellis.*) I'll be right back.

MR. ELLIS: Check to see if the house is empty before dragging him up there.

ALTAGRACIA: Oh, I'm sure it is. (*Yells.*) Hey house, are you empty?! (*Pause.*) I think we're home. (*She makes it up to the porch and lies Primitivo on the floor.*) Now, it's just a matter of getting the door open.

MR. ELLIS: Can you do it?

PRIMITIVO: If she broke me out of a hospital she can break me in to a house. (*Altagracia opens the door.*)

ALTAGRACIA: Please, no applause.

PRIMITIVO: Ah, you just found the key under the mat.

ALTAGRACIA: Shut up and roll your ungrateful little ass in there. (*Primitivo, lying on the porch, rolls his body inside.porch. Mr. Ellis passes the wheelchair to Altagracia who goes into the house. Mr. Ellis goes under the porch.*)

ALTAGRACIA: (*V/O*) It's empty, Mr. Ellis. And so beautiful.

(*the Gloria appears at the bedroom of the other house, she looks out the window. She is a woman of indeterminate age, anywhere from 40 to 60. She is wearing full, theatrical makeup, an over teased bleach blonde hairstyle. Even though she is indoors, she is wearing sunglasses and a long pink net wrapped around her hair and neck to protect her hair style.*)

the GLORIA: I heard something. I distinctly heard someone say the word "beautiful". (*She disappears into her bedroom.*)

(*Altagracia comes out carrying a thermos and two mugs. She places one on the porch for Mr. Ellis. She bangs on the porch floor with her foot and his hand retrieves the cup. He and Betty come out from under the porch. He puts sunglasses on Betty and places her on the beach.*)

MR. ELLIS: You tired?

ALTAGRACIA: Nah, I got my second wind up that third hill. How do you two like it under the porch?

MR. ELLIS: Betty's making a real home out of it.

ALTAGRACIA: Uh huh.

(Altagracia and Mr. Ellis look out on the horizon.)
People actually live like this. And this is like just their vacation home. *(Primitivo rolls himself in, she hands him her cup and sits at his feet. He begins to massage her neck.)* A spare home. Can you stand it?

PRIMITIVO: It doesn't suck.

ALTAGRACIA: *(Enjoying the neck rub.)* Ah, that feels so good. You're the best. You could be a legend on just this alone. *(Primitivo violently shakes his head.)* But of course, the sun is waiting for you. Look at it, it's setting. It's waving goodbye to you. "It's saying, bye, bye Primitivo. See ya tomorrow."

PRIMITIVO: No, I think it's saying, "Altagracia, get a life."

(She playfully hits him.)

ALTAGRACIA: You're my life. I don't need anything else. I really don't like people, you know. I mean, what's to like? *(Primitivo nods. They are quiet. He kisses the top of her head.)* Thank goodness you're a people person, otherwise we would never be invited out.

PRIMITIVO: And when I'm not here?

(Mr. Ellis replaces the mug on the porch. He comes out and begins to dig in the sand next to Betty. He speaks into the hole.)

MR. ELLIS: I'm not staring. I'm not staring. I'm not staring. I'm not staring. Am I staring? I'm not staring. I'm not staring. I'm not staring. Am I staring? I'm not staring. I'm not staring. I'm not staring. I'm not staring. I'm not staring. Oh my God I'm staring.

PRIMITIVO: See, this is the kind of stuff he does that drives me nuts.

ALTAGRACIA: He puts up with your stuff.

PRIMITIVO: I don't have stuff.

ALTAGRACIA: Think again.

PRIMITIVO: Let's go inside.

(Primitivo mocks Mr. Ellis as Altagracia wheels him in.)

MR. ELLIS: I'm not staring. I'm not staring. I'm not staring. I'm not staring. Am I staring? I'm not staring. I'm not staring. I'm not staring. Am I staring? I'm not staring. I'm not staring. I'm not staring. I'm not staring. I'm not staring. Oh my God I'm staring. I'm not staring. I'm not staring. I'm not staring. I'm not staring. Am I staring? I'm not staring. I'm not staring. I'm not staring. Am I staring? I'm not staring. I'm not staring. I'm not staring. I'm not staring. I'm not staring. Oh my God I'm staring. *(He exits under the porch, leaving Betty on the beach.)*

(the Gloria enters her porch. She carries a cellular phone. Note: the Buddy she mentions in the phone call is a hustler that Stan has slept with.)

the GLORIA: Not Gloria, the Gloria. Small "the", Gloria. I'm sure Stan will take my call. Tell him, it's Buddy's friend. *(Pause.)* Tell him, Buddy would want him to talk to me. We go way back. *(Pause.)* Tell him not as far as he and Buddy go. *(Pause.)* Hi, Stan, sweetie honey baby. It's so nice of you to take my call. *(She studies her face in the mirror.)* Well, we've worked together before. You remember. I, I, I, I, did some um bits, ah, cameos, for you and then of course I was in Bed of Roses. Yeah, that was my only feature, how sweet of you to remember. No, it wasn't that long ago, was it? Well, I am currently in between representation and, actually I've been in Europe making some art films with the masters, you know. Well, they have yet to find distribution in the continental USA but you can catch them on cable in Puerto Rico. I don't mean, I don't mean to keep you. Well, you know how it is, since I've, uh, since I've been back I've been going from meeting to meeting and...yes, well...Buddy said he...nothing, huh...well thank you for your time. And...and. Wait, there's a party that I was hoping to go to...Yes. Why, just one little extra blonde wouldn't hurt. Look here, Buddy's a very good friend of mine and...no, of course not. Thanks anyway. Thank you very much. Thanks. *(She hangs up. She stretches her face with her hands.)* Come on. You can give me one more day. You owe me. *(She exits.)*

(Beau, wearing a ski mask that covers most of his face enters. He slows down a bit as he goes past Betty and then starts up the stairs leading to the porch of the house that Altagracia has taken over. Altagracia enters, at first just sees her from the back. When she turns they frighten each other.)

BEAU: Holy Christ!
ALTAGRACIA: Oh, my God!
(Pause.)
ALTAGRACIA & BEAU: I didn't mean to frighten you. *(Beau stares at her face for a second, then looks away.)*

ALTAGRACIA: Either you're repulsed or you're a gentleman; let's go with gentleman.

BEAU: It's...it's not

ALTAGRACIA: my face

BEAU: that. It's just that this house is supposed to be empty.

ALTAGRACIA: Oh, is this your house?

BEAU: No. A friend lent it to me.

ALTAGRACIA: How do I know you're not a burglar? I mean, what's with the mask?

BEAU: Look, this is Frank Hogan's house, isn't it?

ALTAGRACIA: Okay. I mean, yes, of course.

BEAU: Well, he's out of the country

ALTAGRACIA: *(Under her breath.)* Bingo.

BEAU: And, he said I could use it. As in me, alone.

ALTAGRACIA: He must have forgotten to tell you that he told us the same thing.

BEAU: Us? How do you know Frank?

ALTAGRACIA: So, what is the deal with the mask?

BEAU: You don't know him, do you?

ALTAGRACIA: The hell I don't. I'm his mistress.
    (Pause.)
    He's kinkier than you thought, huh.

BEAU: I'm calling the police. *(They stare at each other.)* I mean it.

ALTAGRACIA: So call them. *(Beau begins to climb the stairs. Altagracia stomps on the porch.)* Hey, Mr. E! *(Mr. Ellis comes out from under the porch.)* Primitivo! *(Primitivo awkwardly wheels himself in.)*

BEAU: What is this? How many more of you are there?

PRIMITIVO: *(Pointing to Beau.)* Hey, who's the ugly boy?

ALTAGRACIA: *(To Beau.)* Is that it? Is that why you're wearing that mask? Are you ugly, too?

BEAU: You all gotta get outta here. Right now.

PRIMITIVO: Just how ugly are we talking here?

BEAU: Look, do you folks need money?
    (Primitivo sticks his hand out for the money. Altagracia slaps it away.)

ALTAGRACIA: No, we're fine.

BEAU: Then I'll call you a cab.

ALTAGRACIA: No, I'll call you a cab. Look, I'm willing to share the house with you, because I know Fred wouldn't mind.

BEAU: Frank. You don't even know who the guy is.

ALTAGRACIA: I know...he's in Europe.

PRIMITIVO: Good one.

ALTAGRACIA: *(Making it up as she goes along.)* On business. A big deal. Very hush hush. That's why he lent us the house cause Primitivo, who's a very good friend of—

PRIMITIVO: Frank.

ALTAGRACIA: Frank, thank you. here is in training. I can't interfere with his training. I can't let anything interfere with his training. Training is everything. Our card. *(She pulls a business card from her pocket.)*

BEAU: *(Reading.)* "Primitivo"

ALTAGRACIA: Flip it over.

BEAU: *(He does.)* "Living Legend".

ALTAGRACIA: Can I have the card back? It's our only one.

BEAU: What does this living legend do?

ALTAGRACIA: He swims.

BEAU: He's in a wheelchair.

ALTAGRACIA: So? God blinked. My brother here will swim out into the ocean and when the sun is setting he will reach out and touch the sun. *(Primitivo takes a small bow.)*

BEAU: That's impossible.

ALTAGRACIA: Or so you've been told. Primitivo here knows the possible from the impossible. When he touches the sun history will be made, a legend will be born. We need to be close to the ocean for his training. Twice a day. That's why Frank lent us his house. That and because I'm a great lay. Did you know Frank has a mole by his left teste?

PRIMITIVO: *(To Beau.)* On a scale from one to ten, just how ugly would you say you are?

ALTAGRACIA: You know, you should wear your ugliness like a badge. I do.

MR. ELLIS: He's got ugly eyes, too.

ALTAGRACIA: Does he? I don't think so.

PRIMITIVO: I'm afraid I'm gonna have to go with Mr. E on this one.

BEAU: Would everybody just shut up for a second!? *(Silence. Altagracia pulls Beau aside, she speaks directly to him so Primitivo can't hear them.)*

ALTAGRACIA: There is no reason our ugliness can't coexist under the same roof. Frank would have wanted it that way. Let's do this for him, whaddya say? Look, the second he calls in I'll put him on the phone and you can ask him yourself.

BEAU: I'm here to get away from people.

ALTAGRACIA: We will so totally leave you alone. You won't even know my brother and me are here. Oh, and Mr. Ellis.

MR. ELLIS: And Betty.

BEAU: Who?

(Altagracia points to Betty, who's still basking on the beach.)

ALTAGRACIA: *(Under her breath.)* Don't ask.

BEAU: How long are you gonna stay?

ALTAGRACIA: How long are you gonna stay?

(She returns to Primitivo giving him a thumbs up.)

BEAU: Just keep out of my way.

ALTAGRACIA: Sure, sure. You're a prince among men. A giant. Oh and listen, that bread and peanut butter in the fridge is ours. I don't have to label it, do I?

BEAU: No. *(He goes upstairs to the porch.)* Just keep "the legend" out of the liquor cabinet. *(Points to Primitivo.)*

ALTAGRACIA: Primitivo.

BEAU: Yeah, whatever.

ALTAGRACIA:...Hey, you planning on taking off the mask? *(Beau enters the house. As she is about to enter the house she catches sight of herself in the glass door.)* Damn, it would have to be a bad hair day, wouldn't it?

PRIMITIVO: Yeah. *(Altagracia exits.)* Hey, Mr. E, whaddya think? Axe murderer?

MR. ELLIS: Who?

PRIMITIVO: What's his name?

MR. ELLIS: Of course not.

(He exits under the porch.)

PRIMITIVO: Probably had acid poured all over his face. Involved in some shady deal. Hunted by the police.

MR. ELLIS: *(V/O)* Maybe he's just come to get Altagracia.

(Altagracia enters and gently smooths Primitivo's hair, he is startled.)

ALTAGRACIA: Hey, hey. It's just me. So jumpy. You okay?

PRIMITIVO: I had a little nightmare. You were gone.

ALTAGRACIA: Where would I go? It's not like there's a bidding war going on over me.

PRIMITIVO: There will be.

(Beau enters.)

BEAU: I'm going for a walk.

PRIMITIVO: *(Full stage whisper.)* His name. Get his name.

ALTAGRACIA: Oh, what's your name?

BEAU: Beau.

ALTAGRACIA: Beau. Okay. Altagracia. *(Beau exits.)* Nice to meet you. Bye. I wonder what that smile looks like.

PRIMITIVO: Nightmare.

ALTAGRACIA: Well of course he's ugly, but personality has to count for something. *(Altagracia wheels Primitivo inside.)*

(Enter the Gloria, she stands in a spotlight she has made from her sun lamp and using her hairbrush as a microphone, begins to rehearse movements as if she were singing. She doesn't sing, just soft la la's as she moves.)

the GLORIA: No, let me try that again. *(She does a half spin again.)* Okay, okay. *(She slowly scans the nightclub audience she imagines.)*

the GLORIA: Lose your fear of them. Lose your fear of them. Lose your fear of them. *(She gently touches her forehead.)* Channel the diva, channel the diva, channel the diva. *(She closes her eyes tightly and faces her audience.)* Breathe. *(She takes a deep breath and resumes "chatting".)* Um, so anybody here from my home town? No, huh? I would like to do a little medley of my greatest hits. Feel free to applaud after recognizing each and every one of them. But please, don't sing along, it'll confuse me. *(the Gloria stops. She appears lost. She lowers her head, takes a deep breath. It should appear that she is about to sing.)*...Needs work. *(Applause is heard from under the porch. She panics and enters her house. Lights dim to early evening.)*

(Beau enters, walking back towards the house. Altagracia steps out on the porch, she faces the interior of the house and stands as if she were holding a camera aimed at the room inside.)

ALTAGRACIA: No, Primi, don't smile so much. Remember, these are supposed to be candid shots. I'm the paparazzi, the enemy.

PRIMITIVO: Blood sucking leeches.

ALTAGRACIA: That's better. Good. *(Altagracia enters the house, miming a crazed paparazzi hard at work.)*

(Mr. Ellis enters. He places an empty bowl in front of Betty. He is carrying a letter he is writing. He speaks to Betty.)

MR. ELLIS: How about, "Your magnificence has been an inspiration to one and all," you like that?...Yeah, thought so. *(He runs back under the porch.)*

(Beau has witnessed both little scenes take place. He walks up to Betty. He picks up her bowl and turns it upside down. It is empty. He places it back in front of her and sits next to her.)

BEAU: Come here often? *(He picks her up.)* The scary part is you and me may be the normal ones.

MR. ELLIS: *(Reentering.)* Put her down. *(Beau does.)* Never, ever touch Betty again.

BEAU: Fine.

MR. ELLIS: Sign this. *(He tries to hands a letter to Beau who looks at it quizzically and begins to read it.)* Don't read it just sign it.

BEAU: I don't have to sign something. Trust me, I won't touch her.

MR. ELLIS: It's a fan letter.

BEAU: For who?

MR. ELLIS: Primitivo. I figured now that you're here we can take turns signing them.

BEAU: I'm not signing this. You can all be crazy if you want, but count me out. *(Mr. Ellis, holding Betty by the head, hits Beau with her body as he turns away. Beau whirls around to Mr. Ellis, who is now cradling Betty.)*

MR. ELLIS: The ugly man is very selfish, isn't he?
(Beau grabs at Betty. Both he and Mr. Ellis have a part of her.)

BEAU: Here's the deal. I never touch Betty and you never, ever touch me again. Otherwise you'll wake up one day and Betty will be buried in sand and you won't know where. You got that?
(Mr. Ellis nods. Beau lets go of Betty.)

MR. ELLIS: A different signature would make it look more real. It's just a little favor; something you do for somebody else. I'm sure you got somebody you would do anything for.
(Pause. Beau grabs the paper and signs it.)

BEAU: This doesn't mean anything. *(Mr. Ellis folds the letter and puts it away. Before he turns away he stands behind Beau and reaches at his mask, as if to remove it. Beau speaks without turning around.)* Touch the mask and die.

(Mr. Ellis and Betty disappears under the porch. Altagracia and Primitivo enter the porch.)

ALTAGRACIA: *(As she wheels in Primitivo.)* Okay, you're at dinner, seated on your right is Patty Duke

PRIMITIVO: Loved you in Me, Natalie. *The Patty Duke Show* is a classic. *Valley of the Dolls* was ahead of it's time.

(Beau climbs the stairs, stands watching them.)

ALTAGRACIA: On your left side is John Astin—

PRIMITIVO: Whaddya nuts? They were married, they wouldn't be seated next to each other.

(Altagracia gives him a kiss.)

ALTAGRACIA: Good boy. Okay, you're at a White House dinner and you feel a hand on your knee, realizing it could only be a member of the first family, you

(Primitivo spots Beau and angrily motions to Altagracia to get rid of him.)

ALTAGRACIA: We're really busy right now.

BEAU: Doing what?

ALTAGRACIA: Well, when Primi here becomes famous, you know, he's gonna be invited to all these Hollywood type parties you know so we're just, you know, laying the ground work for conversation, you know. So when he's introduced to all these people, you know, he'll have something to say. You know, small talk. We're practicing.

BEAU: You're practicing small talk? *(Altagracia and Primitivo nod.)* Maybe while you're at it you could practice a reality check. *(Beau tries to walk past Primitivo who suddenly lunges from his chair at Beau, knocking him down, and begins to hit him. Altagracia tries to pull him off.)*

ALTAGRACIA: Whoa! Hey, get off him! Now. Now! *(Beau tries to hold Primitivo's hands. Altagracia grabs Primitivo around the waist and throws herself back, pulling him on top of her. For a moment they all stare at each other.)* We'll get our things together and be out of here by tonight.

BEAU: No. I apologize. *(Silence. To Primitivo:)* I'm sorry, Primitivo.

(Primitivo rolls his body away from Altagracia to the wheelchair. From the side pocket he retrieves a cheap daytimer. He hands it to Beau.)

PRIMITIVO: We're legit. We even got ourselves a...what you call it?

ALTAGRACIA: Schedule.

PRIMITIVO: Yeah, schedule.

(Beau reads from the daytimer.)

BEAU: Eight to ten a.m.— swimming, ten to ten thirty—power breakfast, ten thirty to eleven thirty—grooming, eleven thirty to one—practice interview technique—

(Altagracia rips the daytimer out of Beau's hands.)

PRIMITIVO: Go ahead, tell him.

ALTAGRACIA: One to two thirty—business lunch, two thirty to three—practice autograph signing—*(Beau suppresses a laugh when Altagracia shoots him an angry look.)* Three to four—rehearse candid photo ops, four to five—fine tune Oscar acceptance speech, five to seven—swimming, seven to nine— dinner and small talk class, nine to midnight—free.

PRIMITIVO: But open.

BEAU: That's incredible.

ALTAGRACIA: *(Suspiciously.)* What is?

BEAU: I've never met an Oscar winner before.

PRIMITIVO: *(Smiles.)* Well, not yet.

BEAU: You're a sure thing. Can't lose with Altagracia behind you. Can I have your autograph?

ALTAGRACIA: No.

(Primitivo takes the daytimer from Altagracia. With a great flourish he rips out a page and signs his name.)

ALTAGRACIA: Don't personalize it. It'll have more resale value if it isn't personalized.

BEAU: *(Mocking them.)* Oh, I'd never sell it. Some things are priceless.

ALTAGRACIA: Not priceless, sacred. Some things are sacred.

(Primitivo gives Beau his autograph.)

BEAU: Thank you.

PRIMITIVO: *(Proudly.)* You're very welcome.

ALTAGRACIA: *(To Primitivo.)* Let's go inside, okay?

BEAU: *(To Primitivo.)* Can I help you into the chair?

ALTAGRACIA: No. *(Beau picks up Primitivo and puts him on his chair.)* I said, "no". *(Beau gets behind the chair ready to push it. Altagracia hits him on the arm.)* You haven't earned that yet. *(She motions Beau to step over to her, a few steps away from Primitivo.)* Understand this even if you never understand anything else about us, if you are ever disrespectful to our dreams again I will kill you. *(She goes back to Primitivo.)* All right, Spielberg turns to you and says he loves your work, you say-

PRIMITIVO: What I really want to do is direct.

(Altagracia and Primitivo exit into the house. Mr. Ellis comes out from under the porch.)

MR. ELLIS: You don't ever mess with him when she's around. She's this puny thing but I've seen her attach herself to the back of an orderly like a leech and it takes two full grown men to pull her off.

BEAU: You don't believe he's gonna touch the sun, do you?

MR. ELLIS: Of course not. *(He drags out his suitcase.)* I tried to explain to them that I have all the dreams. In here. And I ain't giving nothing to nobody. But you, I like you, so I'll sell you one. Cheap.

BEAU: I'll pass.

(Mr. Ellis opens his suitcase, slightly.)

MR. ELLIS: Oh come on. Don't you want just one dream?

BEAU: None that you would have in there.

MR. ELLIS: There's nothing you'd wish for? Nothing that would make your life complete? Go ahead, reach inside, take one. I got one with your name on it. Go on. What if you could have any dream but you missed it cause you wouldn't even try? Wouldn't even try. Go on. Go on.

(Beau slowly approaches the suitcase. He is about to place his hand inside when Mr. Ellis snaps the suitcase shut, barely missing him.)

BEAU: Son of a bitch.

(MR. Ellis runs under the porch.)

MR. ELLIS: *(V/O)* Betty, I got another one.

(Altagracia enters.)

BEAU: That guy is outta here. Now.

ALTAGRACIA: He's just *(playing.)*

BEAU: *(Cutting her off.)* He's gone.

ALTAGRACIA: I don't throw people away.

BEAU: I'm not gonna argue with you.

ALTAGRACIA: He stays. This is non-negotiable. There. I said it first. I win.

BEAU: You're lucky I'm letting you stay.

ALTAGRACIA: Excuse me, what was that? Cause I was ready to leave just a second ago. *(She comes downstairs to the beach.)* And please hand over the Primi's autograph.

BEAU: Why?

ALTAGRACIA: You don't deserve it.

(Beau takes it out of his pocket and gives it to her.)

BEAU: I'm sorry I embarrassed you in front of Primitivo.

ALTAGRACIA: I don't get embarrassed. It's a luxury I can't afford. You can't afford it either, bucko, not anymore. *(Silence.)* I know why you wanted me to stay.

BEAU: I don't care if you stay.

ALTAGRACIA: You're hoping I can teach you how to be ugly. I was telling Primi you were new at this ugly thing.

BEAU: How can you tell?

ALTAGRACIA: You don't own it, it still owns you. Your face, I mean. So what was it? Fire, car accident, jealous lover?

BEAU: Car accident. My brother died.

ALTAGRACIA: Sorry.

BEAU: You're a good sister. Mine hated me.

ALTAGRACIA: Why?

BEAU: Something about me being born.

(They laugh a little, relax.)

ALTAGRACIA: I think family's sacred.

BEAU: Where is your family?

ALTAGRACIA: Right here. *(Pause.)* I like big families, you know. I want to have a lot of kids.

(Primitivo wheels himself out on the porch. He sees Beau and Altagracia.)

BEAU: If you had a baby aren't you afraid it would...never mind.

ALTAGRACIA: Look like me?

BEAU: I'm sorry.

ALTAGRACIA: I don't know. It might.

BEAU: Not that that would be a bad thing.

ALTAGRACIA: Oh, of course not.

BEAU: You know,...uh, you have really...pretty...hair.

ALTAGRACIA: Uh huh.

BEAU: And nice ears.

ALTAGRACIA: Nice ears? All the better to hear you with. Yeah, my lobes are the talk of the town.

BEAU: And...

(He looks away.)

ALTAGRACIA: You have to sort of look at them to see them.

(She stares at him. He looks at her.)

BEAU: Beautiful eyes.

ALTAGRACIA: Nice eyes.

BEAU: No. Beautiful eyes.

ALTAGRACIA:...Thank you. So, are you as ugly as I am?

BEAU: Nothing could prepare you for how ugly I am.

ALTAGRACIA: You know, I don't know what anybody told you, but it's not your fault. The way you look, is not. Your. Fault. And you can't control how people are going to respond to it. Learn from me. I'm shameless, I'm guiltless.

(They stare at each other until Mr. Ellis enters. He begins to make a hole in the sand where he will bury some old letters.)

MR. ELLIS: *(Into the hole.)* I'm not staring. I'm not staring. I'm not staring. I'm not staring. Am I staring? *(Softly repeats and fades.)*

PRIMITIVO: Hey!

ALTAGRACIA: Yeah?

PRIMITIVO: You're supposed to interview me.

ALTAGRACIA: Duty calls. *(Altagracia and Beau walk back to the house. She gives him back the autograph.)* Here. Primi's autograph. You better treasure it. Goodnight.

MR. ELLIS: *(Not looking up.)* Goodnight.

ALTAGRACIA: *(Laughs and gently nudges Beau.)* Hey you snooze, you lose.
(Beau stops her before she goes up the stairs.)

BEAU: You would do anything for Primitivo, wouldn't you?

ALTAGRACIA: *(Loudly, so Primitivo can hear her.)* For old meal ticket? Hell yes. *(To Beau.)* I would do anything for him. *(She skips upstairs and begins to wheel Primitivo offstage.)* So, are you sleeping with the president's wife, or not?

PRIMITIVO: Please, I'm an artist. I just want to discuss my work.

(They exit. Beau looks after them. the Gloria enters her porch.)

the GLORIA: Hi.

BEAU: Hi.

the GLORIA: I dropped my telephone on the beach. Do you see it?

BEAU: *(Looks around.)* No.
(While he is looking the other way, the Gloria tosses her phone on the beach.)

the GLORIA: There it is. Can you bring it up? *(Beau climbs her stairs, as he does, the Gloria dims her light and places her net scarf over her head, putting a gauze shell over her face.)* You a skier?

BEAU: No. I have no face.

the GLORIA: That's terrible. What do you see when you look in the mirror? I don't know what I'd do without mine. Not that it hasn't brought me its share of problems. Like, it's so hard for beautiful women like me to have a friend, cause everybody always winds up wanting something from me. Or jealous of me, like it was my fault I was born looking the way I do. Sure I'm gorgeous, but do people see the responsibility? No. Sit. *(Beau is about to.)* No, over there. I look better from over there. *(Beau remains standing.)* You know, stranger

BEAU: Beau.

the GLORIA: No, stay a stranger. I'll be the Gloria, small the, Gloria, and you remain unknown. It'll be easier. How old would you say I am?

BEAU: Hard to tell with that rag on your head.

the GLORIA: *(Defeated.)* Thanks for bringing up my phone.

BEAU: *(Apologetically.)* You look young. Real young.

the GLORIA: *(Big smile.)* Your mama raised you right. You know, I kind of like the fact that you don't have a face, don't have a name. I can have the name and face for both of us. Why don't you kiss me? *(Beau turns to exit. She hands him the phone.)* Here, you can keep it. Just stay. I'm going to this wonderful party, I hope, and I always look better right after, well you know, I do it. Everybody does. You will, too. Your skin glows and your eyes shine and you walk different. *(Beau places the phone on her vanity.)* It's not like I'm using you. It's mutual use. That's okay, isn't it?

BEAU: It would be if you could make me forget, but you can't, so what's the point?

(He exits.)

the GLORIA: If you hear of anything I am currently seeking representation.

(Next day. Altagracia and Beau are on separate ends of the beach. She is holding a towel and watching Primitivo as he swims. Beau is lying on the beach with his arm covering his face; he sits up, looks at the Gloria's house, then at Altagracia who is intently watching Primitivo.)

BEAU: *(Softly.)* What do you see when you look in the mirror?

(Altagracia faces him.)

ALTAGRACIA: What?

BEAU: Nothing.

ALTAGRACIA: Okay. *(Pause.)* Killer eyes. That's what I see when I look in the mirror. Killer eyes.

(Next day. Altagracia enters with a beer can. She pops it open. Mr. Ellis hears the pop and places his hand on the porch, looking for his beer.)

MR. ELLIS: *(V/O)* Can I have one? *(No answer. His hand disappears and returns with an envelope.)* Here's today's fan letter. *(Altalgracia reaches into the kitchen and retrieves another beer that she hands to Mr. Ellis. She takes the letter from him. Primitivo wheels himself onto the porch. He also has a beer. He has a note pad on his lap.)*

PRIMITIVO: Which autograph do you like better?

ALTAGRACIA: Oh gee honey, they're all fine.

PRIMITIVO: I'm trying to work the humility angle with this one.

(He and Altagracia see Beau approaching the house. She gives the fan letter to Primitivo, takes the beer from him and heads towards Beau.)

ALTAGRACIA: Oh, you still here?
(She hands him a beer.)

BEAU: Help yourself to some of my beers.

ALTAGRACIA: Thanks. *(She sips.)* So, just how attractive were you?

BEAU: Does is matter?
(He takes a sip.)

ALTAGRACIA: Just curious. No pictures?

BEAU: Sorry.
(They both sip.)

ALTAGRACIA: I just want to know how much you lost.

BEAU: None of your goddamn business!

ALTAGRACIA: Hey, I am the last person you want to alienate. I know what your future is, bucko. *(Beau turns to leave.)* Ugly 101.
(She blocks his way.)

ALTAGRACIA: I'll teach you. Lesson one; people are evil. If you work from that simple truth everything else is easy. *(She sits on the sand and pulls him down.)* Hey, you really are ugly, aren't you?

BEAU: Yes.

ALTAGRACIA: Say it.

BEAU: I am the ugliest person I know.

ALTAGRACIA: When I was a mere slip of a girl I went to my high school prom. This is not gonna bring up any evil high school memories, is it?

BEAU: No, when I was a mere slip of a girl I skipped the prom.

ALTAGRACIA: I hate you.

BEAU: I hate you worse.

ALTAGRACIA: I hate you best. *(They sip.)* I had no intention of like going but my mother found out the theme was Mardi Gras and that everyone had to wear a mask. She became like a woman possessed. It mattered so much to her that I let myself be talked into it. Let her spend money we didn't have on this beautiful red velvet dress, let her make this gorgeous mask of feathers and sequins. I even let her pay my cousin to take me. She took a polaroid of us and she and Primi waved us off. I thought my heart was gonna pop out of my chest. There I was outside the gymnasium door, and on the other side, everyone who had ever made my life hell for the past twelve years. The doors open, and all eyes turn to face the fairy princess.

(She sips. Beau leans in almost in spite of himself.)

BEAU:...What happened?

ALTAGRACIA: Not a single person recognized me. Not a soul. I was the mystery girl. If I could bottle any moment in my life that would be it. Then somebody figured out who I was. And they all looked away, like they were embarrassed for me. Like I had been caught trying to pull something off. But I fixed them. I took over the prom. I got in the middle of the dance floor with my arms spread out, taking up as much space as I could and I started spinning around. And while I was out there no one else dared to dance. They didn't have the guts to look me in the eye. It became my prom, all mine. *(She drains her beer.)* Sometimes, you just gotta make people feel uncomfortable. Make the golden people look away.

BEAU: You could look away first.

ALTAGRACIA: Why should I? Why should you? *(They stare at each other. She smiles.)* Ugly 101. *(She crushes her beer can.)* Now you were just about to tell me what you looked like.

(Beau takes a sip of his beer. Rises.)

BEAU: Good night.

(He begins to walk away.)

ALTAGRACIA: I made the whole thing up. Everything was a lie.

BEAU: Altagracia, I really don't care.

ALTAGRACIA: You did for a second. I saw it.

(Silence.)

PRIMITIVO: Hey, Altagracia, it's time for my photo ops.

(He wheels himself inside.)

ALTAGRACIA: He's jealous. Thinks you're going to come between us.

BEAU: What do you think will happen when he finds out you've been lying to him.

ALTAGRACIA: Stretch your arm out.

BEAU: Why?

ALTAGRACIA: Stretch your arm out. *(Beau does.)* Try to touch the moon.

BEAU: He gets the sun, I get the moon.

ALTAGRACIA: Men are so competitive; now, close your eyes. *(Beau does.)* Okay, can you feel the moon?

BEAU: Of course not.

ALTAGRACIA: But what if you did it everyday and one day you did? You'd be holding light in your hand. What would that feel like? Hot? Icy? Would it go up from your hand and all through your body to here? *(She gently pats his stomach.)* Or to here. *(She gently touches his heart.)* Or here. *(She touches his face. Beau flinches.)* I'm not gonna take off your mask. So is it here that you feel the light?

(Beau nods.)

PRIMITIVO: *(V/O)* Altagracia!

ALTAGRACIA: Put your hand down. *(Beau does.)* Wouldn't it be scary if no one knew you better than I did?

(Primitivo wheels himself out. Altagracia sees him.)

ALTAGRACIA: I'm on it. I'm on it! *(She takes Beau's beer and finishes it as she walks seductively back up the stairs.)* God, flirting is fun!

(Both Primitivo and Beau stare at her until she disappears into the house.)

PRIMITIVO: Hey, ugly boy, I don't suppose you're much of a dater, you masturbate much? *(Beau starts to leave.)* What do you think about when you do it? Who do you think about? *(Beau stops.)* It better not be Altagracia. *(He goes inside the house.)*

(Next day. Altagracia, Beau and Mr. Ellis are on the beach. Beau is sitting closer to Altagracia, they are both staring at Primitivo who is not having an easy time with his swimming. Mr. Ellis is burying a baby's rattle while softly doing his chant.)

BEAU: Water's pretty choppy today.

ALTAGRACIA: It's fine.

BEAU: Maybe he should come in.

ALTAGRACIA: He's still got another ten minutes.

(Primitivo goes under, both Altagracia and Beau tense up. She involuntarily grabs his hand. They both relax when they see that Primitivo is all right.)

BEAU: He's okay.

ALTAGRACIA: Of course he is. I know what I'm doing.

BEAU: Or maybe you've just been lucky.

ALTAGRACIA: Do I look like the lucky type?

(Beau returns his stare to the ocean, she looks at him. Under her breath.)

Are you falling in love with me yet?

BEAU: What?!

ALTAGRACIA: *(Snapping her attention back to Primitivo.)* Go Primi go!

MR. ELLIS: *(Looking up at Beau and Altagracia.)* Oh my God I'm staring.

(Later. the Gloria holds up her picture to her reflection.)

the GLORIA: This is what I'm supposed to see when I look into you. This is the me that I know.

BEAU: Hi, Miss the Gloria.

the GLORIA: *(She hides her photo.)* Ah, my fan. *(Beau sits watching the Gloria.)* Did I tell you I am currently seeking representation? *(Beau lights a cigarette, he approaches the Gloria who stops him.)* Don't get any closer. Six feet. For your maximum viewing pleasure the Gloria should be seen at a distance no less than six feet.

BEAU: You're very beautiful. You're what I should want. Can I sleep with you tonight?

the GLORIA: As long as you promise to leave the second there is even the faintest glimmer of natural light.

BEAU: I can do that. I can leave.

the GLORIA: Yes, you strike me as the kind that could.

(They kiss. Lights shift to dawn. Primitivo enters and waits for Beau. Beau enters.)

PRIMITIVO: Where were you? *(No response from Beau.)* Mr. E thought you had run off. I knew you hadn't.

BEAU: Why wouldn't I leave? What would keep me here?

(No response from Primitivo.)

PRIMITIVO: What does Mr. Ellis know, he's crazy, but she won't get rid of him. *(Laughs.)* Did he pull the dream thing on you? He does it to everybody. And everybody always falls for it....Why are you here?

(Beau tries to go past him into the house, Primitivo grabs his arm. Altagracia enters the porch.)

ALTAGRACIA: Good, the team's up. I got a good feeling about today. *(To Beau.)* Help me get him downstairs.

PRIMITIVO: He didn't come home last night. *(Silence.)* Did you hear me? He didn't come (home last night.)

ALTAGRACIA: *(Cutting him off.)* And? *(Beau enters the house. Primitivo is silent.)* Is this the part where I care?

(She upends his wheelchair sending him crashing to the floor and storms into the house.)

(the Gloria enters her porch as Primitivo struggles to get up.)

the GLORIA: It's good to see a young man exercising.

PRIMITIVO: What?

the GLORIA: You're doing push ups, aren't you?

PRIMITIVO: Oh, yeah. Ninety eight, ninety nine, one hundred. Yeah, a couple of sets of these babies everyday and, hey, I know you. You're the Gloria.

(He sits facing her, with his legs hanging off the porch.)

the GLORIA: You can't possibly remember me.

PRIMITIVO: Feature film debut in *Bed of Roses*, game show staple and...

the GLORIA: Yes.

PRIMITIVO: I like you a lot.

the GLORIA: Why, thank you.

PRIMITIVO: Wow. the Gloria. You're beautiful.

(the Gloria laughs coquettishly.)

the GLORIA: Just for future reference how far away are we from each other right now?

PRIMITIVO: I'm in the business too.

the GLORIA: Isn't that nice. Do you have any contacts?

PRIMITIVO: Well, no...but I get fan mail.

the GLORIA: No contacts at all?

PRIMITIVO: Not yet.

the GLORIA: I'm trying to get an invite to a party.

PRIMITIVO: Call them.

the GLORIA: I did.

PRIMITIVO: But, you're the Gloria.

the GLORIA: You sound just like my first husband. Just being me should be enough. Wally used to say that his job was to keep the Gloria unaware.

And as long as he was here, I was. Would you like to come over for a drink?

PRIMITIVO: I...I can't.

the GLORIA: In training, huh?

PRIMITIVO: Yeah...What did he keep you unaware about?

the GLORIA: Rain check on that drink? I do so admire the physically fit.

PRIMITIVO: Can I have a picture?

the GLORIA: But of course.

(the Gloria kisses an 8 x 10 photo of herself and tosses it to Primitivo. Mr. Ellis runs out and retrieves it taking it with him under the porch.)

PRIMITIVO: Hey!

(Beau enters with his bag. He puts it down and helps Primitivo back into his chair.)

BEAU: Listen, I think I should leave. This is not working out. It's a little too crowded for me.

PRIMITIVO: Hey, no problem. *(Calls into the house.)* Altagracia!

BEAU: Sssh, no, don't call her.

PRIMITIVO: I knew you wouldn't last. *(Altagracia enters, wearing an apron and drying a dish.)* Beau's leaving. He just wants to say goodbye. *(Altagracia takes off the apron and puts it and the dish on Primitivo's lap as she walks past Beau, totally ignoring him.)* She don't take people leaving too well.

(Altagracia goes to a high spot on the beach where she sits, Beau follows her.)

ALTAGRACIA: Goodbye.

BEAU: I...

ALTAGRACIA: This is the part where you say goodbye. *(Beau turns to leave. Softly.)* Stay.

BEAU: What?

ALTAGRACIA: I'm seeing a movie.

(She points to where she is looking.)

ALTAGRACIA: Over there. They have a big screen TV. It's like being at a drive in. Sometimes I sneak out here when everybody's asleep. It's so quiet. Even I'm quiet. *(Beau again turns to leave.)* You...you can't hear the dialogue so you kind of have to sort of make it up.

(He watches her watch the movie. Silence.)

BEAU: He should leave.

ALTAGRACIA: Why?

BEAU: Anybody can see he's not good enough for her.

ALTAGRACIA: I don't see her complaining.

BEAU: She should. She can do better.

ALTAGRACIA: Maybe. Maybe not. Maybe he thinks he can do better. *(Silence.)* He already has, hasn't he?

BEAU: He probably thought he had. What do you think is gonna happen?

ALTAGRACIA: I don't know. We're making it up as we go along. *(Silence. He fakes a huge yawn so he can put his arm around her, but before he can she places her arms around him. They are the most embarrassed people in the world. He is about to kiss her. She stops him.)* You closed your eyes.

BEAU: No I didn't.

ALTAGRACIA: Yes, you did.

BEAU: If I did it's just cause it's more romantic.

(Altagracia pulls her arm back.)

ALTAGRACIA: Not to me it isn't. Maybe you could have closed your eyes before, but not now. You're not that person anymore. If you're going, go, if not I expect you to get Primitivo to the beach tomorrow morning. If you're there, fine if not that's fine, too.

(She turns and exits. Mr. Ellis comes out from under the porch. He smacks the back of Beau's head.)

MR. ELLIS: You were going, right? What's holding you up? Leave. Go get your bag. But you can only take what you brought in. Don't try to sneak something else out. *(Holding Betty up.)* We'll be watching you.

(Next day. Primitivo wearing a robe, a beret and sunglasses, wheels himself on to the porch. Removing his beret and sunglasses he takes a deep theatrical breath.)

PRIMITIVO: Oh, ugly boy! *(Beau climbs to the porch. Altagracia enters, they avoid eye contact.)* Just one big happy family. The Mansons.

ALTAGRACIA: Could you please help Primitivo to the beach.

PRIMITIVO: *(To Altagracia.)* Oh, and could you get the radio? I got a little surprise for you. *(Altagracia exits. Primitivo extends his arms to Beau, so that he can lift him.)* You may carry me down now. *(Beau grabs his ankles and drags him down the stairs so that Primitivo lands on his rear on every step.)* Hey! Hey! You're supposed to carry me!

(When they reach the bottom Altagracia enters from the house. She is carrying the radio.)

ALTAGRACIA: That was quick.

PRIMITIVO: You have no idea.

(Altagracia kisses Primitivo.)

ALTAGRACIA: Into the water, my darling. *(Altagracia takes his robe, he reaches for the sun with his fingers splayed and half walks, half stumbles into the water. There is an awkward silence between Altagracia and Beau. Altagracia stares intently at Primitivo in the water until she senses Beau staring at her.)* Quit it. Didn't anybody ever teach you that it's impolite to stare.

BEAU: Uh huh.

(He continues staring.)

ALTAGRACIA: So stop.

BEAU: ...I can't.

(Altagracia looks at him, then looks away into the water.)

ALTAGRACIA: Look at him go. He's the best.

BEAU: Even the best can't touch the sun.

ALTAGRACIA: He's in the ocean, isn't he? Swimming, isn't he? And everyday he's doing that I buy another day with him and that's what's important. I could have listened to people like you and just sat back and watched him waste away, but I know what I know and I know my brother is destined for greatness and to hell with the disbelievers. As long as my brother is alive he is on his way to the sun. That is non negotiable. And not you, not you or anyone else can convince me otherwise. Do you think he can, Beau, yes or no, cause I need to know. I need to know if you're willing to go with us. If you can.

(Silence. Beau begins to cheer Primitivo on. Slowly at first and building in power.)

BEAU: Go. Go. Go. Go! Go! Come on, you can do it. You're the best, Primitivo. Nobody like you, Primitivo. Come on, Primitivo, come on. Yes! He isssssss thee one. Pri-mi-ti-vo! Pri-mi-ti-vo! He can feel the sun against his fingertips. So close. So close. He's gonna do it. I'm telling you, I know this for a fact, Primitivo is gonna do it. He's coming back; let's swim out to him.

ALTAGRACIA: I can't. I don't know how.

BEAU: What? Come on.

(He tries to push her into the water. He picks her up.)

ALTAGRACIA: I'm not going into the water. I mean it.

BEAU: *(Still carrying Altagracia.)* Okay, then I'm going in. *(She begins to tickle him, he collapses with her.)* Okay, I give. You win.

(They are laughing and about to kiss when Primitivo enters, soaking wet, he collapses on the sand.)

PRIMITIVO: I suppose a towel is out of the question.

ALTAGRACIA: Oh, oh of course not.

(She dries him.)

BEAU: *(Slapping Primitivo on the back.)* Really looking good out there, Primi.

PRIMITIVO: *(Looking Beau up and down.)* Uh huh. Listen, Altagracia, obviously Beau's medication has finally kicked in so since it's almost time for my interview why doesn't he interview me?

ALTAGRACIA: You really want him to?

PRIMITIVO: Yeah. And while he's doing that I was thinking you could listen to the radio and he could teach you how to dance.

ALTAGRACIA: Oh, no no no no no.

PRIMITIVO: Come on, we're going to be going to all these Hollywood parties and people are going to expect you to dance.

ALTAGRACIA: Primi, maybe Beau doesn't know how to dance.

BEAU: I know

ALTAGRACIA: And maybe I don't want

BEAU: how.

ALTAGRACIA: to learn.

PRIMITIVO: She's never learned cause there's never been anyone

ALTAGRACIA: Hello. I'm here.

PRIMITIVO: she could look at. To dance you have to look into somebody's eyes. And more importantly they have to look back into hers.

ALTAGRACIA: *(To Beau.)* You don't have to.

PRIMITIVO: No, Beau, you don't have to.

(Beau offers his hand to Altagracia.)

ALTAGRACIA: Forget it.

(Beau bows to her, again offering his hand.)

BEAU: If you would do me the honor.

ALTAGRACIA: God, ugly and corny.

PRIMITIVO: Pick some nice music.

(She turns on the radio.)

ALTAGRACIA: Oh, God. Okay I got a ballad going here.

BEAU: Watch my feet.

ALTAGRACIA: Just watch out for mine.

PRIMITIVO: Do the hustle.

BEAU: No. We are going to slow dance. We'll start simple.

ALTAGRACIA: Yeah, whatever. Let's just get this over with. Hey, there's an interview supposed to be happening here.

(She is staring at her feet.)

PRIMITIVO: Lose yourself in the music, Altagracia.

(Altagracia does.)

BEAU: So, any truth to the rumors linking you to that Venezuelan starlet?

PRIMITIVO: Please. I am a gentleman.

BEAU: Your last three films tanked at the box office. Are you on a downward spiral from which your career will never recover?

PRIMITIVO: Dip her. Dip her. *(He makes the obnoxious disco sound.)* Ooooh, ooooh.

BEAU: God, your brother is such an asshole.

ALTAGRACIA: *(Not hearing him.)*...You have such safe eyes. Where did you ever get such safe eyes?

PRIMITIVO: What I really want to do is direct.

BEAU: All right then, let's say you're directing the story of this girl. The film opens and she's...?

PRIMITIVO: I'm directing it?

BEAU: Un filme de Primitivo.

ALTAGRACIA: Look into my eyes.

(She twirls gracefully.)

PRIMITIVO: It would be a fairy tale about how the love of a prince makes her beautiful. How they make each other beautiful.

BEAU: What if they can't? What if he can't?

(Primitivo turns off the radio.)

ALTAGRACIA: What if what can't?

(Primitivo suddenly comes between them.)

PRIMITIVO: You're right. Okay, that's enough.

ALTAGRACIA: *(To Beau.)* Thanks for the dance. *(She stares into his eyes.)*...Can...can I please see your face. I don't care what you looked like before, I just want to see you as you are now.

(She takes Beau's hand.)

BEAU: I'm not good enough for you. I wish I was. I'd give anything if I was, but I'm not. *(She touches his mask. Beau removes his mask. He is the most beautiful man she has ever seen.)* I'm sorry.

(Silence.)

ALTAGRACIA: Oh wow. *(Laughs.)* You're...beautiful. Perfect. Well, you really got me. You fooled the ugly girl, didn't you? I fell, I admit it. Well, no harm done. Come on, Primi.

(Beau tries to touch her.)

BEAU: Forgive me. *(Altagracia whirls on him and begins to beat him. Primitivo tries to hold her and she pushes him away.)* Let her go! Let her go! *(Beau allows himself to be hit until she is spent. She sits next to Primitivo, trying to disappear into him.)*

ALTAGRACIA: Get out.

BEAU: Altagracia.

(Mr. Ellis emerges.)

ALTAGRACIA: Get out. Go back to the golden world where you belong.

MR. ELLIS: What did I tell you kids? I warned you about dreaming?

PRIMITIVO: I knew you weren't good enough for her. You're not good enough for anybody. *(Struggling to stand.)* Why don't you go back and tell all your friends about the losers, about the freaks you fooled?

ALTAGRACIA: Come on.

(Primitivo pushes her off.)

PRIMITIVO: The freaks who trusted you.

(Altagracia pulls Primitivo and they help each other towards the house.)

MR. ELLIS: That's what you get. You pretend you have a right to dream. Who gave you that right? Who the hell are you, either of you, that you should be allowed to dream? And you couldn't dream small, neither, you had to dream big, as if you were worthy, as if you were good enough.

(Beau throws his mask at Mr. Ellis and runs and blocks the way of Altagracia and Primitivo.)

BEAU: I'll race you. I'll race you to the sun.

(Primitivo turns to face Beau, as Altagracia tries to pull him along.)

ALTAGRACIA: Come on he's laughing at us.

(Beau grabs Primitivo's arm.)

BEAU: How about it, Primi, you and me in a swim off to the sun. Think you can take me? Think you can take on the golden world?

ALTAGRACIA: No.

PRIMITIVO: I didn't know bastards could swim.

BEAU: The first one to touch the sun wins.

ALTAGRACIA: Primi, we are not going to jump the gun. We have a lot of pre-press work to do.

BEAU: Friday.

PRIMITIVO: Thursday's sooner.

ALTAGRACIA: Perhaps you two little shits didn't hear me. I said "no".

BEAU: You want to shake on it or does she do that for you too?

(Altagracia pushes Beau away.)

ALTAGRACIA: Okay, we're going inside now. This conversation is over.
(She tries to push Primitivo towards the house but he will not move.)
BEAU: What do you say?
PRIMITIVO: You're on, Beautiful Boy. Shake. *(Primitivo and Beau shake hands.)*

(Early evening. the Gloria enters her porch and looks up at the sky.)

the GLORIA: Star light, star bright
    First star I see tonight
    Wish I may, wish I might
    Have the wish I wish tonight
    (She is about to enter her bedroom, stops.)
    Pretty please.
    (Her phone rings, she runs inside to answer it. Before entering she turns and looks up at the stars.)
    Thank you!
    (She runs indoors.)

(Sunrise. Beau enters from the house, rubbing the sleep from his eyes. Altagracia, Mr. Ellis and Betty are watching Primitivo swim. Mr. Ellis notices Beau.)

MR. ELLIS: He's here.
ALTAGRACIA: The wave.
    (She and Mr. Ellis, holding Betty aloft, wave to Primitivo. Even Beau does from the back.)
BEAU: Wow. How far out is he. *(Silence.)* That's, that's really far, isn't it?
    (He is ignored. Mr. Ellis and Betty head towards the back and resume Mr. Ellis' burial and chant. He is burying house keys.)
MR. ELLIS: I'm not staring. *(Repeats and fades.)*
    (Altagracia walks over to Beau.)
ALTAGRACIA: Look at him as he swims back. So graceful. That's beauty. Earned
    beauty.
BEAU: He's waving at us.
ALTAGRACIA: No, he's giving you the finger.
BEAU: You used to like me when I didn't have a face.
ALTAGRACIA: I knew that person.
    (Primitivo enters from the water. Altagracia lovingly wraps him in a towel.)

PRIMITIVO: I was kind of afraid of you before but not anymore. You're going to become exhausted out there. Your lungs will collapse and they'll fill with water and the only person who can save you will be me, but I'll be too busy touching the sun. *(Pointing to the ocean.)* She's all yours. I'm sure you'll want to practice. I should warn you, she's a little choppy and watch out for her undertow, she doesn't let go easily.

(Primitivo and Altagracia exit. Beau goes to the Gloria. Lights up on the Gloria. She is wearing a facial masque and has a strapped on ice pack around her eyes.)

the GLORIA: Halt, who goes there?

BEAU: It's just me, Miss the Gloria.

the GLORIA: Ah, my fan. But you shouldn't see me like this. I'm a work in progress. Turn away.

BEAU: You look fine.

the GLORIA: Turn away! Have you?

BEAU: Yes.

(He hasn't.)

the GLORIA: I'll have to take your word as a gentleman that indeed you have. *(Beau turns around.)* You're here much too early. the Gloria is best seen under man made illumination. Nonetheless, I'm so glad you're here. I have so much to tell you.

BEAU: Has it ever occurred to you that every time I see you we only talk about you?

the GLORIA: You say that as if it were a bad thing.

BEAU: Do you ever wonder what I look like?

the GLORIA: You're going to give me frown lines. I won't like you anymore if I get frown lines.

BEAU: Do you ever ask yourself, "why you?". "Why are you so beautiful?"

the GLORIA: Massage my feet, please. *(Beau does.)* Because I can handle the stress. Not everyone could, you know. The weight, the burden, the responsibility that comes from being everybody's fantasy.

BEAU: I have my mask off. Do you wanna see me?

the GLORIA: Of course not. I already have my image of you. Whatever you do, whatever it takes, maintain the illusion. It's hard work, it's a full time job, but it's worth it.

BEAU: And what will you do when your beauty is gone?

(Panic stricken, the Gloria stops him.)

the GLORIA: I haven't faded, have I? This is the only currency I have.

BEAU: No, you're still perfect.

the GLORIA: You frightened me. I mean, who would ever want me without my face?

BEAU: Goodbye now.

the GLORIA: Bye bye.

(Beau exits. Mr. Ellis sits on the beach, a pair of baby shoes by his side. He is too tired to dig.)

MR. ELLIS: I'm not staring, I'm not staring, I'm not staring, I'm not staring, am I staring, I'm not staring, I'm not staring, I'm not staring, I'm not staring, I'm...not...I don't like to remember. I don't. *(Beau stops.)* I didn't have a lot. A wife and a child, that's all, and still it was too much for me to keep. *(Beau sits by him and takes his shovel and begins to dig for him. Mr. Ellis grabs his wrists and stops him.)* You weren't invited to help. If you have something you don't want to remember go find your own beach. *(Altagracia brings Primitivo downstairs to the beach.)*

PRIMITIVO: We should be sending out press releases.

ALTAGRACIA: I'm on it.

PRIMITIVO: And we'll need VIP seating.

ALTAGRACIA: Uh huh.

PRIMITIVO: And maybe baton twirlers.

MR. ELLIS: When their parents stopped coming she was there day after day holding his hand. Using her ugliness like a club to get anything he need-ed. But with you she's become weak. That's not good. You take her strength and don't give her anything in return. She's afraid. What do you think his losing will do to her?

BEAU: Are you so sure I'm gonna win?

MR. ELLIS: You're not gonna win. You're just gonna beat him.

BEAU: But if he beat me everything would be perfect.

ALTAGRACIA: I need to talk to you. We need to discuss terms of the race.

PRIMITIVO: The rules.

ALTAGRACIA: Yeah, the rules.

BEAU: We get in the water and swim. One of us wins

PRIMITIVO: Me.

BEAU: and one of us loses.

PRIMITIVO: You.

ALTAGRACIA: Primi, let management manage, okay? That's why I'm getting the big bucks. Why don't you practice your victory speech?

PRIMITIVO: Okay, but don't give away the foreign distribution rights. Remember, I'm right here.

(Altagraica sits on a step.)

ALTAGRACIA: Step into my office.

(Beau sits next to Altagracia who finds herself too close to him so she moves up a step.)

BEAU: So Thursday's the big day, huh? Primitivo seems really excited.

ALTAGRACIA: Yeah.

BEAU: How's that?

ALTAGRACIA: I said "yeah".

BEAU: Are you talking to me or to your feet?

ALTAGRACIA:...You gotta go. Please.

BEAU: I got a race to win.

ALTAGRACIA: Why are you doing this?

BEAU: I thought this is what you wanted.

ALTAGRACIA: I wanted Primitivo to swim.

BEAU: He's not swimming?

ALTAGRACIA: Farther and better than ever. No complaining, either.

BEAU: Then what's the problem? You still believe he can touch the sun? Right?

ALTAGRACIA:...Sure I do.

BEAU: Then you should be grateful I'm staying. I'll give him a chance to prove it.

ALTAGRACIA: You're right.

BEAU: If anybody can, he can. You just lost your faith for a second, that's all.

ALTAGRACIA: Yeah.

BEAU: I guess I should go practice.

(Altagracia grabs his arm.)

ALTAGRACIA: Are you really gonna go through with this? *(Beau nods his head and strips down to his bathing trunks as he goes into the water. Primitivo does his Sun touch, stretched arm with splayed fingers as he watches Beau swimming. Altagracia sits next to Mr. Ellis, who opens his suitcase and retrieves a brooch from it.)* Pretty.

MR. ELLIS: Cheap. My wife's one piece of Christmas jewelry. She'd wear it exactly from December first to January seventh. I didn't even know I had it.

(He drops the broach in the hole and buries it.)

ALTAGRACIA: You know, in the summer, some little kid with a sand shovel is gonna find it.

MR. ELLIS: It might be her. Reincarnated.

ALTAGRACIA: Oh, please.

MR. ELLIS: She'll have a feeling of deja vu.

ALTAGRACIA: I can barely survive going through this once. Let alone over and over again.

MR. ELLIS: Next time it would be different.

ALTAGRACIA: I'd want it in writing, notarized and blessed by the pope.

(She picks up Betty and holds her close.)

MR. ELLIS: We both know you can't control how somebody feels, don't we? *(Altagracia nods.)* I don't want you to get hurt, little girl. Dreams can protect you so no one can hurt you. *(He slowly, seductively offers to open his suitcase.)* I can help you. Cause dreams are my business. Reach in, I'll let you have one on account. Go on. *(Altagracia is unsure. Mr. Ellis points to Beau in the water.)* The beautiful boy is pretty good out there, isn't he?

ALTAGRACIA: I hadn't noticed.

MR. ELLIS: One dream. Any dream at all. Cause you mean so much to me.

(Altagracia is about to reach in when Mr. Ellis suddenly snaps the suitcase shut, barely missing her hand. She hits him and storms upstairs.)

ALTAGRACIA: Asshole!

(She exits.)

MR. ELLIS: Better I should squash your dreams than someone who doesn't love you.

(the Gloria enters her porch, wearing sunglasses and sees Primitivo laying in the sun. Mr. Ellis, upon seeing her, runs under the porch.)

the GLORIA: You were quite the athlete out there.

PRIMITIVO: Miss the Gloria.

the GLORIA: I've never seen anyone swim quite the way you do, with so much passion. Such a handsome boy. Am I making you blush?

PRIMITIVO: Uh, no.

the GLORIA: Yes I am. That's so sweet. Hardly anybody blushes anymore. Come on up for that drink I promised you I have tons of good news. I got invited to the party of the year!

PRIMITIVO: That's great.

the GLORIA: Very last minute, you understand, but what do I care. And I can bring a guest. I'd love to show up with someone as handsome as you on my arm. How about it? It's Wednesday night. We could dance the night away.

PRIMITIVO: I don't dance.

the GLORIA: I can teach you. I can teach anybody.

PRIMITIVO: I'm booked for another party.

the GLORIA: Well, that's a shame. I would have made it a very special evening for you. Maybe I will afterwards.

PRIMITIVO: Yeah, maybe.

the GLORIA: And there's more. I got a part!

PRIMITIVO: You got another feature?

the GLORIA: Yes! Well, actually I'm just doing it as a favor for a friend, it's sort of a, uh sub cameo. I'm in the background but really the entire scene hinges around me. I'm the center of attention. I've decided I'm going to do it all with my eyes.

(She removes her sunglasses.)

PRIMITIVO: Congratulations.

the GLORIA: In lesser hands this would just be a glorified extra, in my hands it's a lock on a best supporting actress nod.

PRIMITIVO: I'm sure you'll be wonderful.

the GLORIA: And beautiful.

PRIMITIVO: Very, very beautiful.

the GLORIA: Come on up and give me a little good luck kiss. Don't be so shy.

PRIMITIVO: I can't.

the GLORIA: *(Not hearing him. Looking out at the ocean.)* Who's that walking this way?

PRIMITIVO: Nobody.

the GLORIA: He's beautiful.

PRIMITIVO: Yeah.

the GLORIA: Don't be jealous. You're both very, very attractive.

PRIMITIVO: Yeah, we're equals.

the GLORIA: I'll see you after the party then?

PRIMITIVO: It's a date. *(the Gloria disappears into her bedroom. Beau enters from the water, he is framed by light.)* I swear the word "Mattel" must be tattooed somewhere on his ass.

(Beau is limping, he crashes on the sand in pain.)

BEAU: Ow ow ow ow ow.

PRIMITIVO: Leg cramp, huh? Must be a bitch.

(*Primitivo drags himself over.*)

BEAU: Don't touch it.

(*Primitivo very gently takes Beau's leg.*)

PRIMITIVO: Don't worry. Slowly. Slowly.

BEAU: Ouch.

(*Primitivo very gently begins to massage Beau's leg.*)

PRIMITIVO: Real soft, see? Very gently. Breathe into it.

BEAU: Ow, ow, ow, oh. (*He exhales.*) Oh God. I'm not used to swimming this much. Especially against such a great competitor.

PRIMITIVO: I'm still gonna beat you. (*Silence.*) Guess it'll be the first time you ever lose at anything, huh?

BEAU:...Yeah. Very first.

PRIMITIVO: I figured...What's it like to be you? To be golden.

BEAU: Perfect. What else could it be?

(*Beau rises and goes towards the house.*)

MR. ELLIS: He didn't have to stay, you know.

PRIMITIVO: What and miss a chance to go head to head with me?

MR. ELLIS: So he's staying just for you?

PRIMITIVO: He doesn't care about my sister.

MR. ELLIS: Maybe he cares for her just a little?

PRIMITIVO: They don't match. They look stupid. He could have anybody, what does he want with Altagracia?

MR. ELLIS: You mean cause she's so ugly? It's not like she could fall in love.

PRIMITIVO: I didn't say that. My earliest memory is of her face. She would tell me she was smiling and she had to tell me cause I couldn't tell. He took from her the one face that she thought smiled like hers.

MR. ELLIS: You're so sure he can't possibly want her?

PRIMITIVO: Not unless he's into science fiction.

MR. ELLIS: And if she wants him?

PRIMITIVO: We got each other. We don't need anybody else.

MR. ELLIS: And of course, you'll never leave.

PRIMITIVO: Would Betty leave?

(*Mr. Ellis drops Betty in the hole he has dug and begins to bury her.*)

MR. ELLIS: She's gone. Maybe to a lot of people she wasn't much but she made me happy. I should have known I wouldn't be able to keep her.

PRIMITIVO: yeah.

(Sunset. Altagracia is on the beach, Beau enters from the house, goes halfway down the stairs and watches her.)

ALTAGRACIA: Go away.

BEAU: You got eyes in the back of your head?

ALTAGRACIA: Wouldn't that complete a pretty picture?

BEAU: Don't turn around. Let's talk without looking at each other. What did you think was under my mask?

ALTAGRACIA: ...I figured, no, I knew that in the accident you had been trapped inside the car with your brother. After the car had turned over a few times it started burning. You got yourself lose from the seat belt and with your feet you managed to break the windshield. Your brother was unconscious so you had to drag him out, cutting your face on the windshield as you struggled to free him. And even though the heat of the flames was so hot it was like your face was melting you kept going. You got his body outside and tried to revive him. Nothing worked, and your tears and your blood fell on him. And you never forgave yourself, and you never will. *(Beau walks away.)* So am I right? *(She turns to where she thinks he is.)* Score one for the ugly girl.

(Primitivo enters.)

PRIMITIVO: I'll get you the next ugly boy. I promise. *(Altagracia walks past him into the house.)* Altagracia.

(Beau runs back to the house.)

PRIMITIVO: Tell me something, when I beat you are you just gonna leave?

BEAU: Yeah.

PRIMITIVO: Alone, right? *(Altagracia enters with a glass of soda, when she sees Beau she is about to go back into the house.)* I said, "Alone, right?"

(Beau grabs Altagracia by the arm.)

BEAU: Look, forget about the race for a second.

PRIMITIVO: Hold up, whaddya mean forget...(about the race).

MR. ELLIS: Primitivo, shut up.

BEAU: Would you marry the person you thought I was?

ALTAGRACIA: What?

BEAU: Would you marry him? That person. Will you marry me?

(The glass falls from Altagracia's hand and shatters.)

ALTAGRACIA: ...No. No thank you. *(She begins to pick up the pieces of the broken glass.)* Anything else?

BEAU: No. Hey, I was just trying to do you a favor, that's all. You don't want to? Fine. Fine! You know what your trouble is? You don't know when to be grateful. You think you're too good for a mercy fuck.

(Altagracia whips around to face him. She has a piece of broken glass in her hand and lunges for his face. She stops herself, but Beau grabs her wrist and tries to force her to cut his face.)

BEAU: Go ahead. Rip it apart. Do it. Do it!

(Altalgracia bites Beau's hand, forcing him to let her go. She begins to heave, then runs into the house. Beau stands there for a moment, looking after her and is about to enter the house.)

PRIMITIVO: Don't. *(Beau holds the door handle.)* Leave it alone.

(Beau comes down the stairs.)

the GLORIA: *(Unheard by the others.)* How can somebody so beautiful be so ugly.

(She disappears back into her bedroom. Her bedroom light goes out.)

PRIMITIVO: You want your face gone? Give me the broken glass. I'll do it. I won't hesitate a second, but then you wouldn't have it to fall back on, would you?

(Beau runs to the Gloria's door, it is locked.)

the GLORIA: *(V/O)* Go away.

(Beau climbs down the steps and sits on the dune. Altagracia comes downstairs and puts her head in Primitivo's lap.)

PRIMITIVO: You okay?

ALTAGRACIA: Heaved my guts out.

PRIMITIVO: That's attractive. *(Pause.)* You don't love him do you?

ALTAGRACIA:...No.

PRIMITIVO: You would tell me if you did, wouldn't you? *(Silence.)* Why would he go and propose the day before the race? *(Altagracia sits up, she realizes Beau had some sort of plan. She goes to him.)* I'll buy a dream from you, Mr. E., make him good enough.

MR. ELLIS: I don't think I have that in my bag.

PRIMITIVO: I want to go to the sun so much.

MR. ELLIS: What about her? If you leave her behind she'll never forgive you.

PRIMITIVO: It's okay if she hates me, it might be good for her. I'm her mask. With me she's not the girl with the ugly face; she's the sister who would do anything for her brother. I have to trust that he sees her the same way

I see her. But I don't know if he does. How do you give up the person you love most in the world?

MR. ELLIS: You don't. You carry her with you for always.

BEAU: I was gonna let him win, you know. I swear to you, I wouldn't beat him. I figured I'd get a leg cramp and he'd have to stop and help me.

ALTAGRACIA: And what if he didn't?

BEAU: He'd have to.

ALTAGRACIA: Would you? Would you give up everything you had ever dreamed of?

BEAU: I had this plan of going to Hollywood to be discovered. So me and my brother stole the family car and took off. Hey, with my looks how could I miss? We were driving on some back road in Texas and I'm massaging Phillip's neck when this jeep pulls up alongside us and I hear someone yell "Faggot!" and this beer bottle comes flying at us. Phillip floors it, turns off the lights and tries to lose them. All the time I'm thinking, "Wait a second, we're not gay. We're brothers. This is a mistake." They force us off the road and drag us out of the car. They shine a flashlight in Phillip's face, then mine. And like an idiot I smile. Hey, my smile was always my secret weapon. Somebody punches me in the stomach and Phillip screams to leave me alone. So they hold me down and beat him. Take out a baseball bat and beat him. They make me kiss the bat with my brother's blood. And I do. Cause I was afraid. Cause I was,.. am a coward. See, that's something you would never have done. You would have let them kill you. You would have found a way to save your brother. I see Phillip die and when they're done with him the gang leader takes my face in his hands. So gently. "Don't cry, you can do better, you're so beautiful.", then he spits in my face and they scatter leaving me to me. My brother lies dead, while you promise yours the sun. See how your eyes fooled you? See how I'm even less than you thought I was?

(Altagracia touches his face.)

ALTAGRACIA:...If you stay, he'll race you. And I can't risk that. I won't. You have to go.

BEAU: Okay. I'll leave before the race.

(He rises.)

ALTAGRACIA:...Beau...

BEAU: Tell him...tell him I chickened out.

(Mr. Ellis goes under the stairs as Beau heads for the stairs.)

PRIMITIVO: So you and Altagracia made up. That's nice. You know, other than that unfortunate last part I thought your proposal went pretty well.

BEAU: You want to take a swing at me?

PRIMITIVO: More than life itself. I'll get my revenge in the water. Can you help me in my chair? Uh, please. *(Beau lifts him.)* Why did you propose to Altagracia? *(Silence.)* There is only one right answer to that question, you know.

BEAU: I know.

PRIMITIVO: You're the one she wants.

BEAU: She said no.

PRIMITIVO: No can mean a lot of things. Look at that. It's gonna be a nice sunset. Buttermilk sky. *(Silence. Points to the sky.)* What do you see up there? In the clouds.

BEAU: Clouds.

PRIMITIVO: Yeah, clouds, but you don't see, maybe a cat? Now, really look.

BEAU: Okay, I see a cat.

PRIMITIVO: And if I say it's a dog?

BEAU: Fine. It's a dog.

PRIMITIVO: No. It's not fine. No. If you see a cat, then that's what you see. Fight for it. You have to fight for what you see. Trust your eyes. Can you do that?

BEAU: Yeah...Can she?

(Beau enters the house as Altagracia approaches.)

PRIMITIVO: Where have you been? I have to work on my victory speech. So few people to thank, so much time.

(They disappear into the house. Mr. Ellis enters with his suitcase. the Gloria enters, her long pink net scarf wrapped around her hairdo. She is a bit tipsy.)

the GLORIA: Excuse me. *(Mr. Ellis stares at her.)* Helloooo. I'm looking for my date. Um, how silly, I don't even know his name. He's a swimmer. He's very young, and very handsome and he's not doing me a favor, you know. I am not his mercy,...date. I wanted to tell him everything that had happened. He has some connections so I'm sure he'll be able to help me. Would you be a love and give him the shortest little message? Can you do that? *(Mr. Ellis nods, he places his suitcase on its side so the Gloria can sit on it.)* Ooooh. A gentleman. They are in scarce supply. This is how a goddess should be treated. Tell him, tell him that the party was fabulous. I was looking wonderful and I had the tiniest little pint of courage, just to steel my nerves and headed to this marvelous A list party. I was in shape, the lights were low and my eyes could still focus. I walked around, sort of knowing people but not really knowing anyone. And then this year's blonde walked in. Lovely girl! Full of shyness and living on promise. Her film has not been released yet but oh the inside buzz is very "promising". She is moist and new. I had been her. I looked at her and surprised myself by not hating her. Her glow. Did I glow like that? Everybody wants to make sure she catches them smiling at her. Just in case she turns out to be the real thing. *(She smiles and winks.)* "Remember I smiled at you. Remember, you owe me." I need to warn her about the burden of possibility. With everyone surrounding her, how can she breathe? I take her a drink. My, this could be some photo op. Yesterday's Blonde and Tomorrow's Blonde. No one wants to give up their space next to her and who can blame them? Her heat was my heat and my heat was fabulous! I am by her side and she takes my hand and shakes it, giving me one of those glazed smiling faces. The one that says, "Thank you for worshipping, now move along." And I toss the drink in her face, followed by the glass, followed by my fist. I was thrown out. I was thrown away. How about that?...How about that? *(She rises.)* Tell him to come over whenever he gets in. But tell him, not the really beautiful one. He's cruel.

(Mr. Ellis takes the suitcase and opens it a bit.)

MR. ELLIS: Would you like a dream for the road? Just for you. Go ahead.

the GLORIA: Oh, I couldn't.

MR. ELLIS: I won't tell a soul.

the GLORIA: Are you sure you can spare one? *(Mr. Ellis nods. the Gloria looks inside the suitcase. She takes off her long, pink net scarf, and with a wink, bunches it up and drops it into the open suitcase.)* I'll trade you.

(Mr. Ellis is stunned. She reaches in and takes a dream.)

the GLORIA: Thanks ever so. *(She takes a few steps, then turns to face him.)* I am too beautiful to live, aren't I?

(the Gloria exits. Mr. Ellis stays staring at her with both his mouth and his suitcase open. Primitivo wheels himself on the porch.)

PRIMITIVO: Hey, Mr. E. *(Mr. Ellis snaps his mouth and the suitcase shut.)* Did a dream get away?

(Mr. Ellis goes under the porch. Primitivo sits on the porch, watching the Gloria go up her stairs and disappear into her bedroom. Altagracia enters, stands behind Primitivo.)

ALTAGRACIA: Look Primi, the first star. Can you reach it for me?

PRIMITIVO: No sweat.

ALTAGRACIA: Who else can do that for me?

(Beau enters. He pulls out a bottle of champagne from behind his back and four goblets.)

BEAU: Ta da! I figured our good friend Frank wouldn't mind us toasting tomorrow's race.

(Beau turns away to open the bottle. Altagracia stares at him, Primitivo stares at her. She catches him.)

ALTAGRACIA: What?

PRIMITIVO: Nothing.

(Corks pops. Beau pours the champagne.)

ALTAGRACIA: Careful. Brother and sisters can read each other's minds.

BEAU: Mr. Ellis!

(Mr. Ellis emerges. He is carrying his suitcase, ready to travel.)

MR. ELLIS: I'm off.

PRIMITIVO: Just finding that out, huh?

MR. ELLIS: I'm leaving.

ALTAGRACIA: What leaving? You can't leave.

MR. ELLIS: Can and must.

ALTAGRACIA: Mr. E I need you. This is not a good time for me. I got this race thing coming up, and, and you're in charge of crowd control and, uh, security. You're my second in command, and and....In fact, we were just gonna have a toast. Weren't we? To the race!

(Mr. Ellis drains his glass in one gulp.)

MR. ELLIS: That's why I'm leaving. I've seen enough people lose, I don't have to see another. I know what that's like. Oh, before I forget. Here *(He puts down his bag and retrieves the Gloria's pink net scarf which he gives to Altagracia.)* This is for you. It's not a dream, but it's almost as good. *(He looks at Beau and Altagracia.)* My, what a lovely couple I leave. Let's see, do I have everything? You can never escape your past. You have to carry it with you, everywhere. But I'm not running from it, I'm taking it with me and as cumbersome and unwelcome as it might get, who would I be without it? *(He kisses Altagracia on her forehead.)* I've wanted to do that for so long.

ALTAGRACIA: Goodbye, Mr. Ellis.

(She turns away, unable to finish.)

MR. ELLIS: You've never gotten used to people leaving, have you?

(Altagracia shakes her head. Mr. Ellis shakes Beau's hand.)

MR. ELLIS: One of us is one too many.

BEAU: Goodbye, Mr. Ellis.

PRIMITIVO: Hey, how about me? *(Mr. Ellis waves up to Primitivo.)* Come on up.

MR. ELLIS: I'm not allowed upstairs.

PRIMITIVO: Hey I know. I made the rule. Come on up.

(Mr. Ellis puts down his bag, and climbs the stairs, counting them as he goes.)

MR. ELLIS: One, two, three, four, five, six, seven, eight, nine, ten, eleven. Oh my, eleven steps. Is that all there was between me and you?

(Primitivo pushes himself up out of his chair and embraces Mr.Ellis.)

PRIMITIVO: See you, Mr. Ellis.

MR. ELLIS: You know, your problem was that you always dreamt so damn big.

PRIMITIVO: What do I want with small dreams?

(They separate. Mr. Ellis goes back downstairs.)

MR. ELLIS: Don't look back. Forward, always forward. I'm not staring. I'm not staring. I'm not staring. I'm not staring. Am I staring? *(He stops and stares at the spot where he buried Betty.)* I'm not staring. I'm not staring. I'm not staring. Am I staring? I'm not staring. I'm not staring. I'm not staring. I'm not staring. I'm not staring. Oh my God, I'm staring.

(He disappears. Silence.)

PRIMITIVO: Hey, is this a party or what? *(Beau raises his glass. Altagracia is silent.)* Well, I guess I'll call it a night. I want to be the first one up. You coming?

ALTAGRACIA: In a minute.

PRIMITIVO: Goodnight beautiful boy...Goodnight beautiful girl. *(He exits.)*

BEAU: *(Beau retrieves the bottle.)* I'd like to make my toast now, come back with me.

ALTAGRACIA: Where? To the real world? There's no place for me and Primitivo there.

BEAU: There is no place for me in what you call the real world. If I don't belong with you and Primitivo then I don't belong anywhere.

ALTAGRACIA: You'd start snapping at Primitivo, then me. You'd stay when what you really want to do was leave, cause you're an honorable man, yes you are. And I would fight as hard as I could but I would begin to blush. I would make up for years of not blushing. Not for me, for you. I would blush for you. For what I would be doing to you. *(She turns to leave.)* I wish I could rip out your heart. I wish I could throw it on the ground and stomp on it. Make it dust, make it disappear. And it would still haunt me forever.

BEAU: Please, can I kiss you goodbye?

ALTAGRACIA: No.

BEAU: Will you kiss me?

(Altagracia takes the scarf and puts it over her face.)

BEAU: No. *(He takes it off her and places it on his face.)* You once loved me without my face.

(They kiss through the scarf. He slowly pulls off the scarf and they kiss again.)

ALTAGRACIA: You kept your eyes open.

BEAU: Can I have one night with you? Please.

ALTAGRACIA: Why?

BEAU: Cause I have never wanted anybody as much as I want you.

(She takes his hand and begins to lead him behind a dune.)

ALTAGRACIA: *(Stopping him.)* When you talk about this, and you better, brag.

(They disappear behind a dune. Primitivo, using the porch guardrail, pulls himself up and takes off his robe. Using the porch handrail he awkwardly makes his way down the stairs to the ocean.)

PRIMITIVO: *(To the sun.)* Okay, so maybe he's not the ideal mate for her. You can match a navy blue sock and a black one and hardly anybody notices. Yes you can. Please let her know that I'm setting her free. And thank her. You better rise nice and slow, Sun. I'm going home. *(As he leaves he picks up the pink scarf, reaches for the sun and drags it out with him.)*

(the Gloria's bedroom light comes up. She looks out, sees Primitivo, smiles and waves to him.)

the GLORIA: Now there's somebody who's going to go the distance. *(She blows him a kiss and disappears back into her room, turning off her bedroom light.)*

(Lights up slowly to sunrise. Beau enters, climbs the stairs and finds Primitivo's robe. Altagracia enters and sees him holding the robe.)

ALTAGRACIA: *(Very small.)* No.
(She pushes past Beau and runs into the house.)
(V/O) Primitivo!
(She runs back out.)
He's not in his room. Primitivo! *(She sees his empty chair on the porch and runs down the stairs followed by Beau.)*

BEAU: Okay, okay, calm down. I'll help

ALTAGRACIA: Primitivo!

BEAU: You look.

ALTAGRACIA: I didn't check up on him *(She looks under the porch.)* one night. The one night. *(She looks out on the horizon.)* Do you see him? Primitivo!

BEAU: He's gone.

ALTAGRACIA: No! No! No. He is not gone. He does not go for a swim without me. I know how far he can go. Primitivo!
(Altagracia runs towards the water, Beau tries to hold her but she breaks free.)

BEAU: He could have started out hours ago.

ALTAGRACIA: Primi! You come back for me! Don't you dare leave me alone. You hear me? Do you hear me?! Primitivo, you have ten seconds, ten, to get your ass out of that water. I'm not kidding with you. Primitivo! Primitivo!
(She takes handfuls of sand and throws them out into the water before collapsing on the beach in defeat.)

BEAU: *(Comforting her.)* Sssh, sssh.

ALTAGRACIA: I sent him out to touch the sun. He's out there trying to do the impossible. Because of me. Cause of me.

BEAU: I'll bring him back to you.
(He begins to strip.)

ALTAGRACIA: Stop it.
(She slaps his hands to make him stop.)

BEAU: It's not impossible. I can take on the sun, the ocean anything you want, for you. If you tell me I can. Tell me like you told him. Tell me.

ALTAGRACIA:...You can.

BEAU: I can what?

ALTAGRACIA: You can touch the sun. You would do this for me?

BEAU: To deserve you I would do anything.

(Altagracia takes his hand.)

ALTAGRACIA: Then wait with me.

(Beau kneels behind Altagracia and holds her. She reaches out with her arm, as Primitivo did, to the sun. Arm stretched, fingers splayed, and then, very slowly she grabs the sun.)

END OF PLAY